"A beautiful, wise, and deep book. The writing invites us to inquire into what it means to teach from a place of embodied mindful presence. It becomes exquisitely clear how facilitating inquiry in mindfulness-based cognitive therapy is a continuation of our mindfulness practice, and requires us to show up in the fullness of our imperfect humanity. This book will be invaluable to new and established teachers of all mindfulness-based programs."

—**Rebecca Crane, PhD**, director of the Centre for Mindfulness Research and Practice at Bangor University, and author of *Mindfulness-Based Cognitive Therapy (CBT Distinctive Features)*

"This book is exceptional, providing a clear and comprehensive guide for anyone who wishes to teach mindfulness. At a practical level, there are transcripts from classes to illustrate the specific skills to be learned, linking these with the themes, rationale, intentions, and practice steps any teacher needs to have close at hand. Then, woven into the practical descriptions are deeper reflections that remind the reader how all of this work explores the most vulnerable yet wisest part of who we are. This is a book that will be used by every mindfulness instructor who wishes to grow in the practice of teaching and training."

—**Mark Williams, DPhil**, emeritus professor in the department of clinical psychology at the University of Oxford

"Having had the opportunity to help train quite a number of mindfulness-based cognitive therapy (MBCT) teachers over the years, I have always been acutely aware of a tremendous need for a definitive, clear, and supportive guide to the art, skill, and science of teaching the program. This is that guide, written by three remarkably talented and wise teacher trainers, in a language that is both articulate and warmly supportive. This is a virtual treasure trove of resources for the teacher of MBCT, presented in a well-organized and thorough manner, in the spirit of MBCT itself. I would strongly recommend that anyone teaching MBCT or adaptations of that program read this book and keep it handy for quick reference in the future."

—**Steven D. Hickman, PsyD**, founding director of the Center for Mindfulness at the University of California, San Diego; executive director of the Center for Mindful Self-Compassion; and clinical psychologist and associate clinical professor at the UC San Diego School of Medicine

"This exquisitely written and beautifully structured book for mindfulness teachers elucidates the often-elusive aspects and art of mindful inquiry and embodied presence. The detailed descriptions and examples of Themes, Rationale, Intentions, and Practice Skills (TRIP) are jewels that offer invaluable guidance and support for those teaching mindfulness-based interventions. This book is a vital contribution to the field of mindfulness and has the power to transform the teachers and teaching of mindfulness."

—**Diane Reibel, PhD**, director of the Myrna Brind Center for Mindfulness, and clinical associate professor in the department of integrative medicine at Thomas Jefferson University Hospitals; coauthor of *Teaching Mindfulness*, and coeditor of *Resources for Teaching Mindfulness*

"In carefully unpacking and illuminating the core elements of mindfulness-based cognitive therapy (MBCT), the authors—who truly know this program from the inside out—provide a great service to current and aspiring teachers. We get to see up close what's unique about MBCT: how in marrying mindfulness to cognitive behavioral therapy, it has created something larger than the sum of its parts. We also come to see what's required to make it effective, including trainers who are committed to a patient process of inquiry that doesn't settle for simple narratives, which may provide temporary comfort but avoid getting to the heart of the matter."

—**Barry Boyce**, editor in chief of *Mindful* magazine and Mindful.org, and editor of *The Mindfulness Revolution*

"This is a wonderful, deep, and practical book about teaching mindfulness-based cognitive therapy (MBCT). It shows the richness of the knowledge, experience, and personal practice of its writers and offers us their insights and skills. It brings together the worlds of cognitive behavioral therapy and Buddhist psychology in a way that can be applied by MBCT teachers all over the world. I am grateful to the authors for their generous sharing of both heartfelt wisdom and detailed practical instructions, as a fellow traveler on our common journey."

—**Anne Speckens, MD**, professor of psychiatry at Radboud University Medical Center, and founder and director of the Radboud University Medical Center for Mindfulness in Nijmegen, Netherlands

Mindfulness-Based Cognitive Therapy

Embodied Presence & Inquiry in Practice

SUSAN L. WOODS, MSW, LICSW
PATRICIA ROCKMAN, MD
EVAN COLLINS, MD

CONTEXT PRESS
An Imprint of New Harbinger Publications, Inc.

Publisher's Note

This publication is designed to provide accurate and authoritative information in regard to the subject matter covered. It is sold with the understanding that the publisher is not engaged in rendering psychological, financial, legal, or other professional services. If expert assistance or counseling is needed, the services of a competent professional should be sought.

NEW HARBINGER PUBLICATIONS is a registered trademark of New Harbinger Publications, Inc.

New Harbinger Publications is an employee-owned company.

Copyright © 2019 by Susan L. Woods, Patricia Rockman, and Evan Collins
                         Context Press
                         An imprint of New Harbinger Publications, Inc.
                         5720 Shattuck Avenue
                         Oakland, CA 94609
                         www.newharbinger.com

Cover design by Sara Christian

Cover photo: Sarah Dorweiler / Unsplash

Acquired by Ryan Buresh

Edited by Gretel Hakanson

Indexed by James Minkin

All Rights Reserved

Library of Congress Cataloging-in-Publication Data on file

Book printed in the United States of America

27   26   25

10   9   8   7

To Andrew, whose love, intellect, and sage counsel is a guiding light in my life.
—SW

To my dearest Bryan Moran; my beloved children: Wakelin, Blair, and Casey; my daughter-in-law Emily; and BFF Hunter.
—PR

To Bryan Hobson.
—EC

Contents

Foreword	vii
Acknowledgments	ix
Introduction	1

Part 1 A Framework for Teaching: Setting the Stage

1	The Mindfulness-Based Cognitive Therapy Program	9
2	The Five Agents of Change	27

Part 2 Skill-Building: Gaining Confidence

3	Practices and Exercises: Using TRIP and the Five Agents of Change	43
4	Group Process in the MBCT Program	63
5	Teaching Competencies, Skills, and Challenges	77

Part 3 Teaching as a Practice: The Inner Landscape

6	Embodied Mindful Presence—The Heart of Teaching	97
7	Expressing and Fostering Embodied Mindful Presence	111
8	Inquiry as Contemplative Dialogue	123
9	Personal and Professional Training and Beyond	137

Afterword	149
Appendices	
Meditation Scripts	152
All-Day Silent Retreat Schedule	181
Frequently Asked Questions	183
How Cognitive Behavior Therapy Informs MBCT	187
References	193
Index	201

Foreword

Put most plainly, this new book by Susan Woods, Patricia Rockman, and Evan Collins, dedicated to exploring inquiry and embodied practice in mindfulness-based cognitive therapy, is essential and exceptional. The topic of inquiry, although touched on in the first edition of the MBCT manual (Segal, Williams, & Teasdale, 2002) and elaborated further in the second edition (Segal, Williams, & Teasdale, 2013) continues to remain opaque to many practitioners, and I am delighted these three leaders in the field have decided to distill their collective practice wisdom and clinical skills into creating this accessible guide.

John Teasdale, Mark Williams, and I realized fairly early on in the process of creating MBCT that the "material" being taught to group members was multifaceted. Viewed from a traditional intervention frame, there were elements of psychoeducation, skill acquisition, self-monitoring, and regular periods of active practice. In many ways, these elements were familiar to us through our formative training as CBT therapists, and so it "seemed" to be fairly logical to deliver MBCT within the same frame. The wrinkle, however, was that in watching skilled mindfulness instructors such as Jon Kabat-Zinn, Saki Santorelli, and Ferris Urbanowski work, we realized that there was a wholly different framework, not completely orthogonal, but nearly so, that informed their teaching. The session content and curriculum were similar, and yet it was being taught to different signposts and with different intentions.

Inquiry and embodied practice are the processes that bridge these two domains. They enable an MBCT teacher to embody the practice of mindfulness regardless of the whether he or she is leading practice, reviewing home practice, discussing negative automatic thoughts, or reviewing the symptoms of depression. This metaframe is deeply informed by the intentional stance one adopts when practicing mindfulness meditation and emphasizes openness, curiosity, approach, kindness, nonjudgment, and tolerance of distress. Such mind states and their development, even germinally throughout MBCT, are especially pertinent to the mind states of rumination, worry, judgment, control, and problem solving that mark mood and other mental health disorders. When MBCT teachers guide inquiry and embody practice in ways that are informed by these intentions, they reduce the risk of reinforcing the habitual ways that group members have of understanding their experience and invite them to discover new and healing internal resources.

And yet, as the authors themselves acknowledge, the process of inquiry is routinely reported as the most challenging part of teaching MBCT. This is why Susan, Pat, and Evan's work is so valuable. They illustrate how, once the elements of the program have been learned, one can move beyond them and into the dynamic and immersive experience of the teaching itself. More concretely, the book is chock full of helpful nuggets that come from years of MBCT mentorship, training, and teaching. One of my favorites is TRIP—the acronym that refers to the Themes, Rationale, Intentions, and Practice Skills for each session and underlines the modular stacking of learning points over the course of the eight-week program. The five agents of change, another helpful invention, allows teachers to link their teaching and guidance to the participants' personal goals.

There are very few books that cover this territory, one that stretches well beyond MBCT, and, as the authors point out, touches into MBSR and mindfulness-based interventions in general. Anyone teaching in these programs will find themselves encountering a choice point in class where a variety of responses will be possible. Reading this book will certainly allow teachers to feel supported in these moments and understand the real-time demands being placed on them with greater skill, clarity, and compassion.

—Zindel Segal, PhD

Acknowledgments

From the three of us:

To Zindel Segal, Mark Williams, and John Teasdale for their seminal work in MBCT; to Jon Kabat-Zinn for his ground-breaking program, mindfulness-based stress reduction (MBSR), paving the way for contemporary mindfulness; to Zindel Segal in particular for all that he has given us as collaborator, colleague, co-teacher, and friend; to Karl Druckman for providing contractual advice; and to our editors Ryan Buresh and Vicraj Gill for their care and thoughtful guidance.

From Susan:

To all my teachers, who over the years have supported me in my journey of awakening. For the love, support, and friendship of Ferris Buck Urbanowski and Gina Sharpe, elders in the field of mindfulness. To Zindel Segal for his wisdom, friendship, and support. To the women of the "Wise Women Club," you know who you are, for all the laughter and moments of irreverence. To my fellow senior trainers around the world who have dedicated themselves to sharing the fruits of mindfulness practice, especially Char Wilkins, Patricia Rockman, and Evan Collins. To Steve Hickman at the Mindfulness-Based Professional Training Institute, UCSD, for having the vision to create the Institute. To my much-loved children, Edward and Carrie; their partners, Sanno and Nick; my adorable grandchildren, Arthur, Monty, and Cole. To my stepchildren, Victoria and Catherine, and their partners, Matthew and Ollie; and my step-grandchildren, William, Thomas, Daisy, Oliver, and Bear; the future is in good hands.

From Patricia:

To Bryan Moran for his incredible support, love, ear, and intellect. To my teachers and mentors of mindfulness and Buddhism including the late Michael Stone, Norman Feldman, Molly Swan, Zindel Segal, Susan Woods, and Pascal Auclair. And to my family and dear friends on the path from whom I continue to learn and to love including Evan Collins, Susan Woods (again), Elaine Smookler, Allison McLay, Jose Silveira, Michael Apollo, Melissa Nigrini, Gwen Morgan, Lee Freedman, Amanda Guthrie, David Denis, and Barry Boyce. Special acknowledgement to Tita Angangco for her vision, collaboration, and support of my development as a human being and teacher. And last but not least to all the staff and faculty at the Centre for Mindfulness Studies for their dedication to bringing mindfulness into the world.

From Evan:

To my partner Bryan for all his support and putting up with me through this process, along with my friends, parents, and family. To my many teachers and fellow wanderers on the mindfulness path including Patricia Rockman, Susan Woods, Zindel Segal, Pascal Auclair, Molly Swan, Norman Feldman, Pat Smith, Kate Partridge, Matthew Church, Rob Pepler, Mary Elliott, Susan Greenwood, and Susan Abbey. And to my colleagues at the Centre for Mindfulness Studies.

Introduction

Our intention, in this book, is to take you through the process necessary to teach the mindfulness-based program (MBP) known as mindfulness-based cognitive therapy (MBCT). We would also like you to consider that to be a mindfulness-based teacher is more than delivering a protocol; it is, essentially, a mindfulness practice, and to capture the essence of teaching mindfulness-based programs (MBPs), we need to talk about *embodying* the practice.

    The foundation of mindfulness-based programs is the delivery of mindfulness meditation practices and their relevance to the reduction of suffering. Every aspect of these programs, from intake to the final session, requires a teacher to embody the practice of mindfulness. Teaching from this stance, especially through the process of inquiry, is the most challenging part of teaching MBCT and other MBPs and the thing trainees say is the hardest to learn. As three clinicians and teachers with a rich collective experience in training and mentoring mindfulness-based teachers, we feel the time is right to explore the elements that go beyond the how-to of delivering a protocol and into the experience of teaching. Furthermore, given its target population of depressed and anxious people, teaching MBCT requires knowledge and skills related to cognitive behavioral therapy (CBT) and other aspects of mental health practice, and we want to give you a book that covers the critical integration of these competencies as well as the experiential and dynamic process that is mindfulness. So, in this book, we will address variables related to teaching, including the protocol of MBCT, and the Themes, Rationale, Intentions, and Practice Skills represented in each session; the agents of change at play throughout the sessions; the skills necessary to achieve competence and best practice in the delivery of the protocol; and above all, what it means to have an embodied mindful presence as you teach, and how this presence can be expressed through the contemplative dialogue of inquiry.

Not a Map, But a Territory

We hope to stimulate a conversation, less about *a map of how to teach* MBCT and more an exploration of *the territory of teaching,* using the experiential as our guide. This allows us to view the teaching of MBCT as a mindfulness practice. We use as our guide the intensive experiential workshops that Susan designed for teachers, but we see this book as applicable to teachers of all levels of experience, from beginner to advanced. And although our focus is on MBCT, we see this book as highly relevant to how one teaches other MBPs.

We have organized this book into three parts. In part 1, "A Framework for Teaching: Setting the Stage," we begin with a description of the MBCT program—to which we add two approaches that Susan developed to assist teachers in their training and learning. These are the Themes, Rationale, Intentions, and Practice Skills (TRIP) one can draw from each session of MBCT and the agents of change that operate in MBCT (and other MBPs) to allow participants to gain insight into the way depression works and learn the skills needed to turn toward the difficult, challenging experiences that stymie them: the protocol of the intervention, the mindfulness practices taught in MBCT, individual learning, group process, and the teacher's embodied mindful presence.

In part 2, "Skill Building: Gaining Confidence," we look more deeply into the skills that an MBCT teacher should work toward in his development. For this, we continue to use TRIP and the five agents of change to explore the various practices and cognitive exercises contained in the curriculum. We then look at group processes and use experiential learning theory to detail the skills, attitudes, and behaviors that comprise the competencies for teaching groups, as well as the common mistakes and developmental challenges we all face as teachers.

In the final section of the book, "Teaching as Practice: The Inner Landscape," we get to the heart of the matter. We explore the foundations and expressions of embodied mindful presence—the attitudinal foundations that inform both an individual's mindfulness practice and the presence an MBCT teacher should bring to the room when leading a therapy group and the insights from Buddhist psychology that inform the skills MBCT is meant to teach—as well as the contemplative dialogue of inquiry we see as so fundamental to MBCT and other MBPs. Finally, we conclude with thoughts on personal and professional training and an afterword about what it has been like to write this book and our hopes for the future.

We recognize the contradiction inherent in *using a book* to encourage a teacher of MBCT to rely on experiential awareness, embodied presence, and teaching as practice. As much as we attempt to intersperse our text with examples, figures, metaphors, and vignettes, it is still a text-based document akin to a two-dimensional map. Perhaps then our book can be like a topographical map that adds an additional dimension, although still limited.

An early working title for this book was *Teaching Practice and the Practice of Teaching*. Although we ended up choosing a less oblique title, what we are trying to convey in this book is contained in that phrase: First, in MBCT, we are teaching people the skills of meditation along with the skills of reflecting on the meditation experience so as to apply them to everyday life. This is *teaching a practice*. Second, teaching mindfulness, or anything else for that matter, is hard and requires skills and competencies developed over time and by repeated practice. This is *teaching takes practice*. Finally, and perhaps most importantly, teaching mindfulness is a mindfulness practice in and of itself that needs to come from a position of embodied mindful presence. This is *teaching as a practice*.

Who Are We?

We are serious students of Buddhist history, philosophy, and psychology, and honor these roots of MBCT and MBSR. All three of us have regular meditation practices in the insight meditation tradition of *vipassana* and regularly go on silent teacher-led retreats (and sometimes lead them). Our work has been informed by our practice and by the contributions of colleagues also involved in the dissemination of training future teachers and of others who have written about teaching mindfulness.

Born in Malaysia and educated in the UK, Susan initially trained and worked as a physiotherapist. In moving to the United States thirty-five years ago, she trained to become a clinical social worker and practiced for many years as a psychotherapist. She was one of the early trainees of Jon Kabat-Zinn and colleagues at the University of Massachusetts–Worcester to teach mindfulness-based stress reduction (MBSR). Then, early on in the development of MBCT, she was recruited by Zindel Segal to lead the groups in one of the early randomized controlled trials of MBCT. She developed a keen interest in how one trains to teach MBSR and MBCT and began to offer workshops and individual mentorship, as well as develop the professional MBSR and MBCT certification training for the University of California, San Diego's Mindfulness-Based Professional Training Institute, and the Centre for Mindfulness Studies in Toronto, among other organizations. As part of her personal practice, Susan studied yoga and is a certified yoga teacher. She also completed the Community Dharma Leaders Program, the teaching program developed by Jack Kornfield, PhD, and others at the Spirit Rock Meditation Center in California.

Patricia is a Canadian and a family physician. After working in family medicine, as well as HIV and palliative care, she focused her practice in mental health specializing in CBT and other psychotherapies and on offering professional training in these modalities. She also worked extensively in developing policy and mentorship programs for family physicians working in mental health, based on a long-standing interest in meditation and other contemplative practices, including being a certified yoga teacher. She trained to teach MBCT and MBSR with Zindel Segal and Susan, among others. She went on to cofound the Centre for Mindfulness Studies (CMS) and developed curricula for MBCT and CBT in Toronto. CMS is a not-for-profit charity offering MBPs in the community as well as to marginalized populations. It is the leading organization in the professional training of MBCT and MBSR in Canada. She is also a freelance writer.

Evan is a psychiatrist who has worked in both community- and hospital-based mental health with multiple populations. He was a student of Zindel Segal, Susan, Patricia, and others in training to teach both MBCT and MBSR, and now delivers training workshops and provides trainee mentorship with them. He is senior faculty at CMS and assists Patricia in curriculum development and administration of both the educational and clinical programs.

A Note on Language and What Has Informed Our Work

While we are serious students of Buddhist psychology, none of us consider ourselves Buddhists; instead, we see the dharma (the teaching of the Buddha) in a wider context, as an expression of contemporary mindfulness that fits alongside our training and practice in mental health. We are aware that many disagree with the idea of non-Buddhists teaching these practices. Indeed, there are many who see MBPs as a dangerous oversimplification of the dharma and question whether it should be taught through institutions of health care, education, and the workforce. In addition to becoming "mindfulness lite" and a commodification of mindfulness (Purser & Loy, 2013), the critique holds that one cannot strip mindfulness from its ethical underpinnings and to do this leads to misinterpretations and misapplications (Monteiro, Musten, & Compson, 2015).

We hold that there is enormous value in offering MBCT and related MBPs, and these are, in fact, embedded in an implicit ethical framework. This framework is supported by the key ethical principles in health care of autonomy (informed decision making), beneficence (promoting the well-being of others), nonmaleficence (do no harm), and respect for human rights. We believe that teachers should understand the origins of the dharma, key principles of Buddhist psychology, and *vipassana* (insight meditation) practice in particular but see MBCT firmly as a contemporary interpretation and practice of mindfulness outside of a religious context.

We have also struggled long and hard about what language to use in talking about the delivery of MBCT. Are we instructors, teachers, facilitators, therapists, or clinicians? Are we delivering education, training, skills development, or psychotherapy? Does MBCT represent a program, a course, a way of being, or an intervention? And are those seeking MBCT participants, students, patients, or clients? In the end, we have stayed with convention and called ourselves *teachers*, with the substitutes of *instructor* and *facilitator* sometimes used to avoid repetition, and those with whom we work *participants*. For a classification of what MBCT is, we continue to use *program*, or MBP, as imperfect as that may be, to convey that it is not a traditional therapy, although therapeutic, and yet not simply education and skills training.

Most importantly, we must, before we begin, acknowledge the founders: Jon Kabat-Zinn, for his work in developing and advancing MBSR, and Zindel Segal, Mark Williams, and John Teasdale, for their development of MBCT, their books and research papers, and their continued study. It is thanks to Jon Kabat-Zinn's vision to bring mindfulness into health care working with stress and distress and to Zindel Segal, Mark Williams, and John Teasdale's extension of this work to depression that we can do the work we do and write this book. We hope that this book can be seen as a worthy continuation of their work.

Beginning the Journey

The commitment we make to building teaching skills in others is a profound responsibility, as it asks of us no less than what we are asking of our trainees. Becoming a teacher of MBCT, MBSR, or other MBPs is about many things but not least bringing a humility and openness to our mistakes, learning from them, and sensing the joy of moments when we have played a small role in alleviating suffering. Whether one is just beginning to train to deliver MBCT or a seasoned teacher with many groups under his belt, we hope this work will be useful.

Bedeviling the Swan

PART I
A Framework for Teaching

Setting the Stage

Chapter 1

The Mindfulness-Based Cognitive Therapy Program

At its most dynamic, teaching MBCT requires a way of structuring one's teaching and developing a set of skills that draw upon one's embodiment of mindfulness. When an MBCT teacher embodies attitudinal characteristics embedded in the practices of mindfulness and understands aspects of Buddhist psychology, the heart of this program comes alive. However, before we can dive into the complexity of being a mindfulness-based teacher, we must first develop a way to broaden and deepen our understanding of what we are teaching. This requires knowledge of the eight-session MBCT protocol as Segal, Williams, and Teasdale (2002, 2013) describe it in *Mindfulness-Based Cognitive Therapy for Depression*—its structure and its modularity—as well as two constructs that we have found useful in furthering teaching skills and developing competence. These consist of five agents of change at play (the *protocol*, the *mindfulness practices, individual learning, group process*, and the *embodied mindful presence of the teacher*) and the Theme, Rationale, Intention, and Practice Skills (TRIP; Woods, Rockman, & Collins, 2016) present in each of MBCT's sessions. These frameworks provide the teacher with an organized approach for exploring the scope of teaching, strengthening best practices, and assisting participants to achieve the changes they are seeking. Teachers are anchored in the core aspects of the program, reducing what can be an overwhelming and anxiety-producing process for the novice—and, for the more experienced teacher, assisting in her development of embodiment and the deepening of inquiry, the contemplative dialogue that follows each mindful practice and cognitive exercise in MBCT.

In this chapter and the next, we'll look first at the MBCT protocol to discuss what is required for the delivery of this program—*how* MBCT is taught. Then, we'll turn to

TRIP—the Theme, Rationale, Intention, and Practice Skills represented in each of the MBCT sessions—to support your understanding and delivery of the MBCT program. Finally, in chapter 2, we will examine each of the agents of change and how they are employed to cover teaching points, guide participants in core practices, and facilitate the acquisition of practice skills for the teacher.

The MBCT Protocol

MBCT is delivered as a group program over the course of eight weeks. The MBCT program brings together mindfulness meditation (with roots in Buddhist practice and psychology) and cognitive behavior therapy and emphasizes an experiential form of teaching and learning. The first half of the MBCT program focuses on stabilizing and strengthening mindful attention and awareness. The second half, building on this foundation, provides various mindfulness practices and cognitive exercises that facilitate participants' learning by helping them turn toward difficult and challenging states of mind and mood prevalent in mental disorders. These skills assist participants to identify personal and specific relapse signatures. The rationale is that, for those vulnerable to depression, by identifying these triggers and habitual ways of thinking that are precursors, skillful action can be taken to stay well. This cultivates a different relationship to unwanted experience, one that does not engage in denial, rumination, worry, avoidance, or distraction, the common and unproductive ways we tend to manage difficulties. Ultimately, the program provides participants with an understanding of the territory of depression, the warning signs of relapse, and, from the practice of mindfulness, the development of a different relationship to low mood and negative thought patterns.

Each of MBCT's weekly sessions is two and a half hours in length and involves teaching a mindfulness practice followed by a discussion between teacher and participants, inquiring into the participants' experience of the exercise, which is known as *inquiry*. It is an interactive process between teacher and participants that requires a teacher to understand the skills she is building from the practice of mindfulness along with her grasp of the important themes of each session. Inquiry has a present-moment focus where the teacher emphasizes what has been noticed, the relationship to what is being observed, and how the experience of the practice might be helpful for reducing distress, preventing depression relapse, and staying well. Included in many of the sessions will be a cognitive exercise that is relevant to that week's theme and includes an investigation on how thoughts reinforce mood and behavior.

What follows is a summary of the MBCT protocol that puts these pieces together. This will be an introduction for those less familiar with the MBCT program and for others, a review.

Preclass Interview or Orientation Session

A preclass interview or orientation session can be conducted individually or through a group orientation with follow-up individual interviews. Participants are given an overview of the MBCT program, and the benefits and risks are discussed. Participants learn about key factors associated with depression and that participating in the program involves hard work and will require persistence and patience. Additionally, time is allotted for the teacher to hear from participants about their experience of depression and any questions they may have about participating in the program. Participants are screened for suitability.

Session 1: Awareness and Automatic Pilot

The teacher welcomes participants, discusses group guidelines, offers a brief review of the MBCT program, and teaches two mindfulness practices: the Raisin Practice (which helps to illuminate automatic pilot by slowing down an action participants would do instantly and mechanically) and the Body Scan Meditation Practice (which begins the process of training attention to the body, a foundational skill in MBCT). After every mindfulness practice, as in every session to come, there is a discussion about what was experienced (inquiry). Home assignments are identified for the coming week, for example to practice the Body Scan Meditation (a formal practice) every day facilitated by listening to an audio recording and to bring a present-moment awareness to a routine activity like brushing the teeth (an informal practice).

Session 2: Living in Our Heads

The teacher facilitates the Body Scan Meditation Practice and inquiry, and reviews home assignments. A cognitive exercise (Walking Down the Street) is discussed, which is followed by a ten-minute sitting meditation with inquiry. The teacher will then assign the home practices for the coming week.

Session 3: Gathering the Scattered Mind

The teacher starts with a five-minute seeing (or hearing) meditation practice and a thirty-minute sitting meditation (Awareness of Breath and Body and instruction about how to work with difficult physical sensations) followed by inquiry. The teacher leads a discussion of the previous week's home assignments followed by a Three-Minute Breathing Space Practice, a Mindful Movement Practice and inquiry, and finally allocates home practice.

Session 4: Recognizing Aversion

The session begins with a five-minute seeing (or hearing) meditation practice with inquiry. A thirty- to forty-minute sitting meditation (Breath, Body, Sounds, Thoughts, and Emotions and Choiceless Awareness Meditation Practice) follows. A poem is read, and then inquiry is facilitated. The previous week's home practices are discussed. The "territory" of depression is reviewed, including the Automatic Thoughts Questionnaire followed by a Three-Minute Breathing Space and inquiry and Mindful Walking and inquiry, and the next week's home assignments are handed out.

Session 5: Allowing and Letting Be

The teacher leads a thirty- to forty-minute sitting meditation (breath and body, where participants are invited to bring up a worry or concern, thus introducing a difficulty within the practice, recognizing its effect in the body, acknowledging and accepting what is present) followed by inquiry. The previous week's home practices are reviewed. A Three-Minute Breathing Space–Responsive and inquiry follow with the reading of a poem, discussion, and home practice is assigned.

Session 6: Thought Are Not Facts

This session begins with a thirty- to forty-minute sitting meditation (Breath, Body, Sounds, Thoughts, and Emotions and Choiceless Awareness and noticing the relationship to thoughts) followed by inquiry. The previous week's home practices are reviewed. Cognitive exercises that highlight that thoughts are not necessarily facts (the Alternative Viewpoints Exercise) and early-warning signs, or relapse signatures, are led. The following week's home practices are assigned.

All-Day Silent Retreat

This day retreat of several hours is held in silence, with the teacher leading participants through the meditation practices that have been practiced over the previous six weeks. These include the Body Scan, Mindful Movement, Walking Meditation, and various sitting practices. A break for lunch is included, which is an opportunity to continue to practice by exploring the relationship to eating by taking the time to notice all the sensations associated with food. Slowing down enhances experience of the senses to be experienced—sight, taste, smell, hearing, and touch—which we normally don't pay much attention to, as we often eat automatically. This reinforces an important theme of the day, which is continuity of practice. The rationale for maintaining silence and the length of this day is to support a moment-to-moment attentional engagement, thus promoting focused attention (paying attention to a primary object of attention, like the breath) and an open-monitoring (a wider frame of reference where a variety of foci are attended to and experienced), both attributes of mindfulness. (See appendix for more detail.)

Session 7: "How Can I Best Take Care of Myself?"

The teacher leads a thirty- to forty-minute sitting meditation (breath, body, and noticing the relationship to the various sensations, sounds, thoughts, emotions, and noting the effect on body) followed by inquiry. The previous week's home practice is discussed. Various cognitive exercises are used to explore self-care behaviors by identifying activities that are nourishing versus depleting and the link between pleasure and mastery. Warning signs of relapse are revisited, and individual action plans are created. The following week's home practice is assigned.

Session 8: Maintaining and Extending New Learning

The teacher leads a Body Scan Meditation followed by inquiry. The previous week's home practices are discussed. The group reflects on the eight-week course along with commentaries about what has been useful. This guides the discussion into preparing for the future around strategies for maintaining practice and review of the action plan from the previous week. A closing ceremony is held.

In bringing together meditation practices with cognitive behavioral exercises, the MBCT program provides a firm foundation and scaffold for learning about how cognitive appraisal, perception, interpretation, and rumination affect mood, and for learning how the practice of mindfulness can help one develop the skills to work with depression and prevent relapse. It is designed to build flexibility of attention, enhance awareness of the relationship one has to experience, promote emotion and behavior regulation, and increase distress tolerance.

Systematic reviews of the research demonstrate that the MBCT program is effective in preventing relapse in recurrent depression (Sorbero et al., 2015). There is also mounting evidence to support its use in more symptomatic depression, anxiety, and mental distress secondary to other illnesses (Goldberg et al., 2018; Eisendrath et al., 2016). Adherence to the protocol is important for the delivery of such participant outcomes. Yet drift over time is common for teachers, especially if they teach in isolation. It can also be difficult, if the established protocol is all you have to rely on, to know how to respond to the unique and unpredictable reactions participants can have in the course of a session. How an MBCT teacher meets participants' challenges and difficulties—whether practice-related or emotional distress—will be an important factor in their learning. She will need to acknowledge these struggles and at the same time encourage a continuing exploration: to support and foster the development of mindfulness-based skills and model a turning toward difficulty, all without needing to be a cheerleader or a caretaker or provide advice. This is where TRIP is helpful.

Themes, Rationale, Intention, Practice Skills (TRIP)

When Woods first began to develop TRIP in 2013, it arose out of reflecting on what was being asked of her as a trainer of other teachers. She felt that, given the multiple variables a teacher must hold when delivering MBCT (and other mindfulness-based programs), teachers needed additional constructs to organize their thinking. This includes a clear understanding of the *Themes* of each session, the session's subject, setting, and context; the *Rationale* for each session or practice, of *why* she is teaching what she is teaching; the *Intention* of a given session or practice, *what* we are teaching to, or the aim; and the *Practice Skills, how* all of this will be delivered: the particular skills teachers need to possess in order to best teach them and the particular skills that participants will need to learn over the course of the program. Together, these elements of TRIP represent a compass that offers clarity and depth by allowing the teacher to understand the goals of each session and how to convey them to participants.

Essentially, the *Themes* point to important topics for instruction in each of the classes, allowing the teacher to understand the continuum and modularity of the participants' learning. The themes anchor each session and help organize a teacher's instructional focus as she fleshes out major teaching considerations specific to each week, ones that will be important to consider highlighting as a guide to building participants' skills. For example, in session 1 (Awareness and Automatic Pilot), these themes provide the teacher with an understanding of what to emphasize by reflecting the mind's tendency to be on automatic pilot and how present-moment awareness allows us to step out of this.

Not only is it important to organize one's teaching with an understanding of the themes of each session, but teaching the MBCT program requires an instructor to be aware of the *Rationale,* the reasoning (the why or the because) for teaching what she is teaching in any given session. In session 1, for example, we learn to recognize the mind's automatic pilot *because* the automaticity of negative thought patterns perpetuates depression and low mood, and we learn about present-moment awareness *because* it permits the intentional focus that allows us to observe what is otherwise automatic. A teacher's understanding of the rationale for a given session or exercise will be affected by a number of factors. These include her personal mindfulness practice (experiential learning) and her past teaching of MBCT, her interactions with colleagues and her reflections from reading on the subject. In addition, science is increasing our knowledge about mindfulness, its impact on difficult mood states, and the absolute and relative contraindications for its use. This emerging research is important for an MBCT teacher to keep up-to-date with, as this evidence base needs to be part of her understanding of what she is facilitating.

Intentions address what we are teaching in each week—in other words, the aim. For example, the intention of the first MBCT class is for the teacher to facilitate, through various practices, an understanding of how often we are on "automatic pilot," failing to pay attention to our internal and external environments as this is a risk for generating negative mind and mood states. The very first exercise, the Raisin Practice, demonstrates this well. The teacher's instruction directs her participants to take the time to "be" with the raisin using a sensorial focus (all five senses) and the sixth sense, that of thinking. Recognizing and categorizing thinking as a sixth sense (which is based on Buddhist psychology) is important, as it relegates thinking to another way of perceiving and acknowledging experience, rather than the sum total of experience. Being with the raisin as an object of interest includes a process of slowing down, which is important, as it counteracts the habitual nature of automatic pilot that assumes it already "knows" what is in front of it. In employing this emphasis on slowing down, participants quickly have access to the thinking mind that is frequently engaged in thoughts unrelated to the current situation. Participants learn how much information is available through the senses and that taking time to notice what is in experience is an important aspect of training attention to each moment.

Practice Skills will be discussed in two ways: (1) the various practices and exercises embedded in each session and (2) what the teacher requires to develop further understanding of a particular practice and how to deliver it. Developing the ability to work with these elements takes time. The good news is that a novice MBCT teacher can take heart that if she adheres to the structure of the MBCT protocol, she will be offering her participants a good entry point to the learning embedded in the program. The more experienced and skilled teacher will demonstrate a deeper understanding of these practice skills, one that offers her participants an embodiment of mindfulness rather than a purely intellectual presentation of the material. This calls attention to the aspect of teaching that goes beyond form and function to where it becomes an extension of mindfulness practice itself.

Practice Skills, for example, in session 1, include the delivery of the Raisin Practice, the Body Scan Meditation Practice, inquiry, and home assignments. For these specific practices, this will include such abilities as offering clear and steady guidance and using language that is simple. It also involves normalizing the movement of attention, bringing awareness to it, and encouraging participants to cultivate the skill of bringing attention back to whatever focus is being used as an anchor. For example, when guiding the Body Scan, a teacher will frequently say, "Noticing when the attention has moved away from body sensations, as best as you are able, gently escorting it back," embodying patience and kindness in her instruction (another practice skill) because this seemingly simple practice of attending to each moment is not so easy and requires effort and practice.

In guiding practices, the teacher's language will convey an invitation to participants to be with all experiences, regardless of whether they are pleasant, unpleasant, or neutral, and she will use words that communicate trust, beginner's mind, nonjudging, acceptance, nonstriving, and letting go: the attitudinal foundations central to mindfulness (Kabat-Zinn, 1990, 2013) that should inform both one's practice of mindfulness and the manner in which it is taught. The MBCT teacher's embodiment of these attitudinal qualities will be a central feature in the delivery of the mindfulness practices for her participants, as they are ones that she is asking them to use as they practice. Moreover, they will inform her choice of words, her pacing of the instructions, and how she is relating to the current understanding of her participants. (We will discuss this in more detail in part 3 of this book.)

An MBCT teacher is also responsible for guiding various cognitive exercises that highlight fundamental ways we process information cognitively and emotionally. The cognitive exercises include the Walking Down the Street Exercise, the Pleasant and Unpleasant Events Calendar, the Territory of Depression and the Automatic Thoughts Questionnaire, Identifying Relapse Signatures, the Office Exercise, the Nourishing and Depleting Exercise, understanding the effect that activities involving pleasure and mastery have on mood, and creating an action plan for self-care. These highlight and reinforce a number of important learning concepts—the parsing of experience into its component parts and the development of a shared focus, vocabulary, and language of experience—that are significant in understanding how to develop and apply a different relationship to mind and mood states throughout the whole MBCT program. The tension for the teacher is ensuring these cognitive exercises are led in an experiential and interactive manner without missing the key teaching points. These exercises have didactic elements, but they should not be taught as lectures. A novice teacher will tend to rely on explaining rather than allowing her participants to explore, reflect, and question the material; a more experienced teacher will know how to guide participants to insight, allowing them to engage with the material and thereby discover the primary teaching points for themselves.

We have discussed how TRIP can be applied generally; now, let's use it to investigate each of the eight sessions. (Note that for the practice skills, for now, we will focus on the skills that the teacher will facilitate. We'll explore in chapter 3 how to teach each practice and exercise.)

Session 1: Awareness and Automatic Pilot

- **Theme:** This session highlights learning to recognize the tendency of the mind to be on automatic pilot and learning about present moment-to-moment awareness and applying that to mindfulness practices and to everyday life.

- **Rationale:** Developing an intentional focus based on the practice of mindfulness helps illuminate automatic pilot and the nature of the habitual movement of attention.

- **Intention:** The aim here is to help participants recognize automaticity by accessing the six senses (the sixth being thinking and emotion) and training attention to the body—senses and sensations. The movement of attention is normalized, with curiosity being brought to all experiences. A *being* mode is contrasted with a *doing* mode of mind. This highlights the idea that being present to experience can be an alternative to always doing something about experience, including depression.

- **Practice Skills:** These will include the Raisin Practice and inquiry, the Body Scan and inquiry, assigning home practices, and a brief breath awareness practice.

Session 2: Living in Our Heads

- **Theme:** This session highlights the persistence of thinking and its influence on perception and interpretation. As a contrast, the theme of focusing on the body or the breath is used as an anchor to the present moment when noticing the tendency of the mind to become overinvolved in thinking.

- **Rationale:** Strengthening an intentional focus on the present moment provides a useful anchor from which we can understand how easy it is to slip into ruminative thinking and worry. Developing a different relationship to experience provides an alternative "view" to the traction of negative thinking patterns.

- **Intention:** The teacher's aim is to cultivate an intention to direct physical experience versus relating to experience through thinking and to continue to support increasing body awareness and a beginning awareness of aversion and attachment. The lens of curiosity is highlighted. She normalizes and welcomes obstacles as they are revealed through mindfulness practice. The intention is to train awareness of the judging mind along with thoughts, emotions, body sensations, and their interactions. Attention is brought to the movement of thought and how beliefs and behavior arise from a subjective interpretation of events.

- **Practice Skills:** In this session, these are the Body Scan Meditation and inquiry, a short sitting practice where the focus is on the breath followed by inquiry, review of the previous week's home practices, the Walking Down the Street exercise and discussion, and assigning home practices for the coming week.

Session 3: Gathering the Scattered Mind

- **Theme:** Understanding the normality of a distracted mind is a key aspect of the learning theme in this session. The other is utilizing the breath and the body (in motion and stillness) as an anchor to stabilize the mind so one can develop a curiosity about what is being experienced.

- **Rationale:** The breath is a primary anchor in training attention and stabilizing the mind to support the investigation of experience. Promoting a "being" mode of mind supports curiosity and investigation of what is arising in experience.

- **Intention:** The teacher emphasizes living in the present, with the recognition that dwelling in the past and future will perpetuate suffering. Cultivating the attitudes of allowing, curiosity, patience, and compassion are allies in this process. The teacher will continue to emphasize the breath and body as an anchor for attention and use challenges in the body as a parallel process for working with difficult emotions. This session introduces practicing mindful attention during movement of the body.

- **Practice Skills:** The teacher facilitates a seeing or hearing meditation; a thirty-minute sitting Meditation—Awareness of Breath and Body—and how to respond and work with intense physical sensations and inquiry, a review of the previous week's home practice, the Three Minute Breathing Space followed by inquiry, and Mindful Movement (based on yoga postures) and inquiry, and assigns home practices for the coming week.

Session 4: Recognizing Aversion

- **Theme:** The theme of this session is the importance of being aware and staying present for the various aspects of aversion, such as avoidance, antipathy, dislike, fear, anger, and hatred. Here, we use the platform of mindfulness meditation practices from which to *see* aversion not as a personal flaw, but as an aspect of *mind* to be observed and explored. The territory of depression is identified as a package, which highlights that depression is a collection of symptoms that can be recognized and used to act as early warning signs of depression relapse.

- **Rationale:** Aversion, avoidance, and wanting things to be other than they are play a major role in depression and other negative mind and mood states. Recognizing these patterns through the experience of mindfulness practice lessens their traction. Emphasizing a *being* mode of mind and developing a different relationship to the contents of the mind offers the opportunity to *view* experience as an observer rather than being connected to a sense of self.

- **Intention:** The intentions of this session are to cultivate the recognition of aversion and meet it with acceptance and compassion, and to recognize that depression can be understood as collection of symptoms that can be fully known. Teachers will promote participants' understanding of the universality of suffering.

- **Practice Skills:** The practice skills are the seeing or hearing meditation; sitting meditation—Breath, Body, Sounds, Thoughts, and Emotions and Choiceless Awareness (Open Monitoring)—and back to the breath followed by inquiry; home practice review; defining the territory of depression using the Automatic Thoughts Questionnaire (ATQ) and diagnostic criteria (*DSM-5*) with discussion; Three-Minute Breathing Space–Responsive with inquiry; Walking Meditation and inquiry; and assigning home practices for the coming week.

Session 5: Allowing and Letting Be

- **Theme:** This section focuses on continuing to emphasize a being mode of mind that incorporates the experience of being present for and investigating all experiences, wanted and unwanted. This is an important aspect of changing the relationship to aversive states, such as negative ruminative thinking and worry, that are so typical of depression and anxiety.

- **Rationale:** Allowing and letting be establishes a different relationship to unwanted thought and mood states. This increases distress tolerance and reduces experiential avoidance. Ongoing mindfulness practices continue to support conditions for mind and mood health as well as emphasizing self-care and self-compassion.

- **Intention:** The teacher will embody allowing for the unwanted, and developing a different relationship to difficulty is valued. Befriending it, nurturing kindness and compassion, creating space to encourage responding rather than reacting, and reinforcing the concept that everything can be held in mindful awareness are primary aims of the teacher.

- **Practice Skills:** The teacher facilitates a thirty- to forty-minute sitting meditation—Awareness of Breath and Body, which includes instruction about being with a difficulty already present or introducing one and how to work with this in the practice. Sometimes, she will include a poem at the end of the practice or later in the class. As always, the meditation practice is followed by inquiry, a home practice review, the Three-Minute Breathing Space—Responsive and inquiry, and assigning home practices for the coming week.

Session 6: Thoughts Are Not Facts

- **Theme:** This session emphasizes that thoughts are not necessarily facts and how emotions play a significant role in determining how we respond to situations and what we think about them.

- **Rationale:** Thoughts are state and context dependent and influenced by mood. Thoughts are mental events (sensations of the mind), no different from attending to and noticing the breath, body sensations, sounds, or emotions. The aim of this session is to continue strengthening attentional training and an open monitoring of all experience as a skill for preventing depression relapse and negative mood states.

- **Intention:** This session uses the platform of mindfulness to loosen identification with negative thinking and low mood and emphasizes multiple ways of experiencing and interpreting events based on mood and context through the discussion from the Alternative Viewpoints Exercise.

- **Practice Skills:** This session includes the sitting meditation practice—Breath, Body, Sounds, Thoughts, and Emotions and Choiceless Awareness—and noticing how we are relating to the thoughts as they arise followed by inquiry, home practice review, Alternative Viewpoints exercise, the Three-Minute Breathing Space with inquiry, and discussion for taking a Three-Minute Breathing Space as a first step to developing a wider view of a triggering situation. This is followed by an exercise—Identifying Relapse Signatures—and assigning home practices.

All-Day Silent Retreat

- **Theme:** The All-Day Silent Retreat provides an extended period of mindfulness practices that supports participants' learning and investigation of a present-moment orientation.

- **Rationale:** The retreat deepens and strengthens practice, allowing for a variety of experiences and increasing awareness and tolerance.

- **Intention:** Here, the teacher's aim is to create a container for practice by offering a variety of modalities for observing the movement of experience on a continuum.

- **Practice Skills:** This will include the Body Scan, Mindful Movement, Walking Meditation, sitting meditations, Mindful Eating Practice, and an introduction to Loving-Kindness practice.

Session 7: "How Can I Best Take Care of Myself?"

- **Theme:** The theme of this session is the importance of self-care and the value of developing a plan of compassionate action for staying well.

- **Rationale:** Reviewing the skills that have been learned and identifying a tangible action plan for the prevention of depression relapse as well as continuing self-care supports and reinforces self-efficacy.

- **Intention:** The aims of this session are instilling hope, encouraging self-care and resilience, preparing for the end of the program, nurturing confidence, introducing the choice of responding with mindful action or a change in attitude as part of the action plan, reviewing relapse signatures, and normalizing the potential for relapse.

- **Practice Skills:** The teacher includes a sitting meditation—breath and body—noticing the reactions to thoughts, emotions, and body sensations, particularly as they reveal themselves in the body followed by inquiry, home practice review, the Nourishing and Depleting Exercise with discussion, exploring the Pleasure and Mastery Activities and their link to mood, the Three-Minute Breathing Space with action steps, and assigning home practices that include action plans.

Session 8: Maintaining and Extending New Learning

- **Theme:** This session offers a review of the eight weeks with a focus on which practices will be used to maintain health and well-being.

- **Rationale:** It is important to continue the practice and maintain the learning as a skill for the prevention of depression relapse and the monitoring of negative mind and mood states for self-care.

- **Intention:** This session is a time for reviewing the eight-week program and developing relapse prevention plans. The teacher's aim is for participants to be able to take the learning into the future, identify what continued practice will look like, and explore what might get in the way.

- **Practice Skills:** The session covers the Body Scan with inquiry, home practice review, reflections on the whole course, and a discussion of how to continue with practice after the program has finished. The teacher distributes a resource list and facilitates a closing exercise.

Having outlined the eight sessions and the all-day silent retreat utilizing TRIP, how can this framework assist a teacher in her teaching?

Using TRIP in Teaching

Consider the following excerpt from the discussion (inquiry) a novice teacher is having with a participant after the Body Scan Meditation Practice in class 1. As a reminder, the *Theme* for this session is awareness and automatic pilot, the *Rationale* is to develop an intentional present-moment focus based on the practice of mindfulness as this supports and helps illuminate automatic pilot and how frequently and automatically our attention moves, and the *Intention* is to recognize this automaticity, bring attention to it, and emphasize how normal it is.

Participant: My mind was all over the place. I had moments of noticing what we were doing, and then I would be thinking about something I need to do. This seemed like it was constant!

From TRIP, the teacher knows that the Theme, Rationale, and Intention for this practice is just what the participant is describing. She responds in a way that normalizes the participant's experience and lets him know that what to him may seem problematic is in fact entirely to be expected.

Teacher: In this practice, we are doing the best we can to pay attention to whatever part of the body we are on. We often notice how our minds have a different agenda! And we begin to see what our minds are up to!

The teacher has here reinforced the Theme, that of automatic pilot, as well as the Rationale for developing a present-moment focus, which supports noticing what the mind is doing.

Participant: It felt like I was fighting with my mind. It made me feel exhausted.

Teacher: It takes a lot of energy to pay attention in this way (continuing to normalize, in keeping with the intention for session 1).

The next example is taken from the second session, in week two ("Living in Our Heads"). A skilled teacher is facilitating inquiry following the Body Scan practice. Unlike the excerpt above, where the participant gave a single response to the teacher's inquiry (which is not uncommon in the first class), this participant provides the teacher with a lot of information. This often presents difficulty for a novice teacher in knowing what to focus on and how to respond. Experience in delivering MBCT and the understanding of the protocol through TRIP can help.

Participant: This was tough.

Teacher: How come?

Participant: I am going to be hopeless with this practice. I couldn't do it. My mind was all over the place. The last time I did this at home, I kept getting interrupted, and I just gave up. I'm useless at this.

The participant has given the teacher a lot of information here, including getting lost in the story and disclosure of a sense of hopelessness. The teacher's knowledge of session 2's rationale and intention helps her see that the participant is also doing a lot of noticing, even if he believes he is a *bad* meditator. She needs to slow things down and bring the participant back to the practice so the participant can see this. As a reminder, the *Theme* for this class is recognizing the persistent nature of the thinking mind and, when noticing that, returning the focus to body and breath sensations. This is because (*Rationale*) a focus on the present moment provides a useful anchor that provides a *break* from ruminative thinking and eventually offers a different perspective on the traction of negative thoughts.

Teacher: I hear you. This practice is not easy (normalizing). It is difficult to train attention in this way because we get in touch with how the attention gets pulled all over the place.

Participant: It doesn't feel good.

This is a potential trap for the teacher. A well-trained psychotherapist will want to ask about the not feeling so good. A skilled MBCT teacher will respond differently, as she will know to explore this from the perspective of supporting awareness and turning toward difficulty. Although turning toward challenging moments is not an identified Theme, Rationale, or Intention of the second class, it is a core learning throughout the program that only by being with difficulty can we alter our relationship to it, and this is reinforced in later sessions. As such, the skilled, experienced teacher will know how to embody this is in her response.

Teacher: Can you tell me a little bit more about this not feeling good? Can you remember when you first noticed it? Where in the body we were?

The teacher is working to steady the participant in the practice of the Body Scan, because anchoring oneself in the practice independently of initial feelings of disappointment and discouragement supports the possibility of acknowledging these emotions but not letting them be the only aspect of the experience. This points to an important feature of what is being taught here, namely that paying attention includes all experience regardless of its charge. This helps loosen the tendency to let an emotional field dictate and changes the nature of the relationship to negative experiences.

Participant: (reflecting) I guess at the knee. I have a lot of pain there after the surgery. I think my mind didn't want to be there.

Teacher: It is hard to pay attention to physical pain (normalizing). Could you describe those sensations?

The teacher is staying with the present moment, in the body, being curious, investigating, and exploring.

Participant: Throbbing, aching, sore. As I am saying this, I am paying attention to the knee, and it feels different.

Teacher: (embodying a key aspect of mindfulness—impermanence) That's interesting…it seems to have changed?

Participant: Yes.

In the above excerpt, we see a teacher skillfully weaving into her inquiry key aspects of session 2 using the tools of TRIP. We can recall that the Theme of this session emphasizes the persistence of thinking and its influence on how we experience something. Here, we see the teacher gently redirecting the participant back to a focus on the body, thereby broadening the lens of attention and using the body as an anchor when noticing the tendency of the mind to become immersed in disappointment and hopelessness. Indeed, by guiding the participant to include other aspects of experience, the teacher is lessening the hold of negative thinking patterns, an important rationale for this session.

And last but not least, this teacher is recognizing that in increasing awareness of aversive moments, one can begin to be with them rather than employ various methods of avoidance and distraction. In this exchange between teacher and participant, this teacher is commenting on her understanding that sensations can be identified and explored, even challenging ones. By bringing this attention to difficult moments, she is staying firmly in a present-moment orientation in her questioning and responses and, in this case, identifying how experience changes. Impermanence is not specifically identified as a core component of TRIP for this session. However, a skilled teacher will be attuned to this aspect when it arises, organically embodying its essential quality through her presence and her speech.

In Closing

Teaching MBCT (and other MBPs) by necessity involves holding many variables in mind. A novice teacher is at risk of becoming overwhelmed by the need to maintain awareness of the structure, logistics (such as time management) and content of a given session, the elements of the guidance and cognitive exercises, the nature of what is occurring in the group, and engaging in the inquiry dialogue. She also needs to remain focused on the key teaching points or themes to be elicited from participants. Given the potentially overwhelming nature of the work for the teacher, using TRIP can enhance the ability to stay on track. For the more experienced teacher, TRIP acts as a reminder of important elements within each session that are needed to support the delivery of the protocol.

In describing TRIP, we emphasize that as a tool, it is intended to serve as a guide for exploration rather than a rigid set of rules. Ultimately, the teacher will need to find her own words to describe the components of TRIP related to each session, without losing their intent, to best use this framework. We note, however, that TRIP has been field-tested over several years in MBCT and MBSR professional training programs. And ultimately, TRIP is just another way of understanding what has always been at the heart of the MBCT protocol.

Once the elements of TRIP become embedded in your teaching, you are free to focus on being open and present, both leading and moving with the flow of the group to fulfill the intentions of the program: to decrease the suffering of your participants.

Having outlined the MBCT protocol using TRIP, in the next chapter, we see that the protocol is just one of the agents of change that inform a teacher's facilitation of the program. Understanding these agents along with TRIP, and knowing how to see and leverage them, gives the MBCT teacher a new degree of fluidity in helping participants train the mind, regulate mood, and ease the suffering depression can cause.

Chapter 2

The Five Agents of Change

At its most dynamic, teaching MBCT requires a way of structuring one's teaching and developing a set of skills that draw upon a teacher's embodiment of mindfulness. When an MBCT teacher embodies attitudinal characteristics embedded in the practices of mindfulness and understands aspects of Buddhist psychology, the heart of this program comes alive. This is one of the significant characteristics of teaching mindfulness-based programs (MBPs), such as MBCT, and one that separates it from other treatment interventions.

There are five agents that we see as foundational for teaching the MBCT program. They are *the protocol of the intervention* (which we explored in the previous chapter), *the mindfulness-based practices, individual learning, group process,* and *the embodied mindful presence of the teacher.* At times, an MBCT teacher will be concentrating on one of them as he teaches, at other times, he will be working with several of them concurrently. Ultimately, it is in recognizing these forces as they emerge in sessions and being able to leverage them that a teacher is adding further depth to the development of proficient teaching skills.

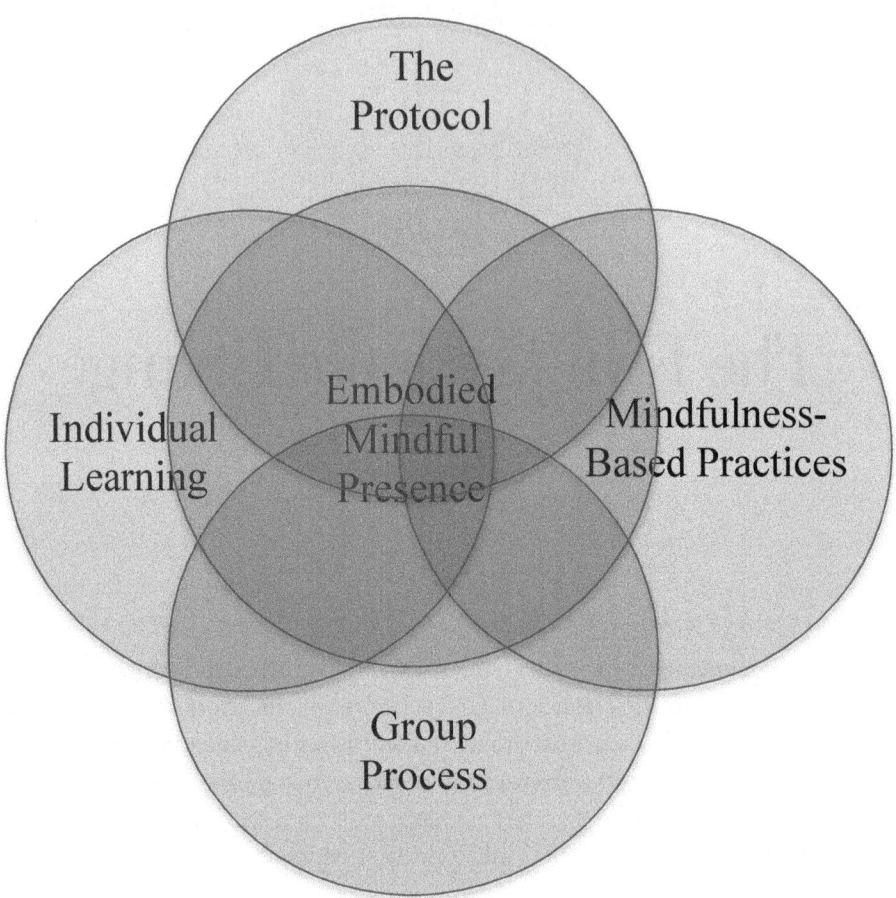

The five agents of change

The Protocol

The protocol—summarized in chapter 1 and detailed in full in *Mindfulness-Based Cognitive Therapy for Depression* (Segal et al., 2013)—provides the MBCT teacher with the curriculum for each of the eight sessions, including the all-day silent retreat, and lays out instruction for the various mindfulness-based practices and the cognitive exercises. Each session builds on the previous one, thus providing a modular approach to skill building. As an agent of change, it is important the MBCT teacher maintains fidelity to and teaches from the protocol, as this will support adherence, participant outcomes, and prevent drift. Knowledge of TRIP—the Themes, Rationale, Intentions, and Practice skills embedded in each session—can increase a teacher's ability to maintain fidelity to the protocol even in the therapy space, which can be unpredictable. In chapters to come, we'll work to apply TRIP to individual practices and exercises within the protocol as well, so teachers continue to understand the knowledge, skills, and values they are delivering to clients.

Mindfulness-Based Practices

The MBCT protocol provides the structure for teaching mindfulness through formal meditation practices, which are undertaken sitting or lying down, and includes mindful movement practices based on basic yoga poses and walking. These practices function as an agent of change because they train attention, increase body awareness, reduce experiential avoidance, expand views, and shift the relationship to experience. We describe this in more detail in chapter 3 and in the appendices, where we have included scripts for a number of the practices.

The MBCT program also employs "informal" meditation practices, which involve being mindful of everyday activities or experiences in daily life. Informal practices offer participants the opportunity to bring the practice of mindfulness to routine activities of daily living that are often completed on automatic pilot (with very little attention paid to what one is doing). A good example of this is washing the dishes or taking out the garbage. Informal practices inform participants of the utility and portability of mindfulness supporting its generalizability into everyday activities. The discipline of the formal practices and the real-world application of the informal practices interact with each other, reinforcing important foundations and skill building for training the mind and regulating mood.

By bringing an intentional awareness and directed focus of attention to the mundane tasks of life, participants learn to check in with what is present in the experiential field, including their emotional states and thinking patterns. They also discover that in attending in this way, the ordinary becomes extraordinary. Repeatedly bringing awareness to everyday activities helps identify negative mind and mood states and negative thought patterns early on before they have gained traction. Instead of avoiding these states (a much more typical response), participants are encouraged to acknowledge them when they are present. Supporting this discernment is an important step toward prevention and self-care. Included in this attention to the everyday, an MBCT teacher will encourage participants to attend to sensations of breathing or body from time to time throughout the day as another practice that provides a way to return to the present moment.

Individual Learning

The third agent of change is individual learning built on the premise that adults learn in different ways and through different means. Some learn visually, others auditorily, and some kinesthetically. If an MBCT teacher incorporates this understanding into his teaching, he will be enhancing the learning of his participants by offering a variety of teaching modalities. Additionally, recognizing that individuals in the group will not be learning the same things at the same time will be an important consideration.

Interestingly, the predominant theories of adult learning fit nicely within the framework of TRIP. These theories suggest that adults learn best when their learning is located within a context (Theme), they understand why they are learning what they are learning (Rationale), they understand the aim of what they are learning (Intention), and they are able to apply and experiment with it on an individual basis, at their own pace (Practice Skills). In addition, the learning needs to be acquired through an experiential process within a coherent model (the protocol of MBCT), and lastly, the timing of the program should be a good "fit" with their other responsibilities.

Malcolm Knowles (1988), an American adult educator, pioneered the principle that adult learning is a process of self-directed investigation that is different from how children learn. He identified that as a person matures, the learning becomes more self-directed and draws on life experiences. With maturity comes a readiness to learn, originating largely from an internal stimulus that is directed toward problem solving. The MBCT program provides many opportunities for self-direction and experiential learning.

Donald Schön (1983, 1987) maintained that solving problems is not solely a question of intellectual knowledge. He asserted that learning is promoted by being a *reflective practitioner* and that through feedback acquired from direct experience, an adult learner continually expands her repertoire of skills. In the MBCT program, the learning is promoted by inquiry, encouraging participants to reflect on the direct experiences resulting from practicing mindfulness. Participants are guided to *become* reflective practitioners. An important condition for the reflective practitioner is that the experience alone is not enough. The *feedback* is what solidifies the knowledge. Specific training is needed for the investigation of, reflection on, and description of experience. In the MBCT program, an instructor teaches a specific attentional training (mindfulness) that encourages the investigation of sensations (breath, body, thoughts, emotions, and behaviors) and uses inquiry to help participants understand the insights that direct experience of such sensations can allow.

David Kolb (2014) discusses the processes of adult learning using a cyclical model that describes four elements: *concrete experience* where the adult learner is experiencing an activity and seeing its effect, *reflective observation* where the learner is reflecting on the experience, *abstract conceptualization* where learning is then used to extrapolate a theory or template of what has been experienced, and finally, *actively experimenting,* or testing out the learning in applied settings. This maps well onto the process that unfolds in MBCT in which participants experience a practice, reflect on it through inquiry, think about its integration, and experiment with it through applying the learning to everyday life. Kolb's theory and its relevance to MBCT are explored further in chapter 5, in which we'll explore how the teacher can recognize these processes in-session and drive them forward.

How do these general theories of adult learning apply to teaching MBCT? First, we know that in the MBCT program, learning is rooted in an experiential, self-directed, and reflective model. Second, we know that the practice of mindfulness is also a self-directed intentional engagement that trains attention to become aware of our relationship to internal experience (thoughts, emotions, body sensations) and to the outer environment. We also know that the MBCT program is modular in its learning trajectory, emphasizing skill acquisition, and that it allows for independent learning, regardless of the theme of the session. Moreover, the teacher encourages the investigation and usefulness of what is being learned, supporting the application of these skills to the intention of the program, namely, working with depression and maintaining well-being.

What does this look like in the class setting? In the following example, a teacher and his group are discussing the previous week's home assignments. A participant is talking about her experience of home practice.

Participant 1: It's been a tough week. The kids and my wife have all been sick. The baby has been particularly ill. To give my wife a break, I looked after the baby for a couple of nights, so when he woke up coughing and crying, I got up. But, wow, am I tired.

Teacher: I am so sorry to hear about your family being sick. How are you doing?

Participant 1: Okay, I guess. The home assignments had to take a back burner. I just didn't have the time. I feel bad about this and got down on myself.

Teacher: Well, it's tough enough to find the time to practice, let alone when you have something like sickness in the family to deal with along with all your other responsibilities. How's the family doing now?

Participant 1: Better.

Teacher: That's good news. I am happy to hear this. I am wondering how getting "down on yourself" showed up?

Participant 1: Usual stuff: Wondering how I am going to cope. Worry, tired.

Teacher: Were these thoughts? Emotions?

Participant 1: Both.

Teacher: So, you were aware of thoughts and emotions?

Participant 1: Um… Yup.

Teacher: Any body sensations?

Participant 1: Tightness, agitation.

Teacher: Anything else?

Participant 1: Well, I do remember thinking, as I was walking up and down with the baby in my arms, trying to soothe him, that this would be good time to do a walking meditation! So, I did a few rounds.

Teacher: How did that work out?

Participant 1: Well, the baby stopped crying, which made me feel better!

Teacher: That's good. And how about you?

Participant 1: Well, I think it was good to focus on my body holding the baby. It sort of settled me, and I think this thing we talked about last week about being with the unpleasant sort of kicked in too. I thought, *This is not fun, but here I am. It's 2:00 a.m., and the baby's not going anywhere and I'm not, so here we are.*

Teacher: So, this is using the practice. Worry, anxiety, and agitation show up, and you thought about doing some walking meditation. That's great!

Participant 1: That counts?

Teacher: Absolutely.

Here, we see the realistic nature of life making its presence known. The teacher is understanding and sympathetic. His questioning captures the essence of the experience from the mindfulness perspective (awareness of thoughts, emotions, and body sensations) and importantly allows the participant to reveal a moment of using what had been worked with in class and its incorporation into a real-life situation. This is an important teaching for this participant, in that it demonstrates and reinforces her individual learning, and for the group to hear, because it demonstrates the practicality and utility of using a mindfulness practice in a difficult experience (group learning). In addition, this exchange is useful, as it illustrates noticing the full range of a trying situation without becoming fixated on thinking or negative affect.

The MBCT teacher is further promoting individual learning that has less to do with a right way and more to do with encouraging curiosity and reflection. This will mean that he is operating more as a guide than from the traditional role of teacher. By directing participants to examine what is being noticed in their experience, he is facilitating their reflective capacity rather than relying on him to have the answers.

Furthermore, a teacher needs to be flexible in his response to each participant and sensitive to what may be most helpful in that moment rather than rigidly adhering to a teaching theme or agenda. For example, if a participant, in reflecting on a practice that just occurred, starts to talk about what happened during the past week, she will be guided back to speaking to her direct experience. Teaching is collaborative, emphasizing interest in what is being noticed and conveying an openness, appreciation, and respect. Making the learning pertinent to the prevention of depression relapse, other difficult states, and to everyday life (an important aspect for adult learning) is an additional potent teaching skill applied to individual learning.

Group Process

Inherent in the MBCT program is a teacher's ability to not only attend to individual learning but also to facilitate the group process. Group process is another dynamic and complex agent of change. In this context, a group can be defined as a collection of people coming together with a defined area of interest or agreement about a goal to be accomplished. Group dynamics will vary depending on how the group has been formed, its size, members, the understanding of the work to be done, and how clearly the intention and rationale for the program is described. For MBCT, the shared experience is mental and emotional distress secondary to a mental health condition, such as depression, and the desire to prevent its relapse.

Considering the sensitivity of such experience, the importance of providing a safe learning container cannot be emphasized enough. In the first two sessions, establishing group norms and appropriate boundaries and attending to safety issues and confidentiality—with reminders in the other classes as needed—are essential for supporting learning.

In addition, participants will need to trust you, as the teacher, to be able to work wisely and safely with difficult mind and mood states. Many of the participants who come to this course will have experienced a sense of isolation and loneliness and of being different from "regular" people. This was poignantly expressed by a participant who said, "I just have a different brain. It doesn't work as well as other people's." It is still true that in many societies, someone who has suffered from depression can feel ostracized and be stigmatized. This sense of isolation can contribute to feelings of not being understood and ultimately to preventing people from reaching out for help and support. Finding themselves in a group with others who have also experienced a mood disorder is comforting and lessens the feelings associated with being an outsider. It is easier to identify with another who has also had mental health problems or chronic illness.

Importantly, the process by which the group goes through MBCT's practices and inquiry together supports a shared humanity that lessens an individually held belief system about who one is. Hearing from others who have similar experiences lessens the view that one is alone or unusual. How others are relating to the presented teaching focus is valuable and helps an individual to disengage from the idea of a fixed self that has only one narrow narrative (for example, "I am worthless"). It is our experience that in feedback given at the end of the course, participants will often say that one of the most helpful things was to be in a room with others with similar experiences.

This aspect of group learning is leveraged as early as the first session. This is illustrated when the teacher opens this session by introducing himself (briefly) and then goes on to give an overview of the MBCT program, and set group norms and safety parameters. The participants are then given the opportunity to introduce themselves to each other. During this process, they are paired with another participant and are asked to address the following questions: what brought them to this eight-week program and what they hope to gain from the experience. (In instructing the class to pair up, the teacher is careful to voice that for some people, talking in a group can be anxiety provoking, but, even if that is the case, to at least introduce themselves.) After some time working in dyads, the teacher reconvenes the larger group and conversation continues. The teacher invites all the group participants to share what they found out in their dyads, which often reveals potent commonalities in their experiences. Participants learn that while their depression feels isolating and can be isolating, there are others with similar histories.

While managing time constraints is a tension for all MBCT teachers, as each session has several important topics to cover, it is vital that a teacher does not shortchange this discussion at the beginning of the first session, as it begins to reduce the sense of isolation and opens the group-sharing process.

Here is a scenario from the introductions in session 1 that further illustrates the poignancy of being in a group of others who have experienced depression and anxiety and other forms of mental distress. (Names have been changed to protect participant privacy.)

Participant 1: Hello everyone. My name is Allan. I'm not sure why I am here. My physician referred me. I have been depressed most of my life. I guess I am desperate. It was helpful to hear about the MBCT program in the orientation. I have some doubts about the mindfulness pieces. But I am willing to have a go.

Teacher: Thank you, Allan.

Participant 2: My name is Jane. I am really hoping this program is going to be helpful. I have had lots of therapy, which was sort of helpful. I am tired of not feeling like other folks. Kind of sad a lot of the time. Sometimes I wake up, and I don't want to get up. But then I do because I must go to work.

Teacher: Thanks, Jane.

Participant 3: I'm Mary. I've heard a lot about mindfulness. I'm curious if it will be helpful. I have been hospitalized for depression. I get anxious easily.

	My mental health therapist thought this program could be helpful. So here I am.
Teacher:	Thanks, Mary.
Participant 4:	I don't think I have been with other people like this… I mean, who have been depressed. It's hard to explain depression to others who have not had it. I was depressed five months ago. I couldn't get out of bed. My husband was really worried, which made me feel worse. He kept telling me to get out of bed and move around and I would feel better. But I had no energy.
Teacher:	(smiles and gently asks) And your name?
Participant 4:	Oh, Angie. And I am happy to be here.
Teacher:	Thanks, Angie.
Participant 5:	I'm Kate. I first got depressed when I was in college. Medication has been helpful. I want to start a family but don't want to be on meds when I am pregnant. I am hoping the MBCT program will let me come off the meds so that I can start trying for a baby. It was great to chat with Lucy in our pair. We have a lot in common.
Teacher:	Thank you, Kate.
Participant 6:	Hi, I'm Lucy. It was so good to chat with Kate. We found out that we live in the same neighborhood. It's good to share about having had depression. Mostly mine shows up as lots of anxiety. I am hoping this program will help me be less anxious.
Teacher:	Welcome, Lucy.
Participant 7:	Hello. I'm George. It feels good to hear from others. I've had depression and chronic pain for many years. I hope we have more opportunities to share. I don't talk to others about how hard it has been. I hope all this mindfulness stuff I am hearing about will help me.
Teacher:	Hi, George.

From these introductions, one of the major themes that is being highlighted is that depression is not a singular, isolated experience. Hearing from others in the group loosens the rigidity of beliefs about the self that coalesce around the view "I am depressed" because they are hearing a range of descriptions about how others have experienced depression, which will most likely be more similar to than different from their own experience.

Another major learning that is dependent on group process is how one's appraisals, context, and state affect perception and interpretation of events. Learning that thoughts are not necessarily facts and that one is not one's depression is more easily identified and accepted in the group setting. One such exercise based on cognitive behavior therapy principles that demonstrates this is the Walking Down the Street exercise taught in session 2 ("Living in Our Heads") in which responses to an ambiguous situation are explored. Participants are presented with a specific scenario: You are walking down a street when you see someone you know coming toward you on the opposite side. You wave, but the person walks on by without acknowledging you. Participants are asked to write down their responses to this. The reactions are then shared in the group. The resulting, often lively, discussion highlights a range of responses from humorous to highly revealing. An MBCT teacher's task will be to use the group to illustrate several important themes.

- First, we are frequently unaware of how we interpret a situation, invariably jumping to conclusions and believing these conclusions are facts.

- Additionally, unidentified thinking patterns exert significant influence on how we come to believe the truth of what is occurring.

- Furthermore, the exercise illustrates the range of differing interpretations suggesting that the "truth of the moment" is highly subjective and commonly personalized.

- Seeing that there is a range of interpretations from the group members lessens the hold of any one interpretation and the recognition that reality is constructed.

Crucially, these learning points are generated by the group and, therefore, have more resonance than if "taught" didactically. Another crucial aspect of learning in the MBCT program that is introduced in this exercise is the insight that the way we feel about something is frequently determined through the meaning we ascribe to a situation. What we often fail to recognize is the thought(s) that links the two and the assumption that our thoughts are true. In depression and anxiety, attending to thoughts is crucial because of their influence on low mood. Indeed, seeing from others in the group that there is a range of possible interpretations lessens the degree of believability of any particular interpretation. This plants the seed that thoughts are not necessarily facts.

Furthermore, the discussion reveals that not only do the interpretations vary from person to person but they are subject to the mood we bring to the situation. This revelation is highlighted by the MBCT teacher asking what might happen to the believability of an interpretation when one is depressed. The overwhelming response is that the held view would be fixed and negative. This question is asked to highlight the influence depression has on what is being believed. Bringing awareness to this is important for participants, as it highlights how depression will influence the adhesion and rigidity of mood-congruent thoughts as well as how they get interpreted.

Embodied Mindful Presence

We have discussed four agents of change, and while they are important, it is our view that embodied mindful presence of the teacher is the key that will influence how all the other agents will be experienced by the participants, for without this active and potent agent, teaching becomes formulaic, without heart.

We should pause here a moment and ask, What constitutes the characteristics of embodiment? Can they be identified? And how do we understand the practice of embodying mindfulness using this rather esoteric description of an embodied mindful presence?

In chapters 6 and 7, we elaborate further on this subject. For our purpose here, we see the following qualities to be representative of embodying mindfulness. A teacher will do his best to represent and bring to his teaching an experiential and working knowledge of the attitudinal foundations of mindfulness—which are patience, trust, beginner's mind, nonjudging, acceptance, nonstriving, and letting go, as well as a sense of curiosity about and compassion for the vicissitudes experience—as well as the insights from Buddhist psychology that inform MBCT's approach to suffering: that experience is impersonal, even though we personalize it; that there is no guarantee life should be perfect and free from pain; that impermanence is a fact of life; and that this applies to both our circumstances and the mind and mood states we experience. This knowledge is fundamental, as it is the catalyst for the translation of the traditional form of the practice into its contemporary form, and that to teach MBCT is a modern-day extension of mindfulness practice. From this discernment, the teacher recognizes the importance of facilitating a present-moment (mindful) orientation in his instructional focus and during the process of inquiry. He appreciates and can communicate the rationale for this focus, encouraging a moment-by-moment experiential versus analytical mode of learning. This entails the skill of noticing and describing various sensations, by which we mean body sensations as well as thoughts and emotions, and using these to support emotional and cognitive resilience. As well as these characteristics, he will model and encourage in his participants an open, receptive attitude to all experiences and an approach that provides an environment of kindness and compassion, particularly when working with difficult moments. We believe the richness of the teaching lies in this ability of an instructor to embody these qualities.

Implementing the Agents of Change

So, what does employing the agents of change look like in a session? As a way of illustrating this, we offer two scenarios. The first example is from session 3 ("Gathering the Scattered Mind") and consists of inquiry with several participants about their experience of the movement practices based on some gentle yoga poses, followed by a walking meditation practice. The teacher is interested in having as many of the participants reflect on how the practice was experienced (using individual learning with group processing).

Participant 1: It felt so good to move.

Teacher: In what way?

Participant 1: Just to move my body. It's been a long time.

Participant 2: I was surprised that I could do some of the poses and that it felt good.

Participant 3: I liked the way we had a focus on the breath. It made me realize I was holding my breath at times.

Teacher: Did you notice holding your breath at any one time?

Participant 3: I think when I wasn't focused on my body.

Teacher: Do you have a sense of what you were focused on?

Participant 3: Thinking! (laughs) At least I am noticing when I go off into thinking.

Participant 4: It felt good to focus on the body, even though I noticed my attention wasn't always on the body. I was thinking, too, at times.

Participant 5: I was feeling a little anxious this evening when we first started, but now I feel differently. I guess moving helps to settle the body. Anyway, I do feel better.

Participant 6: I realized how stiff I am and really beat up on myself.

Teacher: We've heard from several of you about what showed up in this practice. It felt good to move, some surprises, noticing holding the breath at times, some pleasant and unpleasant experiences, a shift in mood, and good old thinking shows up! (laughter from the group) Isn't it interesting how many different reactions there can be from the same practice?

In the above excerpt, the teacher's response at the end summarizes individual reflections, not preferencing one experience over another. In this way, he is supporting individual learning, and through acknowledging the variety of responses, he is modeling the acceptance of all experience.

The next extract is taken from a seasoned MBCT teacher who has just led a discussion on the territory of depression in session 4 ("Recognizing Aversion"). Participants have been talking about the symptoms of depression as identified by the *DSM-5* and have been directed to look at a list of common negative thoughts that are prevalent in depression. As a result, the mood of the group is low. The participants are facing what they have experienced in the past, and this raises sadness and anxiety.

Participant 1: It doesn't feel good to look at this. I mean, why do we have to?

This is a difficult question for a teacher to address. A novice teacher will tend to want to answer the question and explain why. If this is done, the participant is taken away from what she is actually feeling and experiencing and is moved into analyzing the "why," grappling with the content of depression. This doesn't allow the teacher to normalize the feelings of aversion or explore them.

Teacher: It's not easy to face depression. As you look at the list of symptoms and the negative thoughts, might I ask what you are you noticing…thoughts, emotions, body sensations?

This elicits a present-moment orientation along with turning toward the discomfort, an opportunity for individual as well as group learning through exposure. The teacher is embodying a mindful presence that has less to do with fixing or moving away from the unpleasant but more about approaching, staying with, and investigating it. His presence is a steadying influence in directing what is being noticed within the experiential field of thoughts, body sensations, and emotions.

Participant: My body is tense, and I have all these thoughts about what if I make myself depressed by looking at this?

Teacher: Is there a place in the body where you are noticing the tension?

Participant: My chest and my shoulders.

Teacher: Could you name those sensations of tension?

Participant: Tight, sore, achy…

Teacher: Would it be possible to bring a sense of the breath to these areas, exploring them?

(The participant sits up and takes a few breaths; shoulders release.)

In this excerpt, the teacher does not address the content of the teaching module of the moment (the territory of depression) directly but stays with the exploration of this participant's worry and concern. Indirectly, yet importantly, he is embodying a crucial theme of the program—that of turning toward and staying with challenging moments and investigating them through sensations in the body. Part of embodiment is demonstrating that it is possible to safely endure and move through difficulty. This is an important teaching moment for an individual—and for the group, as it allows the experience of one group member to inform the others. Here, the teacher's embodied mindful presence automatically brings two other agents, individual learning and group process, to life—and the agents of the practices and the protocol are present as well.

In Closing

In this chapter, we have considered five agents of change: the protocol, the mindfulness practices, individual learning, and group process, along with the mindful presence and embodiment of the teacher. By understanding their influence and working with them, a teacher adds depth to his teaching and enhances his skill set. Teaching MBCT thus becomes an organic practice.

While we believe embodiment is the most essential component for delivering the program, it does take time to develop; it is based on experience gained from teaching the MBCT program, attending MBCT trainings, a commitment to a personal mindfulness practice, mentorship by a skilled MBCT teacher, and ongoing professional development. However, during the period of a teacher's growth, he can be reassured that the learning of his participants and his teaching of the MBCT program will be supported by the other four agents of change.

Now that we have established TRIP and the five agents of change, we will examine, in part 2, how these constructs can help teachers build their skills and their confidence in teaching specific practices and exercises, guiding MBCT groups through the therapy, and leading participants through the experiential, reflective process by which participants learn to stabilize and strengthen their mindful attention and awareness and turn toward difficult and challenging states of mind and mood.

PART 2
Skill-Building
Gaining Confidence

Chapter 3

Practices and Exercises: Using TRIP and the Five Agents of Change

Our intention in this chapter is to use the framework of TRIP (Themes, Rationales, Intentions, Practice Skills) and the five agents of change to orient, explore, and deepen your understanding of the essential elements of the mindfulness-based practices and cognitive exercises (referred to collectively as the "practices" wherever possible) that are embedded in each of the eight sessions of the MBCT program. TRIP can be applied not only to each session, as we outlined in the previous chapter, but also to the individual exercises and practices within each session. Our hope is that this chapter will serve as a useful tool for both novice and experienced teachers of MBCT. Scripts for many of the practices can be found in the appendix.

TRIP as Applied to the Practices and Exercises

As a reminder, the *Themes* (the message, subject, and context), the *Rationale* (why we are doing what we are doing), the *Intentions* (what we are doing and its aim), and the *Practice Skills* (how to elicit or convey inherent key teachings) allow a teacher to more easily identify what is needed in any given moment as she guides participants through MBCT. Teachers tend to deliver in a didactic manner the knowledge, values, skills, and competencies they are trying to pass on. In MBCT, much of our teaching is *elicited or implied,* and this is supported by TRIP.

The teachers' *Practice Skills* are those that enhance and facilitate the skills participants are learning. This means the teacher is acquiring and using specific skills so the participants can more readily develop theirs. Not surprisingly, at times, there is commonality between them, but below, we distinguish between the two.

In this chapter, we use TRIP to explore selected practices and cognitive exercises. Keep in mind that TRIP is generalizable to all the practices. We have chosen those we think most exemplify what we are trying to illustrate.

The Raisin Practice

The practice skills in session 1 begin with the Raisin Practice as soon as the teacher hands the raisins out. She instructs the participants to hold this "object," or raisin, in their palm and invites them to, with a beginner's mind, bring attention to it using the sense of sight, exploring its various qualities. Using periods of silence to assist participants in their personal investigation, she guides them systematically and slowly around the senses of touch, hearing, smelling, and tasting before they finally chew and swallow the raisin. From time to time during the practice, she will remind the group to notice if attention has been pulled away from direct experience into thinking, with a gentle reminder to return to the task at hand, which is the investigation of a raisin.

Theme: Attending to experience and learning about automatic pilot through the senses

Rationale: To develop mindful attention and awareness using an external, accessible, and familiar object and activity

Intentions:

1. Cultivating direct experience using the senses

2. Directing attention sequentially through each of the senses

3. Beginning to develop an awareness of the tendency to interrupt direct experience with thinking, for example through comparison, evaluation, preference, associations, images, memories, explanations, or conclusions

Practice Skills: For the Teacher

1. As with all the practices, she balances verbal guidance with her own immersion in the practice (embodied mindful presence) while monitoring participants for auditory and visual cues that relate to how they are experiencing the practice.

2. Clearly and systematically, she directs the group's attention to the individual senses in the following order: seeing, touching, hearing, smelling, tracing the raisin along the lips as a prelude to taste, and finally, tasting, chewing, and swallowing.

3. The language of guidance is invitational, although directive, and entails the use of present participles (-*ing* verbs) and a minimal use of questions. This enhances the ability of the teacher and her participants to stay in the experiential flow of the practice versus engaging in an internal cognitive dialogue. There is also little use of personal and possessive pronouns *(you, yours, yourself)* to emphasize the impersonal nature of experience. Examples of using present participles during guidance include *bringing attention to…, noticing qualities of…, attending to sound…, examining texture…, moving the arm…*

4. Various qualities of the raisin are described to assist the group in the development of a common experiential vocabulary and enhanced sensorial awareness: color, shape, transparency, opacity, texture, edges, roughness, smoothness, ridges, weight, soft, hard, sound, aroma, saliva, flavor. *And of course, if there is no sensation, noticing that!*

5. The teacher provides the conditions that allow participants to bring attention to whatever they are experiencing. Delivery of the guidance is measured and by necessity includes periods of silence. Too much speaking by the teacher results in participants mostly attending to the teacher's voice rather than to whatever is arising for them.

6. Participants are assisted in developing attention regulation by the teacher's references to the noticing of "the pulling of attention" or "wandering mind" that highlights the habitual tendency of attention to move to thoughts, emotions, sensations, or impulses. She then invites them to return their focus to the sense being explored.

Teacher: What did you notice about the raisin?

Participant: When I looked at it, it looked like mouse poop, and I couldn't eat it because it was disgusting.

Teacher: Oh, so you had a thought, an association, along with an emotion of disgust? What qualities about the raisin brought that association and emotion to mind?

Participant: It was brown, small, and wrinkled…

Teacher: Thank you. What did other people notice?

7. The teacher aims to enhance participants' experiential reflective capacity by discussing the practice immediately after it ends. This is the inquiry process, which we'll discuss in detail later in this book.

Practice Skills: For the Participant

1. To train the placing, investigating, and shifting or releasing of attention using the senses as a vehicle

2. To explore and articulate direct experience

3. To increase the noticing of experience and step out of doing mode

4. To notice how direct experience is disrupted by thinking and other pulls of attention

Body Scan Meditation Practice

The Body Scan is the first formal meditation practice taught in MBCT. Participants are asked to get into a comfortable posture, lying on their backs or sitting, and instructed that sleepiness may come, but that this is not the purpose of the Body Scan. The teacher will also suggest, depending upon the constituency of the group, that participants with a history of trauma, dissociation, or intense anxiety may wish to cover themselves with a blanket (if lying on the back elicits too much vulnerability), and, should they become too distressed, are free to open their eyes, sit up, or let go of the practice and either attend to the breath or the soles of the feet as acts of self-care. The teacher guides participants in bringing attention to the entire body and its points of contact. She initially directs participants to attend to the sensations of breathing. After a few minutes, she assists them in focusing their attention, beginning at the feet (or head) and moving attention in a systematic order around the body to investigate sensations as they arrive, persist, and pass.

The Body Scan is thirty-five to forty minutes in length. Novice teachers and participants often ask why it's this long, because they perceive it as boring, sleep inducing, agitating, or pointless. Again, keeping the framework of TRIP in mind can help the teacher elucidate the primary Theme, Rationale, Intentions, and Practice Skills as she introduces and conducts the practice, helping answer this frequently asked question along the way.

Theme: Becoming aware of and exploring sensations in the body

Rationale: To identify bodily sensation as source of information and an anchor for attention

Intentions:

1. Reinforcing attentional training and mindful awareness through systematically and sequentially directing attention to different parts of the body, exploring what is present (body sensations), and then shifting to the next part (a parallel process for dealing with future difficult mind and mood states)

2. Training attention to and cultivating awareness of *all* experience, whether pleasant, unpleasant, or neutral

3. Recognizing and becoming familiar with obstacles, resistance, and reactivity to present-moment experience using the body—this is the beginning of meta-awareness, to be developed and generalized to dealing with distress during difficult states

4. Reinforcing that obstacles that may arise, including agitation, restlessness, frustration, rage, doubt: "Is this for me?", wanting or not wanting (wanting things to be other than they are), experiences, people, things, sleepiness, boredom, impatience

Practice Skills: For the Teacher

1. The teacher guides the group to develop a vocabulary of the qualities of sensations. The guidance and inquiry emphasize the participants' use of sensorial language to later be able to link thinking, emotion, and impulses or behavior to the body. Body sensations may include numbness, tingling, pressure, tension, warmth, coolness, moisture, heavy, light, coming and going of sensation, and if there's no sensation, noticing that!

2. Participants are trained in placing, releasing, and sifting their attention while directing it in an organized manner from one end of the body to the other.

3. The teacher guides with equanimity and calm, conveying implicitly that no experience is to be privileged over another. The duration of the practice allows for a variety of experiences to emerge for the participant: the wanted, the unwanted, and the neutral, to which we are usually indifferent. This disrupts participants' common expectations that the body scan is for relaxation or "to feel less stress." Participants are asked to stay with difficult experience or to employ self-care. This introduces the skill of discerning what is needed in any given moment.

4. In inquiry, the teacher elicits from participants the naming of various bodily sensations, modeling openness and curiosity to all experience. Participants' reactions to this practice and the teacher's inquiry into them begin to bring into awareness what happens when we are faced with what we do and don't like—sensations we like, we often want more of, and those we don't, we frequently try to avoid.

Practice Skills: For the Participant

1. To experience and describe body sensations and the variety of mind and mood states that may arise in this long practice

2. To reinforce and expand an intentional focus on the body

3. The develop the skill of tracking experience, including the pull of attention away from the intended object of focus

Awareness of Breathing and Challenging Physical Sensations Meditation Practice

In session 3, the teacher guides participants in a sitting meditation practice with instructions about how to skillfully work with challenging sensations. She first brings attention to posture while sitting, assisting them to embody a state of wakefulness and ease as best they can. She guides the group in the practice of bringing a focus to the physical sensations of breathing in a chosen area of the body: nostrils, chest, or abdomen. After approximately ten minutes, participants are invited to bring an open and receptive attention to the entire body and to sensations as they present themselves. They are then asked to notice and explore any intense physical sensations that may be present, engaging in self-care if required (for example, by changing position), and then returning to their original posture.

Theme: Anchoring to and being with sensations of breath and body, turning toward and exploring challenging physical sensations

Rationale: To use the sensations of breathing and other bodily phenomena to provide a present-moment focus and alternative vantage point (other than the voice in our heads) from which we can explore difficulty—the body will alert us to what is salient or challenging

Intentions:

1. Cultivating and supporting a focus of attention on the sensations of breathing and body

2. Reducing experiential avoidance and decreasing habitual reactivity by using challenging physical sensations to acclimatize to this process

Practice Skills: For the Teacher

1. The teacher directs participants to focus on sensations of breathing where they are felt most prominently in the body, bringing an investigative curiosity to each new breath as it comes and goes.

2. The teacher will normalize the movement of attention, reminding participants that in noticing this, they have the capacity to choose to return attention back to the breath or body without judgment or struggle. Mindfulness is equally about waking up to the movement of attention as it is to a sustained concentration on one object of focus.

3. During the guidance, participants are directed to expand their attention to the entire body to explore sensations as they arise and pass away.

4. When encountering challenging physical sensations, participants are invited to explore them with an investigative curiosity, using the breath as a support, and offered the choice, if necessary, of intentionally shifting position and (if and when ready) returning to the original posture. Through exposure, this is a means of training distress tolerance and skillful responses to difficulty versus automatic reactivity or avoidance.

5. In inquiry—the contemplative dialogue that follows this and every practice in MBCT—the teacher will assist participants in describing the experience of breath in the body, bodily sensations, how they responded to the instructions to bring attention to intense physical sensations, and the movement of attention from moment to moment. Through her questions and reflections, the teacher guides the group in investigating the experience. When dealing with intense sensations, this is particularly relevant and highlights what happens when we turn toward and explore difficulty versus when we avoid.

Practice Skills: For the Participant

1. To develop primary attention on salient sensations of breathing and body

2. To cultivate awareness of the movement of attention away from the chosen focus and deliberately returning to it with equanimity and kindness

3. To approach and investigate the qualities of intense physical sensations as a support for being with, instead of turning away from, difficulty

4. To bring into awareness when self-care is needed to address difficulty

Mindful Movement Practice

In session 3, the teacher guides participants through a series of yoga postures at a pace that allows them to attend to the body and what it reveals while in motion. She reminds them to attend to sensations during the practice and to notice thoughts when they arise and then return to a focus on body.

Human beings are meant to move. Yet, so often we are sedentary, ignoring and diminishing the importance of body in favor of thinking. Mindful movement reminds us that we have a body, and it comes with us wherever we go. Depression, a state of hypo-arousal, often results in less activity, while anxiety, a state of hyper-arousal, may manifest through increased movement. The body in motion or stillness provides us with signals that can be significant in the management of depression and anxiety.

Movement can be an accessible and tangible practice for participants. However, it may spontaneously activate difficult emotions through comparative and judgmental thinking when we are faced with physical limitations. The teacher will need to be aware of this and respond with practice skills such as normalizing aversive experiences that participants might share.

Theme: Bringing awareness to, and being with, the body in motion

Rationale: To use the body in motion as another focus of present-moment attention—participants are offered an additional platform for working with the mind, as the tendency to judge, compare, make assumptions, and draw conclusions is common during this practice

Intentions:

1. Cultivating attention to the moving body

2. Bringing awareness to the transition from one posture to another to assist in the development of mindfulness of every moment

3. Heightening attention to bodily sensations that are often ignored, unnoticed, or overridden to increase the ability to register various mind and mood states

Practice Skills: For the Teacher

1. The teacher instructs participants to attend to the sensations of the body, staying comfortably within their limits, engaging in self-care when needed.

2. The teacher conveys that mindful movement is not a competition or an attempt to build a better body but is another focus for attention—discouraging a focus on

a particular goal or result by privileging the principle of attention to experience. Movement occurs with the only goal being attending to experience as it is. Participants are reminded that they may notice thoughts related to achievement, comparisons with others, or self-judgment arising, and that if this happens, to simply return attention to the body.

3. Inquiry helps participants develop the skill of noticing the relationship between an event (in this case movement), associated thoughts and emotions, and ultimately, the recognition of their relationship to downward mood and anxiety spirals.

Practice Skills: For the Participant

1. To develop the language of direct experience in the moving body with appreciation of boundaries, limitations, and the use of movement for hyper- and hypo-arousal

2. To make salient being and noticing versus doing and striving

Three-Minute Breathing Space (Regular and Responsive)

The Three-Minute Breathing Space–Regular and the Three-Minute Breathing Space–Responsive are core practices of the MBCT program and are introduced in sessions 3 and 4 respectively. They have different uses and need to be taught in an explicit manner. There is often confusion differentiating them and their applications partly because of how they are described, and they have different names in the two editions of *Mindfulness-Based Cognitive Therapy for Depression* (Segal et al., 2002, 2013). For the sake of clarity, we will be using the terms *Regular* and *Responsive* to distinguish between the two practices.

The Three-Minute Breathing Space–Regular

The Three-Minute Breathing Space–Regular is a formal daily practice used to train participants to engage in repeated short mindful moments that bring attention and focus to what is present and to check in with whatever is happening.

This practice takes place over three steps of approximately one minute each, explicitly naming them in the guidance. The teacher asks participants to adopt an alert sitting posture and to bring attention to whatever is current in thoughts, emotions, and body sensations. During the second step, the teacher asks the group to narrow and shift attention to the physical sensations of breathing at the belly. The third step involves bringing attention to the entire body, around the breath, and a more spacious awareness to experience. It is an accessible and portable practice often reported to be the one most used following completion of the MBCT program.

Theme: Checking in with current experience

Rationale: To be able to quickly direct attention to the cognitive, emotional, and bodily components of experience, practicing mindfulness in any given moment

Intention: Taking a moment to check in with what is current and step out of automatic pilot

Practice Skills: For the Teacher

1. The teacher is guiding participants to quickly check in and identify what is present in thoughts, emotions, and body sensations—wanted, unwanted, or neutral (step one)—to practice the skill of gathering attention to sensations of breathing at the belly (step two), and then to expand attention to the entire body (step three).

2. The inquiry focuses on the three steps of this practice, ensuring participants understand its stages. The emphasis is on the use of the Three-Minute Breathing Space as a support for being with what is present. The tension here is that participants can confuse it as a "quick fix" or escape from distress, and this should be listened for and discussed during the inquiry process. Participants are also asked to identify when and how this practice could be used in everyday life.

Practice Skills: For the Participant

1. To develop the skill of bringing awareness to experience, focusing, and then expanding attention

2. To quickly bring mindful attention to any situation while learning to shift to and from focused attention to open-monitoring as a tool to step out of automatic pilot

Three-Minute Breathing Space–Responsive

In this variation of the practice, in the session, the teacher asks participants to bring to mind a difficulty or concern and notice what thoughts, emotions, and body sensations arise. They are asked to name emotions if present and then directed to explore for a period any associated body sensations. Participants are invited to use the breath or specific phrases to help support being with sensations associated with emotion. They are then directed to the sensations of breathing at the belly and finally to bring attention to the entire body.

The Three-Minute Breathing Space–Responsive is vital for teaching participants the skill of bringing their attention to difficult emotional states and discovering that they can be with and explore them. They are asked to practice this in response to difficulties in real time, allowing them to learn more skillful ways of responding rather than ways of reacting that are often resistant, maladaptive, or avoidant. The body is an essential focus for this practice, as it provides an additional way to be with challenging experience. Participants learn that difficult states pass and that they can process them in an experiential and intentional manner in healthier and more skillful ways.

Theme: Turning toward, being with, and embracing difficulty

Rationale: To decrease reactive behavior and build distress tolerance, acceptance, and responsive choice

Intentions:

1. Bringing awareness to whatever is in experience that is associated with a difficulty (thinking, emotions, and body sensations)

2. Using bodily sensations as a vantage point during difficult thoughts and emotions versus narration and problem solving

Practice Skills: For the Teacher

1. Participants are instructed to intentionally bring attention and kindness to a manageable difficulty in a safe setting.

2. The teacher guides participants to identify thoughts, emotions, and body sensations associated with the difficulty. As part of this, she helps participants name emotions and their sensorial manifestations.

3. Instructions are directed at shifting and holding attention on the exploration of bodily sensations when the unwanted is present.

4. As a part of guidance, should the emotional and physical reaction be overwhelming, participants are invited to use the breath or specific phrases to help support being with the difficulty.

5. The teacher then guides participants to intentionally focus, shift, and expand attention.

6. The inquiry, led by the teacher, helps participants track their experience, learning the difference between experiential avoidance and exposure (turning toward the

difficult). It also elicits the changing nature of experience: that what is experienced in one way may be different at a different time, and that difficulties pass or can be tolerated. Lastly, the dialogue between participants and teacher demonstrates that there is often a skillful way to respond to the unwanted.

Practice Skills: For the Participant

1. To recognize and identify when distress is present

2. To learn to identify and label emotions in a less personalized (decentered) manner

3. To develop willingness and the ability to compassionately turn toward and stay with difficulty as it is expressed as sensation without prioritizing content

4. To shift attention to the entire body to enhance decentering and to discern a skillful next step

Breath, Body, Sounds, Thoughts, and Emotions and Choiceless Awareness Meditation Practice

This longer sitting practice is taught in session 4. It is subsequently modified in later sessions to introduce working with emotionally charged situations similar to the Three-Minute Breathing Space–Responsive. The practice begins with guidance around posture and then moves to the sensations of breathing. After a few minutes, the teacher guides participants to shift attention to a focus on the body and subsequently to the bare sensations of hearing, receptive to sounds as they come and go. Participants are then invited to focus on thoughts and emotions as objects of attention and finally to bring an open and receptive stance to the entirety of experience (choiceless awareness/open-monitoring). The practice closes with a few minutes of attending to the breath in the body.

Theme: Moving from focused concentration to receptive attention then to open-monitoring of all experience

Rationale: To develop an attentional focus on the entirety of experience (internal and external) with an increasingly receptive and nonjudgmental awareness. This cultivates equanimity and the ability to identify difficult mind and mood states early.

Intention: Recognizing internal and external sensations as a bridge to working with thoughts and emotions and developing an open stance to whatever is arising.

Practice Skills: For the Teacher

1. Guidance is clear and explicit in moving attention between specific foci while increasingly widening the attentional field.

2. The teacher promotes the participants' discovery that thoughts may be viewed akin to sound or any other sensation, external to self, reducing one's identification with them.

3. Inquiry highlights the ability to shift attention between different foci and notice how thoughts are like sounds—sensations or events that come and go. In addition, the broadening of awareness to include all experiences is explored.

Practice Skills: For the Participant

1. To strengthen attentional focus and cultivate open and receptive attention

2. To develop the capacity to approach thoughts and emotions as sensations of the mind with their own specific qualities

3. To recognize and shift from focused attention to open-monitoring

TRIP as Applied to the Cognitive Exercises

The cognitive exercises in MBCT—the Walking Down the Street (session 2), Automatic Thoughts and the Territory of Depression (session 4), Alternative Viewpoints Exercise (session 6), Identifying Relapse Signatures (and developing an action plan in sessions 6 and 7), and the Nourishing and Depleting Exercise (session 7)—assist the participant in developing an observational stance to, and be less identified with, experience. This allows for more skillful and conscious responses, in particular to difficulty, while decreasing the duration and intensity associated with reactivity. TRIP can be applied to the cognitive exercises embedded in the MBCT program to help the teacher stay focused on the relevant teaching points.

For ease of discussion, we will begin by exploring the Themes, Rationales, and Intentions for the cognitive exercises, followed by the Practice Skills for the cognitive exercises in general, because there is significant overlap between exercises. It is beyond our scope in this chapter to explicitly apply TRIP to all the cognitive exercises, but as we have previously pointed out, this tool is generalizable. It would be a useful exercise for the reader to apply TRIP to some of the other exercises not mentioned below for the development of teaching skills.

Walking Down the Street

The teacher guides participants to imagine an ambiguous event in which they smile and wave at someone they know coming toward them on the opposite side of the street who doesn't seem to notice and walks by. They are then instructed to write down their responses to the situation.

Theme: Recognizing that reality is a construct and open to interpretation

Rationale: To decrease fusion with our interpretations and to recognize them as a view

Intention: Elucidating the varied responses (thoughts, emotions, body sensations, behaviors, and impulses to act) to an ambiguous event—thoughts are emphasized as interpretations and not necessarily facts

Automatic Thoughts Questionnaire

The teacher provides participants with a list of automatic depressive thoughts (variation includes a list of anxious thoughts) and asks them to identify the three thoughts that most resonate with them, particularly when they are depressed or anxious. The teacher then facilitates a discussion around these thoughts, their universality and impersonal nature, and how they may be more or less believable dependent upon mood.

Theme: Externalizing thoughts from self

Rationale: To recognize that there are signature thoughts for depression that are universal and perpetuate symptoms through rumination

Intention: Illustrating how depressive and anxious thoughts are common, affected by state, and not personal

Territory of Depression

Participants are asked to identify common thoughts, emotions, body sensations, and behaviors associated with depression. These can be recorded on a whiteboard for discussion. The teacher then elicits from participants the value in recognizing and externalizing these symptoms and how they are often viewed as a moral failing rather than a set of symptoms that belong to a condition.

Theme: Recognizing that depression is a constellation of different signs and symptoms

Rationale: To increase the understanding of depression as states of illness separate from one's character, making them more manageable

Intention: Identifying the components of difficult mind and mood states, their familiarity, and universality

Practice Skills for the Above Cognitive Exercises

The following practice skills will be relevant for each of these exercises.

For the Teacher

1. The teacher introduces, explains, and concisely guides the cognitive exercises, ensuring the group discovers the primary teaching points of each.

2. The teacher elicits, conveys, and reinforces that experience consists of discrete and interrelated components, regardless of affective charge.

3. The teacher guides the group in the discovery of the contingent nature of events and how this can affect thinking, emotions, sensations, behaviors, and impulses.

4. The teacher helps participants integrate the knowledge acquired into ways to manage depressive relapse or anxiety.

5. The teacher emphasizes how difficult experiences, including depression and anxiety, are common, shared, and impersonal.

For the Participant

1. To develop the ability to parse experience into its components

2. To identify and externalize the various aspects of depression in early and later stages of relapse

3. To understand how context and state affect the believability of a thought (disidentification), the negative emotional charge or interpretation attached to a view of an event (decentering), and the appraisal of and behavior or impulse to act that follows an event (interrelatedness of experience)

There are several ways to facilitate the participant reflections in these various exercises. Some teachers use a whiteboard as a collaborative endeavor to elicit from participants relevant teaching points that are visually reinforced. This assists in the externalizing of difficult mind and mood states, emphasizing their universality. Other teachers will process the exercises as a general conversation, drawing upon participant responses and normalizing them as needed. In both formats, the teacher asks participants what they see in or notice about the various responses. A discussion ensues in which the teacher uses open-ended questions to help participants investigate their understanding and utility of these exercises. A sample of the kinds of questions we would use are: What did we do in this exercise? Why write this down? What do you make of the responses? What do you think of the fact you were able to come up with all of this so easily? What does this tell us?

Nourishing and Depleting Exercise

The Nourishing and Depleting Exercise (session 7, "How Can I Best Take Care of Myself?"), while also conceptual, is separated from the others above because it is also behavioral and somewhat solution focused. The Practice Skills are directly tied to activation, attitudinal shifts, and self-care behaviors. The Nourishing and Depleting Exercise asks participants to document their activities during a typical day and whether they experience an activity as nourishing, depleting, or neutral. TRIP can inform this practice, helping the teacher remain focused on the practice intentions of awareness and self-care rather than becoming sidetracked by the participant narrative.

Theme: Identifying nourishing and depleting activities

Rationale: To build awareness of daily activities and their effect on energy and mood

Intention: Deconstructing a typical day to bring insight to what activities increase or decrease energy and to shift behaviors or attitudes in the interest of self-care

Practice Skills: For the Teacher

1. The teacher highlights the effect of activities on thoughts, emotions (mood and anxiety), and body.

2. The teacher gently emphasizes skillful self-care through shifting the relationship to that which cannot be changed, decreasing depleting activities or increasing nourishing activities when able.

3. The teacher guides participants in operationalizing self-care where possible (making it concrete, behavioral, and manageable).

Practice Skills: For the Participant

1. To be able to sequentially describe the activities of a typical day, building the capacity to track, experience, and identify the feeling tone of activities and their effect on mood

2. To be able to divide nourishing activities into *mastery* activities that bring a sense of accomplishment and *pleasurable* activities that are simply pleasurable without an end goal

3. To internalize the knowledge that not all depleting activities or difficulties can be changed, and that a shift in one's relationship to this may bring a new perspective

We have outlined how TRIP can be applied to both formal meditation practices and the exercises derived from cognitive behavior therapy. This is important so that the teacher has a clear understanding and foundation from which to teach. TRIP allows the teacher to know what she is teaching, why she is teaching it, and what ultimately it is in the service of—the amelioration of suffering.

The Five Agents of Change: A Return to the Raisin

As mentioned at the beginning of this chapter and in chapter 1, the five agents of change are another frame of reference to maintain adherence to the assumptions, principles, and practices of the program. As a reminder, these include the *protocol*, the specific *practices (mindfulness-based meditation practices* and *cognitive exercises),* the participant's *individual learning,* the *group process,* and the *teacher's embodiment of mindfulness* that includes the inquiry process. The Raisin Practice is used here as an example of how the agents of change can assist the teacher with both this adherence and maintenance of coherence throughout the eight-week MBCT program.

The Protocol

Trainees and teachers tend to drift from or add to the protocol when they begin teaching. We believe it is essential to adhere to the protocol for an extended period before one considers any additions to or subtractions from the program. However, minor adaptations or modifications may be required, depending upon the population with whom one is working. And each teacher will, in time, develop her own voice, language, and style of teaching. Ultimately, there is a specific structure to follow when teaching the Raisin Practice or any other practice—*and* flexibility of response to the needs of the moment within a given session is important.

Looking at the protocol, using the lens of the raisin, we see how this practice serves as an entry point into training participants in mindfulness skills that evolve throughout the program. Eating is a familiar activity to which we can relate easily. Second, it is an activity that highlights automatic pilot by using an external object to employ the senses. This provides easy access to mindfulness practice for the beginner. Following the practice with inquiry is an important aspect of the protocol. The teacher emphasizes experiential learning, reflection, and integration of what is learned into everyday life.

The Mindfulness-Based Practices

All practices have their own specific form and structure. The teacher will use language that has a clear focus and a well-defined beginning, middle, and end with very little preamble. In guiding the Raisin Practice, the teacher will focus on the senses. In other practices, there will be an emphasis on other foci, but she will always include the unintentional movement of attention into thinking with a reminder to return. The teacher engages in the practice, including eating the raisin, while guiding participants. Guiding from her own practice is an aspect of embodiment essential to all practices.

Her language is invitational, clear, and concise. As with all practices, she will use present participle ("*placing* the object on the tongue") and a lack of questions to enhance the ability to stay in the experiential flow of the practice. The language of guidance describes in broad terms various qualities of the raisin (shape, texture, color, flavor, and so forth) to assist the group in the development of the vocabulary of experience and enhanced sensorial awareness. Another aim is to heighten participants' noticing of their experience as it arises. Her delivery includes periods of silence to allow participants to bring attention to whatever they are experiencing in the body and mind.

Individual Learning

A teacher who uses individual learning as an agent of change will recognize that every participant has his own learning trajectory. In all practices, including the Raisin Practice, the teacher will be interested in eliciting a range of responses about the practice. One learns throughout the program from this continuous interplay between practice, self-reflection, insights, information, and descriptions from the group members in what is an iterative process. Each participant's dialogue with the teacher also enhances individual learning and the participant's ability to describe the experience. In this way, the skill becomes generalized.

For example, following the practice, a woman said, "I hate raisins, and when I realized that we were going to eat it, I felt kind of sick and revolted but decided to do it anyway. I was surprised at the burst of flavor and that it wasn't so bad!" The teacher can then simply say, "Oh, so things didn't turn out as you expected." The participant then discovers that there may be a difference between expectation and outcome and that to be open to new experience may influence what happens next. This has a direct relationship to depressive states, where one often comes to expect that this mood will never change or will only get worse, and can highlight that what we look for is what we see. This curiosity and knowledge become experientially embodied by the participant allowing for the possibility of a different relationship with a low mood the next time it rears its head.

Group Process

Group learning is an integral part of the program and is reciprocal with individual learning. For example, as the group discusses the raisin, this facilitates the learning of a common language that reinforces description over analysis. The teacher aims for a breadth of response from several participants, to gather as many adjectives of the sensory experience as possible. The teacher ensures during the discussion that all experiences are included, regardless of whether they are pleasurable. This normalizes to the group that both are worthy of attention and that it is safe to discuss them.

The teacher elicits from the group the relevance of eating a raisin to the intention of preventing depression relapse and anxiety. This aids development of an understanding of the work to follow and enhances commitment to the practice. Reflections from participants are likely to hold more resonance than those explicitly taught by the teacher.

Embodied Mindful Presence

In guiding the practice and the inquiry that follows, the teacher demonstrates embodiment of mindfulness through her body language, by maintaining an attentive and open physical stance, and speech which is clear, concise, and focused in the present moment. In these ways, she expresses an understanding of the potential impact that nonverbal cues and reactions can have. She also embodies attitudinal foundations such as curiosity, kindness, and beginner's mind during guidance and inquiry. Her interest in and curiosity about her participants' experience with the raisin help model beginner's mind around a mundane and common experience. The teacher is embodying the practice while guiding, allowing it to flow from her own experience of the raisin.

Inquiry is, again, the contemplative dialogue that takes place between teacher and participants to assist the latter in their development of observing and describing sensorial, cognitive, affective, and behavioral components of experience. It is a complex and layered process that involves both concrete skills and an embodied mindful presence. The teacher's use of inquiry supports participants to reflect on the Raisin Practice (and all the future mindfulness practices and cognitive exercises) and to integrate the learning into everyday life.

In conducting inquiry for the Raisin Practice, the teacher elicits from the group, gathering from as many people as possible (horizontal inquiry), the naming of the fruit's qualities (for example, brown, oval, rough, heavy or light, sweetness, woody, aromatic). Associated thoughts, memories, struggles, and preferences (I like this; I don't like this; "I remember those little red boxes of raisins my mother would put in my lunch when I was a kid!"), emotions (for example, desire, disgust, surprise), and impulses to act (such as to eat or not to eat) are highlighted as they present themselves. Comparing and contrasting this way of eating with our habitual eating patterns takes place during the post practice dialogue.

Linking this eating practice to managing depressive relapse and anxious states is essential because it can be quite a stretch for participants to see the relationship to eating this tiny dried fruit and their suffering. In fact, the raisin exercise can seem absurd without this necessary link being skillfully extracted from the group. Embodied mindful presence and inquiry are inextricably linked throughout the MBCT program. (We will discuss how best to achieve the mindful presence necessary to conduct inquiry successfully in more detail in part 3 of this book.) Just as we have used the five agents of change to elucidate the Raisin Practice, so too could the other meditation practices and cognitive exercises be viewed in the same way.

In Closing

Applying TRIP and the five agents of change helps the teacher hold the many variables inherent to teaching the program, such as the teaching points, logistics, time management, and other factors. The teacher needs to remain focused on and attentive to drawing out key teaching points or themes to be elicited from participants. Eliciting rather than telling is a core practice skill for the teacher to develop to optimize experiential learning for participants. This takes time to learn and requires the element of trusting the process. Given the potentially overwhelming nature of the work for the teacher, using TRIP and keeping the agents of change in mind can enhance the ability to stay open and present to fulfill the intentions of the program.

Chapter 4

Group Process in the MBCT Program

One of the distinct features of MBCT, as it is most commonly practiced, is that it takes place in a group. When Kabat-Zinn developed MBSR and Segal, Williams, and Teasdale developed MBCT, they saw the group format as a cost-effective, powerful, and supportive learning environment.

While there is long-standing literature around group counseling and psychotherapy, relatively little has been researched or written about the role of the group in MBCT (or in other MBPs) even though as discussed, we see it as an essential agent of change. This is because group members work together to discover commonalities in their experience of depression and, with the teacher's guidance, arrive at a given session's teaching points. And, as Pedulla (2017) states, whereas the goals of traditional group psychotherapy are learning how to better relate to others, in MBCT, the goals are relating to one's personal experience more skillfully, which in turn affects one's relationship with others. Therefore, the MBCT process is both intra- and interpersonal.

Each MBCT group is different, created between the participants with their varied personalities and needs, and the teacher's personal strengths, weaknesses, and teaching style. Where MBSR groups can be large, up to thirty-five people, MBCT groups tend to be smaller, between twelve and eighteen participants. MBCT's group size is due to the perceived vulnerability of the depressed population, although the optimal group size for MBCT has never been formally researched. The teacher will determine group size using a number of factors including the facilities that are available, recruitment, screening, and his expertise. The teacher creates a learning environment, or container for holding the group, that ensures safety and support. As the group forms and evolves over the eight-week program, the teacher attends to the changing needs of the individual participants while mindful of the whole group and its learning trajectory. Above all, the teacher allows the group to teach itself and downplays traditional forms of education and skill development, such as lecturing and an expert stance; he promotes learning that arises from participants' experiences of mindfulness practice and its relevance to the universal experience of suffering.

In this chapter, we will explore some key theories around group process and development and map them onto MBCT. This is in aid of a teacher understanding this powerful and undersung agent of change. These include the therapeutic factors at play in a group-based intervention, considerations around group composition, and the life cycle or developmental stages of a group. We will pay particular attention to the orientation and assessment necessary to form a successful MBCT group. We will then explore some of the leadership skills important for an MBCT teacher. As part of this discussion, we will introduce common group situations that teachers must address.

Therapeutic Group Factors

Yalom and Leszcz (2005) studied in detail the therapeutic factors that are at the core of any group experience focused on personal transformation. They originally proposed eleven elemental factors they saw as therapeutic, while subsequent researchers have added others. Some of the key factors with relevance to MBCT are

- instilling hope
- universality
- group cohesion
- self-understanding
- identification with other group members and the teacher
- existential factors (the human condition)
- catharsis
- imparting information
- guidance
- altruism.

We will now explore each of these factors as it relates to MBCT.

Instilling hope. Instilling hope, as a therapeutic factor, is the encouragement that recovery and healing are possible. The placebo effect of any therapeutic intervention demonstrates how strong the role of expectation can be. However, participants suffering from depression, anxiety, or other forms of distress come to a new group hopeful but cautious, if not skeptical, about how this new modality might help them. In the orientation session, the teacher discusses realistic expectations by talking about what MBCT is, what is involved in participating in the group, the home assignments, and finally, the research that supports MBCT's efficacy. As the eight weeks unfold, he will—through the delivery of the protocol and embodiment of his own personal experience of mindfulness—demonstrate attitudinal qualities of the practice that further build group confidence in the effectiveness of the group process. Further, during periods of doubt and struggle, participants will look to other group members who are likewise struggling but hanging in for encouragement and hope. If participants express skepticism, frustration, or doubt, the teacher normalizes these thoughts and feelings and encourages a sense of being present and accepting them as part of the process.

Universality. Another important therapeutic factor is universality, the realization that we all suffer and that this is part of our common humanity. Given the isolation that many with depression and other mental health and chronic conditions endure, it is not unusual for participants to share how liberating it is to be in the company of others who have struggled with similar experiences to their own. For many, it is the first time they've shared their experience of distress and realized that they are not alone, their suffering is not unique, and there is relief.

Group cohesion. Group cohesion is a critical therapeutic factor in all forms of group therapy, including MBCT. As Yalom and Leszcz (2005) state, "cohesiveness is the group therapy analogue to relationship in individual therapy" (p. 53). Although researchers, therapists, teachers, and group members can easily recognize the nature of cohesion in groups, it is hard to define and measure. Elements include a sense of safety and trust, and feelings of belonging, warmth, empathic understanding, and acceptance. Of note, this is not just between participants and the facilitator but also between participants and the whole group. Yalom and Leszcz (2005) call this sense of solidarity a "we-ness" or "esprit de corps." Cohesiveness is one of the factors most strongly correlated to positive outcomes in a variety of group modalities, as well as to attendance and completion. In MBCT, cohesion usually develops because of the group's common experience and shared desire to skillfully manage distress, and in part by a teacher's promotion of group interaction and his embodiment of the attitudinal foundations of mindfulness. Cohesion is further supported by the teacher creating an environment of safety and acceptance from the orientation on and reaffirmed in each session. Factors include welcoming of diversity regardless of ethnicity and culture, socioeconomic status, gender, and ability; a commitment to confidentiality and boundaries; and an open acceptance of all experience with curiosity and kindness.

Self-understanding. Self-understanding *is* the insight that arises from participants being encouraged to reflect on and question (individually and within the group) what they are being exposed to through the trajectory of the program, mindfulness-based practices, and the cognitive exercises. It is the understanding of one's personal patterns of behavior and views about self, others, and the world that color depression, anxiety, and distress. A shift in attitude and approach that arises from the practice of mindfulness can change the participants' relationship to their difficulties. Facing the lessons of universal suffering, impermanence, and the impersonality of experience, self-understanding comes from learning that avoidance and being overly attached perpetuates suffering, and that, through acceptance of suffering, it can be reduced. This is an intrapersonal process witnessed by and shared in the group through mutual reinforcement.

Identification with other group members and the teacher. Often called *imitative behavior* in group therapy, identification is the process of adopting attitudes and approaches demonstrated by others and learning from their successes and failures. From each other, group members learn that risk taking and being vulnerable can result in new experiences that don't conform to their expectations. From the embodied teacher, group members learn acceptance, equanimity, and compassion.

Existential factors. Existential factors arise in a group from the recognition that suffering is universal; there can be no escape from pain, sickness, and aging (and ultimately death); and that life is at times unfair and unjust. In recognizing these realities, we can face life more honestly and be truer to our values. There is liberation in discovering this and realizing that it is not that we are flawed but rather that life itself is challenging.

Catharsis. Catharsis is the expression of emotions, be they positive, negative, or neutral, in a goal-directed and responsible way. Within MBCT, this starts by learning to identify and parse experience into its component parts of emotions, thoughts, body sensations, and behaviors or impulses to act. As the course progresses, the participant develops awareness of which components show up most noticeably when she is struggling; she builds tolerance for distress and learns to turn toward the difficult with attitudes of willingness, allowing, and letting be. Again, this happens in the presence of, and is supported by, others experiencing similar challenges.

Imparting information. Despite the bulk of the learning in MBCT being from direct experience and reflecting on it, imparting of information by the teacher and other group members is a constant. The teacher initiates discussions on the how-to of meditation and navigating its obstacles. The nature of depression, anxiety, distress, and coping skills are also discussed. The teacher, wherever possible, will support awareness of and reflection on experience over a didactic instructional focus. Teachers tend to be reliant on lecturing when what is to be cultivated is a receptive and reflective stance. As such, the imparting of information, while necessary, will be carefully balanced.

Guidance. Another recognized therapeutic factor is guidance, which in this context means the offer of support, advice, or assistance by the teacher. Although a core feature of many therapeutic group interventions, advice-giving runs counter to the essence of MBCT. An MBCT teacher will of course provide such support, but a theme of the program is to turn toward challenging mental and emotional states. Even the most well-intentioned verbal expressions of advice in these instances can be rescuing and reinforce avoidance and dependence on the teacher. As much as possible, the teacher maintains a "being" mode of mind, over the "doing" mode of problem solving and offering solace.

It will be important to remember that there will be times when a teacher will need to offer support and reassurance. Equally, there will be times when problems or issues need addressing. In most cases, it will be enough for him to communicate empathic support, self-kindness, and investigative curiosity to whatever is arising through his presence. The same holds for a participant's offering of advice or support to other group members, often described as cross-talk. This is to be gently discouraged by the teacher in service of modelling the welcoming of all experience and the encouragement of participants speaking to and from their own experience. This is addressed directly in the orientation session and is revisited when necessary.

Altruism. Although altruism in other therapeutic modalities is expressed through advice and reassurance between participants, it is different in MBCT, although no less important. In MBPs, it is expressed through the group's acceptance of individual participants' experiences without needing to change them. Altruism is demonstrated through the kindness members show to each other as well as the direct support offered before and after the group. Participants get to know each other and show interest, kindness, and care, which has its own therapeutic properties, especially for the distressed participant who has turned inward, feels isolated, and is self-involved. It is interesting to note that when researchers asked participants of traditional group therapy the most helpful therapeutic factors for them, guidance and altruism ranked among the least important (Yalom, Tinklenberg, & Giula, 1970), which may provide an evidence base for holding these lightly in MBCT.

Group Composition

As mentioned, MBCT was originally designed for people with histories of recurrent, episodic depression who were well enough to learn skills to prevent future depressive relapse. Over time, this has broadened to other mental health challenges, including other forms of depression and anxiety, as well as mental distress secondary to physical illness. Although groups are commonly advertised for depression, or depression and anxiety, in the community, a much wider range of people seek MBCT. It is important to ensure that the group is comprised predominantly of people where the presenting condition is identified as depression. MBCT has a narrow focus on depression and, therefore, if people wish to attend without a history of this, they should be referred to MBSR, which has a wider frame of reference.

Another issue around group composition is the growing importance of diversity in MBPs. The general perception is that most MBCT and MBSR participants, and most teachers, are white, middle-class, female, and middle-aged, and that in Western mindfulness communities, people of color are significantly underrepresented (Magee, 2016). There is little formal research around this, although in the largest clinical trial to date of MBCT (Kuyken et al., 2015), of 424 recruited participants, 99 percent identified as white. Reasons for this lack of diversity are unclear but may include lack of access availability, cultural barriers, and economic issues posed by fee-based MBPs that bias participation toward white, middle-class, and older participants.

It is beyond the scope of this chapter to explore the critical issue of diversity in depth. However, it behooves us as mindfulness teachers to at least acknowledge that this is a concern. We encourage teachers of MBCT and other MBPs to ensure that their programs are welcoming and safe for all people, regardless of race and ethnicity, as well as sex, sexual orientation, gender expression, age, physical ability, and religion. Teachers should be especially sensitive when participants who are members of minority or marginalized groups are in the room to ensure an environment of safety, inclusion, and cultural competence for all. As Magee (2016) argues, it is not enough to be "color-blind" and pretend contemporary mindfulness is beyond race. We need to acknowledge that there are differences among participants in a culture and health care system that often accentuates those differences through privilege and exclusion.

Developmental Stages, or Life Cycle, of the Group

It is useful for a teacher to understand the developmental stages of a group. This knowledge will help a teacher have a better grasp of the group process and appreciate its normal phases from beginning to end. In Tuckman's model (Tuckman & Jensen, 1977), there are five stages that characterize group development—a group is defined here as any constellation of people coming together for a purpose, whether therapeutic or task-oriented, time limited, or open-ended. These are forming, storming, norming, performing, and adjourning.

- Forming, or the stage setting, is the coming-together of the group.

- Storming, the inevitable next stage of group development, is characterized by feelings like ambivalence, doubt, and resistance as the demands of the group and expectations for change become clear.

- Norming and performing is when group cohesion is established and members begin to realize its aims.

- Adjourning is the stage in which the group comes to an end.

In this section, we discuss these stages as they relate to MBCT.

Forming

In this stage of the group's life, the activity is to orient to the task at hand. In the case of MBCT, the tasks are learning meditation and how cognitions and interpretations relate to mood. Early group behaviors tend to reflect dependence upon the leader because members don't know what to expect and the setting is unfamiliar. They may also test boundaries to learn what is expected and acceptable in the group.

In MBCT, boundaries and appropriate safety parameters are established during the orientation and intake and codified in the first few sessions. Given that group formation is highly dependent on steps taken before the group even starts, we will elaborate on this process here.

In MBCT groups, there is an initial assessment interview to screen prospective participants and to orient them to what's involved. Some teachers do individual screening coupled with a group orientation or written handouts communicating the nuts and bolts of the program. The intention is to establish contact and build confidence in the teacher and modality, ensure suitability to MBCT and group participation in general, discuss risks and benefits, and establish informed consent. The preclass participant interview and assessment can be performed in person or by telephone and gives the opportunity for the teacher to get to know the prospective participant, and vice versa. Using an open-ended question like, "What brings you here?" a teacher tries to draw out the motivation for the participant to take the program now and begin to assess suitability and fit.

Traditionally, contraindications for participation in MBCT include severe depression or anxiety that would limit participation, suicidal behavior, active drug or alcohol use, psychosis, and unresolved history of trauma with emotional dysregulation or dissociation. For our part, we recognize that MBCT is not risk free. However, we tend to see these contraindications as more relative than absolute and something that needs to be discussed with the participant and individualized.

Currently, there is discussion about the risks of meditation and consideration of the relative contraindications in taking an MBP (Dobkin, Irving, & Amar, 2011; Lindahl, Fisher, Cooper, Rosen, & Britton, 2017). The field is seeing some backlash against the universal adoption of mindfulness meditation practice. One example of this is the increased attention to the potential adverse effects of meditation. This is particularly relevant for people who have a history of unprocessed trauma. One such prominent study addresses long-term meditators and Buddhist teachers in a retrospective methodology (Lindahl et al., 2017). This research has generated interest in our field although (a) it is addressing long-term meditators, (b) their exposure to meditation is greater than what our participants receive, and (c) the research is in its infancy, and therefore, it is too early to make the claims they are making.

For example, someone with active depression may have limited energy and concentration that puts her ability to attend class or do home practice at risk. However, in discussion, it may become clear that she is highly motivated and has strategies in place to ensure compliance with attendance, such as a supportive partner who will drive her to class and remind her to do the home practice. This, plus the research showing benefit of MBCT even in severely depressed patients (Eisendrath et al., 2016), may allow participation in the group. Similarly, with past or current suicidal ideation, it may be that more acute treatment is needed rather than MBCT. Although if the participant has other clinical care, social supports, and protective factors in place and is highly motivated, and the teacher has knowledge of adaptations of MBCT for people at risk of suicide (Williams, Fennell, Barnhofer, Crane, & Silverton, 2017) and is clinically competent in this area, the teacher may allow participation.

Likewise, active drug or alcohol abuse is a concern. In addition to alcohol being a depressant and anxiety provoking, the active use or withdrawal of any recreational substances are likely to compromise MBCT adherence. In addition, any intoxicated behavior will be disruptive to the group. For this reason, many teachers try to ensure a period of abstinence before undertaking MBCT. However, our personal experience is that abstinence is not always required as long as participants are motivated, willing to strategize around their use, and can commit to not coming to class intoxicated. If upon assessment, the participant reveals that she is currently using drugs or drinking, further questions need to be asked to ascertain risk. Understandably, active psychosis would also limit someone's understanding of the material and may lead to disruptive behavior in the group, hampering other participants' experience. However, in the case of psychosis in remission or with residual symptoms, participating in the program can be a successful experience for the participant and group alike.

Untreated trauma is the last commonly cited contraindication for fear that the meditation experience will precipitate a dissociative crisis or that extreme emotional dysregulation will be highly disruptive to other participants. Again, our approach is to engage in frank conversation with the prospective participant about the risks. If it's clear that the person is motivated, has done past integrative psychotherapeutic work, has learned techniques to manage instability, and has a psychotherapist to help support her through any reemergence of symptoms, then participation may be indicated. Participants may be advised to engage in specific "grounding" exercises should symptoms related to trauma arise, as well as to inform the MBCT teacher of what is happening so that practices may be modified, and group suitability reassessed. In addition, the teacher should have professional experience with this clinical population. Of interest is the aforementioned large trial of MBCT (Kuyken et al., 2016), in which those with histories of childhood adversities tended to do better than those without trauma with MBCT in preventing the relapse of depression, although this is not clearly understood.

In general, with these relative contraindications and other concerns around participation, our approach is to

- be open about the risks and benefits of MBCT

- communicate that any participant, irrespective of baseline mental health, may experience worsening of symptoms with the mindfulness-based meditation practices and that the participant should alert the teacher if there are concerns

- emphasize the importance of class attendance and home practice and ensure the participant's physical and mental health conditions, or current life situation, will not undermine this (If there is a concern, decide whether there is enough motivation and realistic strategies in place to compensate.)

- advise participants not to consider medication changes for the duration of the group without the advice of a primary care practitioner and to inform the teacher if such changes are made

- emphasize that MBCT can always be reconsidered at another time, if there are insurmountable concerns

- secure and document informed consent for MBCT, an understanding of other treatments available, and acknowledgment of any potential risks around worsening of mental health and physical risk with mindful movement practice

- establish confidentiality and its limits (for example, intention to harm self or others).

As mentioned, in addition to screening for suitability for MBCT, the formation of the group entails an understanding of what MBCT consists of and what the participant is getting into. This is done in the preclass interview and the group orientation and is reiterated in session 1. Key points include:

- what MBCT is, which may include a little on the history, theory, mechanisms, current research, and so on

- a discussion of mindfulness and the practices and how it may help reduce depressive relapse, mental distress, and moderate anxiety and depression

- the attitudinal foundations of mindfulness—especially nonstriving, in that all participants want relief from suffering, but overattachment to outcome undermines the being mode of mind we are practicing

- the importance of attending weekly classes and engaging in home practice

- the logistics of the course (session dates, timing, missed classes, dropping out, how to get in touch with the teacher) and other practical arrangements

- challenges to taking MBCT (for example, doubt, not "getting it," temporarily feeling worse, risk of drop out, and so on)

- key elements of group participation including: (1) the importance of confidentiality and its limits, (2) voluntary participation in group discussions, (3) respectful listening and speaking, and (4) discouragement of cross-talk and allowing all participants to have their own experience.

Storming

Storming—the next stage of group development and an inevitable one—manifests as struggles with practices, course material, other group members, or the teacher. This can manifest in group members as internally or externally expressed ambivalence, doubt, or rebellion; behaviors like missing sessions; or other forms of resistance. In classical group therapy, the focus of storming is usually on interpersonal conflict between group members or with the teacher. While this can certainly happen in MBCT, and needs to be managed, usually, the conflict is intrapersonal and focused on challenges related to difficulties with meditation practice, doubt in its usefulness, and barriers to practicing at home. This is a theme revisited throughout the course but is especially current in sessions 2 and 3 and can lead to frustration, discouragement, and attrition.

In classic meditation instruction, intrapersonal struggles are described as "the hindrances" and in MBCT, as obstacles or barriers. These include *restlessness* (difficulties with concentrating, sitting still, the habitual movement of attention, and other mental or physical agitation), *sloth and torpor* (sleepiness, sluggishness, lack of energy, or motivation), *doubt* (doubt in oneself, as expressed by "I am not good at this," doubt in the process as in "MBCT is not for me," and doubt in the teacher as in "he doesn't understand me"), *wanting* (wanting the meditation to end, to be free of pain, or things to be different than they are), and *aversion* (feelings of dislike, rejection, avoidance, hatred, or boredom). The teacher's approach to these is to remember that challenges are normal and to be expected. Chiefly, through inquiry into the participants' practice in the session and at home, he reinforces the normalcy of these struggles not by relying on advice, problem solving, or reassurance, but by modeling how to be with these challenges that arise with kindness, acceptance, and patience and taking action when required. This may be as simple as asking the whole group who else had challenges with the home practice, implying that this is a normal part of the process and to be explored.

It is important to recognize that sometimes when a participant is expressing struggles, this may be more than "obstacles or barriers" and may be legitimate in that the group may not be right for a participant for a variety of reasons, for instance, a participant who is angry, dysregulated, or extremely socially anxious. It is also worth noting that at times, participants may take issue with something the teacher says or they may not like the recordings, home practice, or other aspects of the course. Importantly, the teacher should not personalize such criticisms but maintain the same stance of curiosity and acceptance that he would bring to anything coming up in the group. This of course does not include abuse or events that put the teacher or other participants at risk.

Norming and Performing

In the next stage of group development, cohesion is established by the teacher's skillful response to storming and as participants are socialized to the modality. Trust in the process and the teacher develops along with a sense of belonging to the group. This is paralleled in personal practice as confidence builds in the method of mindfully paying attention to the present moment and the approach of being with challenges. An experiential understanding of mindfulness starts to take place, leading into the fourth stage of performing. This stage has more relevance to task-oriented groups that are focused on finding a solution to a problem or completing a project. For MBCT, it is a continuation of norming in which cohesion is strengthened. Personal practice deepens and develops a rhythm, and participants begin to apply insights to day-to-day struggles, fluctuations in mood, and interpersonal relations outside of group. The role of the teacher is to step back even further and let group members teach themselves through their reports on practice and insights into its relevance and integration into daily life. In the example below, the group is discussing home practice.

Teacher: Who had a chance to practice?

Participant 1: I didn't have a chance to do the formal practices, but I remembered when I was getting irritated with the kids to take a breath.

Participant 2: I can relate. I had to work late every day this week, but I found myself using the Three-Minute Breathing Space. It was really helpful.

Participant 3: I also found it difficult to practice this week but found myself remembering when I started to get down on myself that it was just a thought.

Teacher: So, lots of working with the practice when you can.

Adjourning

The final stage is adjourning and is described by some as mourning. Any group will meet the prospect of ending with anxiety about separation, a sense of sadness, and strong feelings toward the teacher and other group members. It is no different in MBCT.

The MBCT teacher's role is to remind participants that the end is approaching in session 7 and to spend session 8 reflecting on lessons learned and preparing for life after the group ends in terms of maintaining practice and how to apply strategies learned when mental distress reemerges. The teacher may speak about this ending as a beginning of what is to come. Finally, a closing ceremony marks the end.

A common expression in the group as it ends is the desire to continue. This may show up through the creation of an email list, a social gathering, or a peer-led graduate group for meditation practice. In our experience, although the intention is sincere, these groups usually peter out unless they are organized and structured by a teacher. Still, they can be helpful, and participants' desire to organize them reflects how healing and intimate an MBCT group can become.

How can the MBCT teacher hold the group learning environment through these stages while promoting the therapeutic factors that help participants strengthen and stabilize their mindful attention and turn toward what is difficult and challenging in their lives? In the next section, we'll present particular skills that can help teachers bring this knowledge to their teaching.

Group Teaching Skills

There are many ways to consider the functions of the teacher in leading the MBCT group and the skills needed to fulfill this role. We think of the teacher, above all, as a guide. This means that he is a facilitator of the protocol and a leader who points the way by responding to the needs of the group members. He uses the structure of the program and embodies mindfulness as a platform to explore the difficulties a group may face. Holding the group will be essential.

Thus, there are eight key teaching skills relevant to the group.

1. Conveying group guidelines and norms (as discussed above). The aim is to create a culture of safety for participants to take risks and grow in their learning.

2. Maintaining appropriate boundaries for individuals and the group. These boundaries delineate an MBCT group as different from a traditional therapy or a support group, with the emphasis on the attention to present-moment experience. A key boundary is making clear the limits of the teacher's responsibilities and availability between classes and after the program ends.

3. Managing all stages of the group from introduction and formation to ongoing development and closing, while attending to the trajectory of the eight-week curriculum and managing agendas for each session. (Knowledge of TRIP can be useful here.)

4. Holding a leadership role that comes with a sense of authority. This is in contrast to McCown's (2016) ideal of the cocreated group and of the mindfulness teacher as a member of the group, equal to the others, with additional responsibilities. While he will try not to dictate behavior or impose his views on others, the MBCT teacher is still, by definition, a leader who group members look to for direction and guidance. He is also, usually, a clinician with a professional designation and as such has responsibilities regulated by his profession. The key is for the teacher to be an authority who is not authoritative in his presentation. He will take responsibility for guiding the group through the agenda and through practices and inquiry, but he will lead the group *as* a guide, allowing them space to investigate and arrive at their own insights.

5. Drawing out key learning points from the group whenever possible. This means that over time, the teacher aspires to speak less in inquiry and group discussion, and lets the group engage in a process of discovery and teach itself.

6. Monitoring the group's energy, engagement, and emotional tone; extending or shortening an inquiry or practice as needed; shifting the agenda; or revisiting a theme as called for. The protocol acts as a guide, but by necessity, it is held with a light touch, depending on the needs of and what is arising in the group.

7. Engaging with individual participants while keeping the other group members in awareness, and, in guiding mindfulness practice, keeping his attention on his own practice while guiding and monitoring the group.

8. Embodying mindful presence and the key attitudes that support it so as to create a safe environment in which participants can take risks, adopt new relationships to experience, and deepen their practice.

In Closing

The group is a critical agent of change in MBCT and other group-based MBPs. An understanding of group process supports a teacher's ability to facilitate the delivery of the MBCT program. It also promotes the group's ability to teach itself and to develop individual and group autonomy. In this chapter, we have highlighted some of the important group dynamics at work. The group is greater than the sum of its parts. The teacher is the leader and promotes group learning through reflection on experience over the didactic delivery of information. The teacher holds the learning environment while attending to individuals and the group as a whole. By attending to the therapeutic factors of any group, its composition and stages of development, and group-related teaching skills, the teacher is supporting each participant through the MBCT journey.

Chapter 5

Teaching Competencies, Skills, and Challenges

As we've previously established, the teacher in the room is an agent of change who will have an impact on the learning trajectory of her participants. The learning in MBCT is founded on the deconstruction of the components of experience (thoughts, emotions, body sensations, and behaviors). In addition, participants develop awareness of the interaction between internal experience and the environment and that habitual attentional pulls (automatic pilot) are normal. Recognizing this can lead to a stabilization of attention, allowing participants to cultivate a different relationship to experience, wanted and unwanted. This learning is largely acquired through an experiential and reflective process. This demands that a teacher, in addition to her embodiment of mindfulness and knowledge of the protocol, understands this and how to best encourage these traits in her participants through a defined set of competencies and skills. In addition, teaching mindfulness requires that a teacher be aware of common challenges and be open to her continuing development, bringing awareness to her teaching strengths and limitations and how to work with them.

The terms "skills" and "competencies" are commonly used interchangeably but really reflect different ideas related to the learning process and its expression. The word "competency" is defined in a variety of ways. Here, we are using it to discuss the capacity to do something well. The faculty of competency depends on several factors: acquired theoretical and factual knowledge, technical and cognitive skills, key attitudes, and the abilities (or behaviors) that are tied to performance quality and improvement. All of these are relevant to the teaching of MBCT and other MBPs. In this chapter, we explore the acquisition of these teaching skills as they contribute to competency as well as the common mistakes we make as teachers regardless of experience. By bringing awareness to these variables, we commit to our continuous personal and professional growth and learning.

Experiential Learning

How can we generate the building blocks for developing competency in MBCT? We propose using some of the conceptual models of experiential learning theory to describe and discuss the skills, their acquisition, and the competencies needed for teaching MBCT. As introduced in chapter 2, the adult experiential learning model of Kolb (2014) sees learning as a "process whereby knowledge is created through the transformation of experience" (p. 49). It is most applicable to adult education, the workplace, and personal development. Kolb's adult learning model is based on Kurt Lewin's experiential learning model (Kolb & Fry, 1975), which sees learning, change, and growth as a cyclical process. In this simple learning model, a concrete experience is followed by a process of reflecting upon it. From these reflections, new ideas or theories are developed, which are then tested out in practice, thereby leading to more experiences. This differs from traditional educational models that rely on the unidirectional transmission of information with the student as tabula rasa, or blank slate, waiting to be filled with knowledge by the teacher.

In Kolb's influential adaptation of Lewin's cycle to individual learning, Kolb called the four stages concrete experience, reflective observation, abstract conceptualization, and active experimentation. In its simplest form, an experience is processed through the questions: What just happened? So what? Now what? Underlying this theory, Kolb saw learning as a means of resolving discordance between old perceived models of understanding the self and the world and new disconfirming ideas resulting from interactions between a person and the environment. He viewed the model as holistic and iterative, encompassing creativity, problem solving, decision making, performance, and development (Kolb, 2014). Finally, learning, as Kolb describes it, is a continuous process in which experimentation leads to new concrete experiences, deepening learning as one continues. It is also a lifelong process. This is a constructive way of viewing how participants learn in MBCT and other MBPs, how teachers can support this learning, and how teachers themselves learn to teach.

We have mapped on to Kolb's cyclical model and present an adaptation of this in the figure below. Concrete experience becomes *facilitating experience* (through guiding meditations, cognitive exercises, and inquiry), reflective observation becomes *facilitating reflective observation* (and description of experience), abstract conceptualization becomes *facilitating abstract conceptualization* (and generalization of experience), and active experimentation becomes *facilitating active experimentation* (and application of learning). To this, we add *constructing and maintaining the MBCT learning environment* as an additional key competency that supports the others. As in Kolb's original cycle of learning, the flow in our adaptation is unidirectional. We realize this is simplistic and does not consider the complexity of learning. Finally, we add that at the heart of learning to be an MBCT teacher is *embodied mindful presence*. In keeping with the definition of competencies offered above, the teacher will need to develop the necessary knowledge base, abilities, behaviors, attitudes, and relevant skills for each domain.

We will begin with the first key competency, the construction and maintenance of the learning environment.

Constructing and Maintaining the MBCT Learning Environment

The first competency to be developed is creating the learning container in a deliberate way that facilitates experiential learning. This would include the logistics, from organizing and running a group to marketing and physical space. It would also entail enrollment and screening for suitability and socializing members of the group to MBCT through orientation, as detailed in chapter 4. A key factor here is creating a space that is safe and accepting for both individual and group learning so that issues of confidentiality, privacy, informed consent, self-care, and voluntary participation are discussed, as well as the foundational attitudes of mindfulness.

In the orientation, the process and context of experiential learning is introduced by saying that different from other forms of education where one talks about something and then practices it, we will practice first and then talk about it. By commencing each session of the program with a practice, this model is reinforced.

Once constructed, care must be taken to maintain a conducive experiential learning environment throughout the eight weeks. For the MBCT facilitator, the necessary skills for maintaining the learning environment relate both to effective communication and basic counseling techniques. Crane et al. (2012b), in the "Mindfulness-Based Intervention: Teaching Assessment Criteria (MBI:TAC)," call them *relational skills* and details key features as (1) *authenticity and potency*, a manner that conveys genuineness, honesty, and confidence; (2) *connection and acceptance*, actively attending to participants and conveying back empathic understanding; (3) *compassion and warmth*, showing sensitivity, appreciation, and warmth to participants and their experience; (4) *curiosity and respect*, the conveyance of interest in participants' experience while respecting boundaries, emotional vulnerabilities, and the need for privacy; and (5) *mutuality*, working with participants collaboratively. These relational skills mirror the counseling conditions of Rogers (1942) and others, including genuineness, unconditional positive regard, empathic understanding, therapeutic alliance, and congruence.

Many of the specific skills that arise from the conditions we have outlined are detailed in the section on reflective listening below and in other chapters. To these, we might add the communication skills of speaking clearly and loudly, gently interrupting, and use of silence, as well as the broader skill of cultural sensitivity. The latter relates to

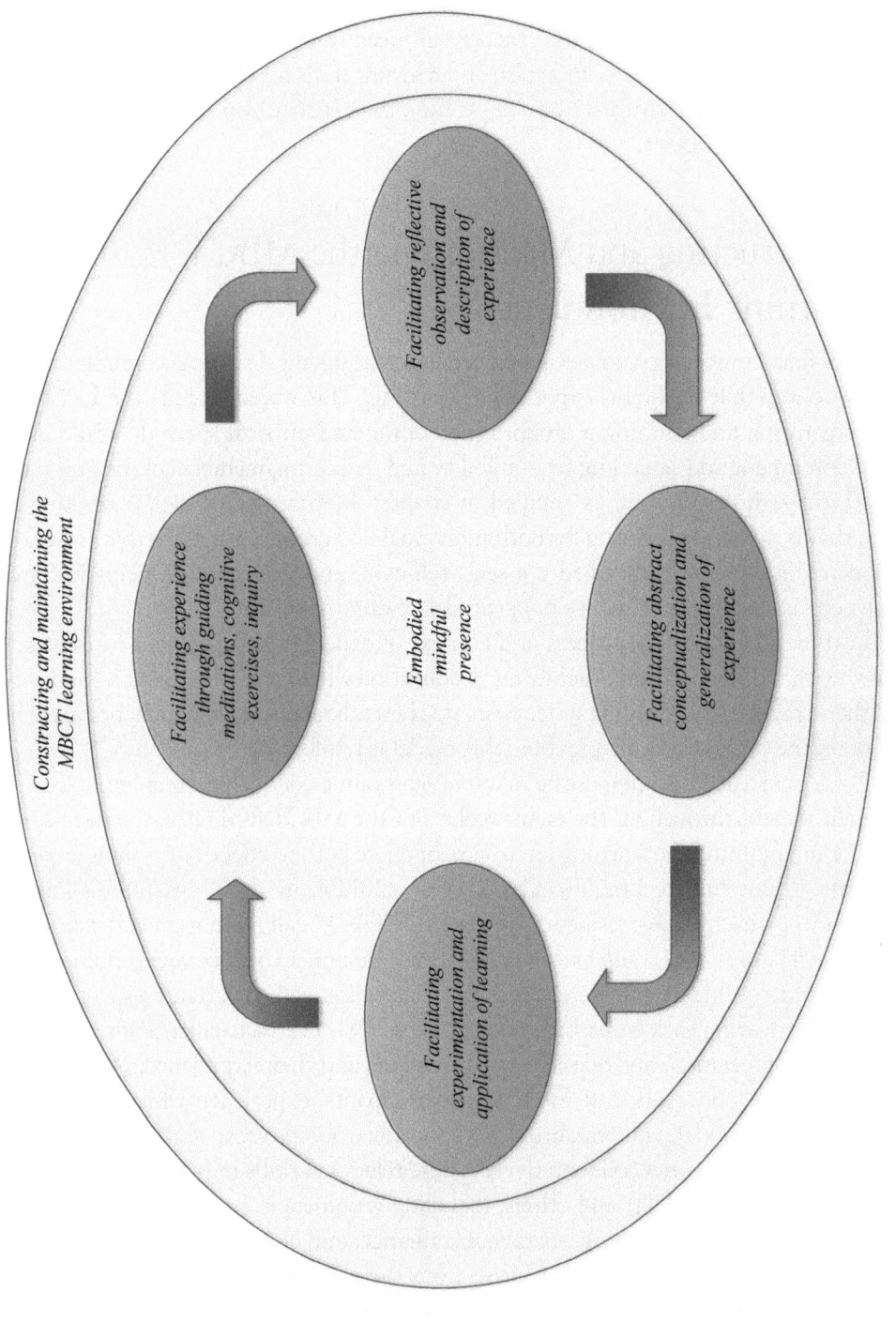

MBCT competencies from an experiential learning perspective

the need in our increasingly multicultural society to bring awareness to and respect differences in race, ethnicity, religion, language, ability, age, identity, and culture and how they may influence customs, beliefs, and behaviors. The knowledge base to support this and all the other competencies includes the teacher's understanding of the protocol and its theoretical premises—the agents of change and Themes, Rationale, Intentions, and Practice Skills—and her ability to embody mindfulness.

Pitfalls and challenges include lack of attention to logistics, such as recruitment, physical space, handouts, and so forth, as well as running a group in a population beyond the teacher's scope or insufficient screening of prospective participants so that people who are not suitable for MBCT are accepted. Additionally, insufficient orientation, such as not making explicit expectations for participants and guidelines for group interactions, is also an issue that leads to dropouts and other consequences. For example, active participation in the group process is encouraged but not coerced, and a challenge for the teacher may be the desire to "pick on" a quiet participant to elicit his experience, especially if the group seems slow to express itself. It is important that the teacher maintain consistency with the guidelines she has set at the outset around voluntary participation.

Although MBSR has a tradition of nonclinicians training to be facilitators, MBCT is by and large offered to a clinical population, usually within the health care system. Therefore, most teachers will be clinicians with experience working in mental health. If not, lack of training and understanding about issues such as confidentiality, informed consent, boundaries, managing emotional crises, and chart keeping may lead to ethical, clinical, or legal problems for the teacher.

Facilitating Experience Through Guiding Meditations, Cognitive Exercises, and Inquiry

This second competency entails the guiding of meditations and cognitive exercises and use of inquiry in a way that maximizes concrete and direct experiences for the participant. The skills start with how a teacher fosters in participants beginner's mind, openness, and the loosening of biases and expectations to allow for new experiences to unfold. Some of this is evident in the setup for each practice, exercise, and the inquiry that follows, and some of this is in the actual embodiment of the teacher: her use of clear and invitational language, the present participle, and silence in guidance, as well as her pacing. She must ensure her language is employed to direct and enhance the participants' attention to experience as it unfolds (and not to lecture or tell them how their experience should be). Another important skill in guidance is the minimal use of personal and possessive pronouns to support disidentification with, and impersonality of, experience, so a teacher might guide to bring attention to "the breath" as opposed to "your breath." It is interesting to note that numerous studies show that the use of personal pronouns is more common in the language of people with depression and anxiety (Brockmeyer et al., 2015), which may indicate an increased tendency to personalize experience. This has relevance and utility for the skills that are being developed in both teacher and participant. Some of these skills are highlighted in the example below of part of a guided movement practice in session 3 of MBCT ("Gathering the Scattered Mind").

Teacher: We'll be moving to a mindful movement practice of gentle stretching, so the invitation is to roll out your mat on the floor. (Teacher pauses as the group follows these instructions.)

Now, coming to a standing position with feet hip-width apart, the knees slightly bent, and bringing into awareness what is being noticed in the body as you stand. Perhaps noticing that even in stillness, there are subtle movements of swaying or vibration in the body, or other sensations present.

Here the teacher is starting the practice with minimal introduction to set context. The teacher engages in the practice with the participants to both demonstrate and embody it.

Teacher: We are setting an intention for this practice to use the body in motion as a focus of attention. Remembering that different from other forms of exercise, this is not about striving for flexibility, strength, or physical fitness. We are bringing attention to physical sensations while moving. Critical to this practice is knowing your physical limitations and only doing what feels possible. Stretching only as far as feels right and even imagining a particular movement instead of doing it physically to limit injury or pain. Knowing that it is an act of self-care to work within one's limits, while noticing habitual patterns of mind around striving or comparison with others.

As part of the instructional focus, the teacher emphasizes the intentions of the practice, self-care, and the attitude of nonjudgment.

Teacher: And on an in-breath, slowly lifting the arms until they are parallel to the floor and holding them here for a moment, breathing normally. On another in-breath, continuing to mindfully lift both arms until they come together above the head and breathing here…feeling the tension in the muscles and joints required to make the movement and holding the stretch. Then allowing the breath to move in and out at its own pace while stretching upward, first with one arm and then the other, as if picking something from a high tree branch…noticing whatever bodily

> sensations are arising while doing this stretch and noticing when the attention is pulled away into thoughts or sounds in the room…then on an exhale, slowly lowering the arms back down, paying attention to whatever sensation is present, perhaps even the sensation of the air on the arms as they move.

The teacher is using invitational language and present participles to encourage a present-moment orientation and providing periods of silence to allow participants to experience the practice and reminders to return attention to the primary object of focus, which in this case is the body. The mindful movement practice continues in this manner through a series of poses using the body in motion as a focus of attention and as a bridge to informal mindfulness.

Common pitfalls in guidance start with giving too much explanation about the practice and its purpose before commencing, reading from a script, problems with pacing, not using the invitational present participle, speaking too softly, not allowing enough silence, or using a "meditation" voice different from one's normal speaking voice. Given that one should guide from the practice, it is important that one is monitoring the group. If one is too much in the practice, one can begin to speak too softly or fail to notice when participants might be struggling. Too little in the practice, and teachers can guide from autopilot and sound inauthentic.

Likely the biggest challenge is the tendency to talk too much in guidance, whether motivated by nervousness or the need to make things clear for participants, because we get overinvested in our own words and voice, or for our own entertainment. All guidance requires periods of silence for participants to experience the practice themselves so that they can encounter a range of sensations, including challenging ones. By and large, as the course progresses, more silence in guidance is provided.

A final pitfall is in closing the practice. This should be deliberate and clear, expressing the transition that is about to happen. Commonly, trainees say, "Opening your eyes and coming back to the room," which is neither precise nor true (participants have not left the room!) and may be an example of a teacher not understanding that transitions are very much part of practice or being on automatic pilot and unaware of what they are saying. Rather, "In a moment, we will be coming to the end of this practice, taking a moment before opening your eyes or widening the gaze and taking in the surroundings of the room."

Facilitating Reflective Observation and Description of Experience

As has been stated, integral to any meditation practice or cognitive exercise, the MBCT teacher facilitates participant reflection chiefly through the contemplative dialogue of inquiry. This is a prelude to participants using this for self-inquiry. Inquiry aligns with the second stage of Kolb's experiential learning model, reflective observation. As a process, it is supported by adoption of the observational stance introduced in meditation. One is encouraged to notice and observe, reflect on one's experience in a decentered way, and describe it, as opposed to getting lost or immersed in analysis or one's ideas or conclusions about the experience. As part of this, the teacher models an attitude of investigative curiosity, expressing a valuing of direct experience and its description, essential for developing the skill of decentering.

Inquiry supports reflective observation through its use of a dialogue between teacher and participant, beginning with a primary question such as, "What did you notice?" or "What stood out for you in this practice?" Responses are initially elicited in a horizontal fashion (gathering input from as many people as possible, going for breadth versus depth) to reinforce and enhance the acquisition of reflective skills even for those who don't partake in the conversation. As the program unfolds, when a participant is struggling, the teacher will ask more questions of that one participant to support staying with, and the sequential tracking of, experience (vertical inquiry). As part of this, a vocabulary of experience is cultivated that parses intrapersonal phenomena into the somatosensory and perceptual (body sensations), the cognitive (thoughts, memories, and mental images), the emotional (moods and feelings), and the behavioral (actions and impulses to act). Therefore, reflective observation entails the teacher training participants to develop the skills of being able to notice, stay with, track, and describe experience from moment to moment. To this end the teacher needs to ensure that her inquiry is consistent with these intentions.

As a core feature of any helping relationship, professional or otherwise, one must employ *reflective listening*, a process of attending and responding to what a speaker shares that is derived from the active, or empathic, listening first described by the humanistic psychologist Carl Rogers (1942). Reflective listening is a process that helps the listener understand what the other is saying and to not make assumptions, while allowing the speaker to feel heard (Katz & McNulty, 1994). Further, it can help the speaker clarify for himself what is being said, better understand the content and emotions connected to the communication, and plan a course of action. In a mindfulness context, it helps the participant differentiate direct experience from narrative and anatomizes the experience into body sensations, thoughts, emotions, and behavior.

As a mindfulness skill, reflective listening is about communicating attunement between teacher and participant. It starts with *attending to* the speaker conveyed through body language (eye contact, a posture of leaning in, and so forth) and a focus on what the person is saying (not busy formulating a response), verbally and nonverbally. This may include a judicious use of positive verbal clues that you are listening (for example, "uh huh," "I see," "okay,") or subtle body gestures (such as head nodding), although by and large these gestures and verbal cues are kept to a minimum to convey a neutrality and acceptance of whatever is being expressed by the speaker.

The second part of this process entails *responding* when appropriate. This may include asking clarifying questions, emphasizing what was said, reframing, normalizing, summarizing, and thanking. The teacher may ask *clarifying* questions to ensure understanding and avoiding assumptions while communicating a sense of curiosity. As part of this, the teacher may need to ask what a participant meant when he used a particular word (such as "upset," "good," "works"). Also, the teacher needs to clarify when a particular experience happened to ensure it was part of the experience being reflected upon versus an idea, insight, explanation of what happened, or memory of something that happened in the more distant past.

A response may include *emphasizing* a nugget or essential piece of what the person is saying by repeating, or subtly rephrasing in the teacher's own words, while avoiding it sounding like parroting. Usually these responses are prefaced by a qualifying statement like, "If I heard you correctly..." or "It sounds like you're saying..." in order to avoid assumptions or putting words in the mouth of the participant. These simple reflections ensure the participant feels heard and understood, highlights learning, and reinforces the individual and group's ability to reflect upon, sequentially track, and describe the components of experience. There is a tendency to overuse reflections as a default response rather than identifying what is needed in that moment or essential to where one is in the program.

As part of the above rephrasing, or as a separate response, the MBCT teacher will sometimes *reframe* what has been said to distill direct experience from the extraneous storytelling that we can all get caught up in. This at times may require gentle interruption. Reframing will emphasize important teaching points the participant is making of which he or others in the group may be unaware. This will sometimes include parsing the person's experience into body sensations, thoughts, and moods to convey the language of experience used in MBCT.

Frequently, the teacher needs to *normalize* the experience when a participant reports a challenge with meditation often expressed as self-judgment. It is important not to offer reassurance by explicitly saying, "Don't worry." Rather, there will be times when the teacher will say something like, "That's normal, that sometimes happens in meditation, and then what happened?" moving through the process. Alternatively, she might occasionally, after hearing a few responses, look to the group and say, "Did anyone else struggle?" and inevitably when many hands go up, she might say, "Well, I guess that's a pretty common experience." In this way, the teacher embodies equanimity, treating all participant responses equally, whether they are describing a joyful or a challenging experience.

The teacher *summarizes* in a succinct manner and if appropriate subtly emphasizes a key learning point relevant to the practice or session theme, particularly when it has been elicited from other group members. At times there is no need to summarize or indeed to say anything if the person's reflection is clear. Finally, she ends by *thanking* the participant for his contribution.

The example below illustrates this through an inquiry following the sitting meditation practice where participants are being instructed how to work safely with challenging physical sensations in session 3.

Teacher: I am curious to hear about people's experience during this meditation. (Conveying both curiosity and a focus on the meditation experience.)

Participant: I had difficulty staying still. My legs and my mind were all over the place.

Teacher: So, there was physical and mental restlessness during the meditation?

The teacher is using simple reflection, subtly rephrased as a question.

Participant: Yeah. As I said, my legs have been jumpy and achy. I've recently returned to the gym because my therapist says it will help my depression. I suppose it's good, but it's really hard on my body. I remember once I went back to the gym after a long time and overdid it and ended up with a bad injury.

Teacher: So, your legs were aching, and you moved a lot, and then you had an idea that it's because you've been back to the gym. Did that explanatory thought occur during the meditation or after?

Here the teacher is bringing the participant back to the experience, reflecting what was somatic and what was cognitive, and tracking its sequence.

Participant: I guess during the meditation. Do you think it would help if I sat a different way?

Teacher: I'm not sure; perhaps you can experiment with that. Coming back to today's experience, it sounds like you had awareness of what was happening in the body and your mind. Thank you. Others? What else did you notice?

Here the teacher does not get sidetracked into a discussion of sitting posture and instead returns to reflection. She summarizes in a short, encouraging way while reinforcing the value of awareness and depersonalizing experience.

During the initial stages of the program, she moves from a question like, "What did you notice?" to a question that asks for further reflection, such as, "How might this way of paying attention be different from usual?" This helps direct participants to compare and contrast mindful ways of attending with more habitual ways, making mindful attention salient. She employs the same listening skills as above, although with less need for rephrasing to allow responses to speak for themselves and be the teaching points for the group. At times there is a need to ask for clarification, especially if it seems the response is vague, shows partial understanding, or the teacher recognizes she is making assumptions about what was said.

As described in more detail in chapter 8 ("Inquiry as Contemplative Dialogue"), this comparative question is dropped after the first few sessions of the program, and emphasis is then placed on tracking a participant's experience as it unfolds. With questions like, "And then what happened?" "And then?" a participant's experience is further dissected with emphasis on how the different components of experience flow and are contingent on one another. For example, how the sensation of a mild ache in the leg during a sitting practice might lead to the thought, *What if it gets worse and I can't hack it?*, which leads to a feeling of worry manifest in the body as constricted breathing and then to abandoning the meditation altogether with the concluding judgment, "I can't meditate." The teacher's tracking of these experiences from body sensation to thought and emotion, and then back to body, leading to more thoughts, helps to bring awareness to the process that occurs between a trigger and end behavior or mood. This is applicable to how, in someone with a history of depression, a minor negative thought might cascade out of control and lead to a spiraling downward mood. Tracking may also help the participant see the habitual tendency to focus on that which supports a mood-congruent (often negative) view versus one that does not.

Some of the pitfalls for the teacher in facilitating reflection are by and large errors of commission. Teachers tend to talk too much, probe too much, teach too much (by lecturing or explaining), perform too much (through jokes or poetry or self-disclosure), or try too hard to ensure a learning point is made or heard. Whether in guidance or inquiry, less is more (or as has been said: "Don't just do something, stand there!"). In facilitating reflection, a teacher's primary role is to listen and judiciously use reflection and reframing to enhance the learning. She must hold lightly her need for participants to "get it" and allow them to lead the conversation, learning at their own pace. A pitfall is allowing participants to delve into their narrative without interrupting them and bringing them back to the experience or question at hand. Interruption should be used with discrimination, and the teacher must be careful not to interrupt simply because she has the impulse to speak.

Another common challenge for the teacher is to use body language or verbal expressions that send a message preferencing positive comments by participants related to their experience and learning. For example, if a participant says, "I really felt calm during that meditation," the teacher might automatically say, "That's great!" Whereas if the next participant says, "That was a struggle for me," the teacher might reflexively respond with concern, reassurance, or advice saying something along the lines of, "I'm sorry to hear that. Would it help to change your position or take a deep breath?" What we are highlighting here is that all experience is welcome, and the language the teacher uses needs to reflect this in her response to any participant comment, whether positive or negative—for example, by using similar or the same words in responding to a participant reporting on a pleasant or challenging experience.

As teacher trainers, we often notice distinct teaching styles that can be both strengths and challenges, and we default to these out of habit or when we are vulnerable (such as when we are fatigued or triggered by a participant's distress). Some of us are *professors* and most comfortable with lecturing or explaining; others are by nature *caretakers* and want to nurture or rescue people who are suffering; some teachers are *coaches* and default to encouragement, support, and even cheerleading; many of us are by training *therapists* and want to analyze or problem solve; and others are *performers* who tell jokes, read poetry, or tell personal stories about themselves. Other variations of these archetypes include the *dharma teacher*, who draws everything back to Buddhist teachings; the *scientist*, who talks too much about research and neuroscience; and the *evangelist* who proselytizes (and sometimes oversells) mindfulness and its benefits. Again, nothing is wrong with these styles per se if used judiciously, but it is helpful to recognize which styles we identify and are most comfortable with and notice when we are triggered and rely too heavily upon them.

Facilitating Abstract Conceptualization and Generalization of Experience

The question, "What relevance does this practice have to preventing depressive relapse, depression, or anxiety, and why we are here?" may sometimes be asked in inquiry as it highlights the movement from reflective observation to supporting participants to conceptualize what is being learned from their observations and to generalize them to life "off the cushion." It continues to hone an observational and curious stance to experience but supports an understanding of where the practice is leading, how it can serve us, and why we do it. This helps resolve discordance between old models of understanding experience related to negative moods states with new, disconfirming ideas and ways of being while building understanding, insight, and reasons for continuing to practice and apply the learning to real-world situations.

The teacher must maintain a present-moment orientation on what participants are saying and not get caught up in her ideas about what points need to be made. If the participant's answer seems to manifest an embodied understanding of the teaching point, the teacher might say nothing or offer a simple reflection by repeating or rephrasing what has been said. Sometimes one needs to use a complex reflection to guide the group to a more nuanced or deeper understanding of key learnings. Complex reflections are questions or statements that explore implicit meaning or intention (Miller & Rollnick, 2013). This is not the same as a psychological interpretation that tries to uncover or explain unconscious motivations, one's core beliefs, or hidden reasons behind a statement, but more an expansion or reworking of the person's words to help clarify meaning.

Commonly, a participant's reflections do not need a response on the part of the teacher. This is especially true in later sessions when the teacher needs to say less and less and allow the learning points to come from group members without embellishment. Other times, a participant response may reflect understanding or skill development but is somewhat unclear with respect to the utility of what is being learned as it relates to the intentions of the MBCT program. In that case, the teacher should resist the temptation to explain to the participant and instead follow-up with a question like, "Okay, so how would what you say be relevant for staying well?" This gently clarifies what is being said, creating the bridge between practice, learning, and application and making it explicit for all group members.

An example of an inquiry following the Three-Minute Breathing Space–Responsive in session 5 and requiring the participant to bring to mind a manageable difficulty, worry, or concern during the practice follows.

Teacher: How many of you were able to bring up a difficulty? Show of hands? I'm interested to hear what happened.

Participant 1: I got completely overwhelmed by the problem and wasn't able to do anything with the practice. I got really dizzy, shaky, and sweaty.

Teacher: Okay, when did you notice those sensations? (The teacher is calmly staying with a reflective observation of the practice and tracking.)

Participant 1: As soon as the problem came up.

Teacher: And what happened when asked to identify the emotion and body sensations?

Participant 1: Well, that's when I noticed feeling yucky and shaky.

Teacher: So, you stayed with the practice. And then what happened when you were instructed to bring attention to the breath at the belly and then to the entire body?

Participant 1: I felt some relief, but I still had tension in my stomach, and my hands were sweating. It's still there.

After hearing from several other participants about their experience with this practice, she turns to the whole group.

Teacher: Given how unpleasant this can be, what could be the relevance of this practice, which is to be present with difficult and challenging mind and mood states?

The teacher is trying to build an abstract conceptualization of what's happening in the practice and a rationale and elicit a case for its utility.

Participant 2: So, you get to know your patterns?

Teacher: And why might that be helpful?

Here, the teacher is getting more specific and concrete.

Participant 2: Maybe with awareness of the patterns, I might have the option of approaching things differently rather than just running away or distracting myself.

Teacher: Well, many might say that running away is a good thing. Why stay with this if it is unpleasant?

The teacher is using a paradoxical question to encourage a new way of dealing with difficulty.

Participant 3: Yeah, but often what we run from just continues or gets bigger. And sometimes you find out if you stay with it, it's not so bad, and you can survive and move through it.

Teacher: Ah, so sometimes avoidance and distraction might make things worse, and sometimes you discover it's not as bad as your feared. That's interesting isn't it?

The teacher is allowing a participant to generate the teaching point but offering new labels (avoidance and distraction) and giving it emphasis.

Teacher: So, I'll be asking you to experiment with this practice when a real difficulty arises. Next week, we'll talk about how it went and what you discovered when you stayed with a challenging moment.

The teacher is reinforcing the importance of experimenting with this in real life as home practice and reporting back to the group.

This case demonstrates the simple and complex reflections used through statements and questions that foster abstract conceptualization of the practice and reasons for testing it out in the real world. She tries to generate from participants an acceptable and believable rationale, consistent with their goals, while valuing and supporting further formal and informal practice.

At this stage of abstract conceptualization and generalization, the greatest challenge for the teacher is to resist telling versus eliciting from the group the links and benefits of the work. Although complex reflections and some summarization may be required, as much as possible, her inquiry must let the group come up with its own theories as to the relevance, generalizability, and rationale for the practice, thus teaching themselves. This process takes time. Yet often, as teachers, we are eager for participants to "get it" because we have an agenda, forgetting that people learn at different rates and that the themes are repeated throughout the course of the program. Further, trainees often do not trust in the wisdom of the group to generate the key teaching points for themselves.

A particular risk is in sessions 4 and 5 when participants begin recognizing habitual patterns of aversion and realize the practice is about turning toward, staying with difficulty, and building tolerance instead of engaging in avoidance. Given how counterintuitive this is, people often struggle or become distressed, and the teacher is tempted to fall back on rescuing, lecturing, or convincing them. Whether this comes from the teacher's own discomfort with difficult emotions or her desire to relieve suffering, rescuing, reassurance, and lecturing may subtly reinforce the same avoidance that is being challenged by the practice. It also sends the message that these emotions should not be tolerated but rather quickly managed. As part of this, she can be overinvested in participants getting relief in a way that often hinders instead of facilitates understanding. The teacher needs to learn how to treat all experience equally, modelling equanimity.

Facilitating Active Experimentation and Application of Learning

After having had the concrete experience in class, observed and reflected on it, and then explored its relevance to depression, anxiety, and other distress using a new mode of mind (not dependent on problem solving), the participant is then asked to go home, practice, reflect, and experiment with what has been learned. This enhances the skills of concentration, shifting attention, and a decentered stance, and helps participants see how these skills can be employed during stressful and depressogenic moments in life.

The term *home practice* is intentional as it is thought to be less provocative than calling it *homework*, particularly for those participants who have negative associations or memories of school. Further, it emphasizes the practice and skill development aspect of what is being asked. Home practice is highlighted from the beginning as a critical part of the program to reinforce and extend the learning that takes place during each session. The intentions of home practice include the application of concepts, assumptions, and principles of the MBCT program, as well as the formal and informal mindfulness practices to everyday life. Research may even be cited that suggests the amount of home practice is associated with positive outcomes in both MBCT and MBSR (Parsons, Crane, Parsons, Fjorback, & Kuyken, 2017).

In assigning home practice, its importance is often reiterated, and care is taken to ensure participants understand what is being expected. Handouts are given at the end of every class with relevant readings but also with a written list of the home practice assignment and recording log to encourage adherence. This log is valuable to continue the process of reflective observation on experience as well as externalizing it and reinforcing its accuracy in reporting back. This package can also be emailed to participants who missed that session to ensure they know what was covered and keep up with the practice. Time is allotted in every session to review the previous week's home practice and at the end to assign new work. The teacher needs to ensure that there is adequate time devoted to the home practice review in order to deal with its challenges and motivate the group to do it. Given the density of the program, the review of home practice may get short shrift. It is essential that it receive as much attention as other components of the program.

In the first few sessions when taking up home practice, the group explores obstacles to practice to both identify and normalize them. The group quickly generates strategies for dealing with these barriers. During discussion, it can be helpful to revisit the attitudinal foundations as relevant to home practice, including patience, trust, kindness, nonstriving, and curiosity. As with any aspect of teaching MBCT, a question like, "What attitudes might be important to support home practice?" will facilitate this learning better than just telling the group which attitudes to adopt. In subsequent sessions, discussion centers less on overcoming obstacles and more on the home practice experiences and insights that grow from them. Every experience is an opportunity for learning regardless of whether there is ease or struggle and whether a group member completed the home practice or not.

The home practice, in addition to various formal meditations, includes readings and exercises such as the Pleasant and Unpleasant Events Calendars, Identifying Relapse Signatures, and action plans for when depression and anxiety manifest. These are intended to help integrate and internalize the learning into daily life in both scheduled and ad hoc ways.

Not devoting enough time to the home practice review in each class not only misses critical learning opportunities but also may telegraph that home practice is an afterthought. Another mistake when dealing with obstacles is defaulting to always giving advice instead of allowing the group members to generate their own strategies for overcoming barriers when they can. There is always a balance between encouragement to do the practice, even if difficult, and encouraging self-care. Sometimes it is necessary to explicitly offer guidance and direction to the group. One must juggle a position of holding people accountable while at the same time maintaining an attitude of compassion and acceptance that this is not easy.

With the home practice logs and the events calendars, people are encouraged to read directly from these when reporting on their efforts. This emphasizes the importance of the home practice assignments, keeps the discussion located within the parsed components of experience, and reinforces the reflective observation of experiences outside of class. This also limits the tendency for participants to engage in excessive narration.

Of note, home practice review is not about exploring someone's experience using the inquiry one would use immediately following a meditation practice. Rather, its primary intention is about assisting an individual and the group to support the continuation of practice and applying the learning outside the session. This entails dealing with challenges and successes that come from practicing at home. It is necessary to make the doing of the home practice relevant, generalizing it beyond the stated intent of the MBCT program to a broader intention of staying well and increasing self-efficacy.

In Closing

In this chapter, we've identified teaching competence as a combination of knowledge, attitudes, skills, and behaviors. We reviewed Kolb's experiential learning model and offered it as another way to unpack MBCT teaching competencies and their components. Along with creating and maintaining a safe and supportive learning environment, we explored how teachers can facilitate direct experience, support reflective observation and abstract conceptualization, and assist participants in experimentation and practice. Within each competency, we detailed some of the necessary skills, attitudes and behaviors, and challenges and pitfalls for the teacher. In the coming chapters, we turn to embodied mindful presence as the heart of teaching mindfulness, thereby transforming these competencies from a list of attributes to something alive—from teaching as something to do and deliver to teaching as a practice.

PART 3
Teaching as a Practice

The Inner Landscape

Chapter 6

Embodied Mindful Presence— The Heart of Teaching

Part 1 covered certain foundations for broadening our understanding of teaching MBCT. We introduced the five agents of change and TRIP and applied those constructs to the MBCT protocol. In part 2, we looked at ways we can further deepen our teaching by applying TRIP to specific mindfulness practices and cognitive exercises. We then discussed group process from the unique lens of a mindfulness-based program and ended that section by considering teaching competencies, skills, and challenges. In this final part of the book, we will move more deeply into the foundations that inform teaching MBCT—addressing not just the skills you will need to teach MBCT, but the essence of teaching this program as a practice.

We will begin with the embodied mindful presence of the teacher, a critical aspect of teaching MBPs. Our focus will be on developing clarity around what is seen as an esoteric process of communicating mindfulness through the teacher's presence and instruction. Embodiment has a significant part to play in enriching our teaching and underpinning best practices and competence in the delivery of MBCT as well as other MBPs.

Neither fully an educational model of teaching nor a psychotherapy, facilitating MBCT endeavors to be a mindfulness practice itself, a process of understanding how we (the teacher and participant) can develop a different relationship to the concepts of suffering, impermanence, and our sense of self. In highlighting these three, we are emphasizing what we addressed earlier in the book—that to teach MBCT, we are facilitating a contemporary form of meditation practice. Therefore, teaching mindfulness of necessity requires a teacher to have an experiential understanding of these garnered from his own practice. This will entail an awareness of one's own suffering and how we have come to understand the roots of that suffering—which, in the Buddhist context, are greed (wanting things to fulfill us and give us lasting satisfaction or wanting things to be different than they are), hatred (anger, dislike, aversion, ill will), and delusion (a confused or a wrong understanding of reality). This understanding will have grown from a practice in insight meditation, a training that is a means of investigating internal and external experience (regardless of whether it is pleasant, unpleasant, or neutral) by bringing a present-moment, nonjudgmental, and compassionate awareness to whatever is occurring in any given moment.

In this chapter, we will explore attitudinal foundations of mindfulness and include an appreciation and understanding of key teachings of Buddhist psychology as central to the development of a teacher's embodied mindful presence. In the next chapter, we will expand on these foundations to discuss how these are expressed and translate into teaching. This translation requires a present-moment orientation involving the ability to teach bare attention (an intentional focus on the present), the capacity to demonstrate an open receptivity (open-monitoring or meta-awareness), and the ability to convey that how we relate to experience can be a choice that will inform our behaviors through discernment and skillful action. Having knowledge of these elements as well as a mindfulness practice of your own allows you to embody and instruct others in these practices. Therefore, teaching MBCT will be a mindfulness practice as well as a way of being.

Attitudinal Foundations of Mindfulness

The attitudinal foundations (Kabat-Zinn, 1990, 2013) are a helpful start for our discussion on embodiment because they offer specific ways for the teacher to engage with mindfulness practices and to model them for his participants. These attitudes are expressed through the teacher's nonverbal behavior, instruction, and inquiry. It is through the lived experience and felt sense of these attitudes that a teacher strengthens the possibility of embodying mindfulness, which in turn facilitates the learning and reinforces the everyday relevance of these practices for his participants. These are the ability to express and embody patience, trust, beginner's mind, nonjudging, acceptance, nonstriving, and letting go (Kabat-Zinn, 1990, 2013). It is our understanding that the original attitudinal foundations outlined by Kabat-Zinn were never meant to be exhaustive but rather were meant to emphasize that there are specific qualities inherent to mindfulness. Although, for the sake of clarity in the discussion that follows, we have separated these attitudes, in reality they overlap; for example, nonstriving requires patience and letting go and nonjudging require beginner's mind. We have added curiosity and compassion as two additional foundations because we think they are essential to both embodied mindful presence and in teaching.

The MBCT teacher, in emphasizing paying attention to all experiences, will convey and express the attitudes of patience, trust, and beginner's mind as ways of approaching what is being noticed. Furthermore, he will model nonjudgment, acceptance, and nonstriving to his participants—tapping into a being mode of mind that fosters resilience and the ability to move with experience rather than resisting what isn't wanted (which will invite suffering).

Two other attitudinal foundations are those of curiosity (investigating experience with interest before acknowledging its disappearance) and compassion (a kind-hearted and tender approach to each moment, allowing it to be present, even if it is difficult or painful). A teacher who embodies these qualities leads participants to explore experience with interest; he guides them to develop an awareness of and interest in the how, what, where, and when of experience rather than just the why. In this way, attention is drawn to investigating the present moment and not to the narrative of past experiences or predictions for the future. Compassion is an essential component in meeting the moments of self-judgment, which helps disrupt the negative view of self that perpetuates depression. The compassionate teacher conveys an empathic attunement and warm acceptance of all experience, the antidote to critical and judgmental thinking.

These are also the qualities our participants need to cultivate. Our focus here is on how these attitudes inform the development of teaching skills that illuminate the embodiment of the practice and how the teacher encourages them in his participants. What follows will be a general explanation of each attitude and how a teacher can intentionally embody it. We will then explore some of these attitudes in action by following a teacher facilitating a discussion after a session 3 practice.

Patience. Most of us move fast, driven by a sense of needing to get things accomplished quickly before moving on to the next thing. In addition, it's not unusual to be juggling several projects at one time. The practice of mindfulness presents us with the option of slowing down or stopping and the wisdom to know when to do so. It takes patience to reset the busyness of the mind and allow things to reveal themselves in their own time.

For the teacher, this means embodying patience as an attitudinal quality by demonstrating and modeling to group participants the understanding that it can take time to settle, learn about what it means to be with oneself, and attend to what is being met.

Trust. Trust in this context is the basic trust in one's own intuition and authority. It is turning toward the experience of the moment, being present for what is arising, and allowing for what is being noticed. The realization that we can trust ourselves to do this is an essential part of the teaching.

For the teacher, this means expressing interest in what participants are experiencing as they engage in mindfulness practices and conveying a sense of confidence and trust in their exploration.

Beginner's mind. Beginner's mind is a key aspect of mindfulness practice. It prompts us to recognize when the mind has wandered off and escort it back with a commitment to begin again. It also allows us to be open to what the program has to offer, unfiltered by preconceived notions and judgments about mindfulness. And it allows us to let each moment be a fresh one, unfettered by the past or the future.

For the teacher, it means maintaining an openness to each moment and recognizing that he will not necessarily know how it will present itself. It will also mean the dropping of expectations about how, what, and when learning will unfold for each individual and for the group. By embodying a gentle presence that understands the many modes of mind and behaviors that take us away from the present, a teacher articulates the process of beginning again.

Nonjudging. Nonjudging is the suspension of the mode of comparing, evaluating, and expressing preference. We are often most harsh toward ourselves and critical of how we measure up, especially if we are prone to or struggling with depression and anxiety. Awareness of our judging minds, and the ability to be with our experience without judgment, is key.

For the teacher, it is the practice of embodying a friendly curiosity without immediately rushing to judgment, comparison, or evaluation. He embodies steadiness and patience through personal knowledge of the frequent intolerant cognitive modes of self-criticism, disparagement, and blame. A sense of kindness accompanies nonjudgment because meeting the judging mind with more judging makes things much worse.

Acceptance. When we get in touch with the contents of the mind and heart, aspects of ourselves that are difficult or unwanted can be revealed. Acceptance is the befriending of these challenges, finding a way to give them as much space as they need, and allowing them to be known just as they are. This acceptance is neither passive nor resigned, and does not require us to like our experience, but requires a compassionate courage to witness what is arising and to act only when needed.

For the teacher, it is embodying a presence that models permission, kindness, spaciousness, and gratitude while gently holding what the practice is pointing to, namely that there is no aspect of ourselves that is not worth loving and taking care of. This is of significance throughout the MBCT program and is a core aspect of teaching and embodiment for the teacher.

Nonstriving. Much of our lives involve taking responsibility for all the tasks of daily living, and of course this is important. But this doing mode of mind is inevitably goal directed and attached to outcome, which has problematic consequences when we view our internal experiences in this way. The idea of being with the unfolding nature of each moment liberates us from the constant need to be always doing something. Nonstriving supports us in being present, stimulating curiosity about what is being observed, tuning in, and turning toward various sensations regardless of how they are being experienced.

For the teacher, it is modeling calm, gentleness, and compassion. A teacher will have experienced his own habitual urges to avoid uncomfortable or challenging experiences. Appreciating when they appear in his participants' responses requires an understanding of the release that can come when he surrenders to what is being experienced. The teacher can then see clearly what, if anything, is needed in that moment.

Letting go. This is perhaps the most difficult of all the attitudinal foundations. We are inclined to want things to be a certain way. We grasp for what we want and often want more of what we like and think we need. And we tend to hold on to things long after they have ended. Interestingly, we have an equal propensity to hold on to negative situations as much as positive ones. In mindfulness practice, by turning toward difficulty, we get to see how grasping will increase suffering. By observing this many, many times with kindness and gentleness, we are eventually released from this tendency, simply by seeing and understanding the suffering that results.

For the teacher, it means modeling a gentle, kind acceptance of the tendency to repeatedly ruminate on what has just happened. Embodying a compassionate evenness in these moments, the teacher supports for himself and promotes in the participants an awareness that encourages an understanding of how painful rumination and clinging can be and how freeing it is to let go.

Curiosity. Bringing curiosity to each moment is an essential component to exploring experience from an observational stance. This is a critical skill to develop in MBCT as it allows one to be less immersed in experience and to develop a different relationship to it that is less reactive, allowing for a wider range of responses. Being interested in what is occuring in any given moment requires an active engagement in exploring the field of experience. By bringing curiosity to these moments, it is possible to notice the arrival of a particular sensation (here defined as any component of that experience— thought, emotion, body sensation), investigate it, and acknowledge its disappearance when and if it does.

For the teacher, it means embodying a steadiness and interest in what a participant is discovering in experience and directing attention to not only what is being noticed but to following how that shifts and changes.

Compassion. Compassion grows through the experience of allowing and meeting each moment, even if difficult or painful, without judgment. Mindfulness practices in the MBCT program encourage being with (noticing, accepting) and tuning in (acknowledging, being curious, exploring) to the difficult. This encourages understanding that how we relate to the difficult or unwanted can be a choice.

For the teacher, novel learning for participants comes from a teacher's embodying a willingness to turn toward moments of struggle, resting in whatever is arising, with whatever degree of compassion is available in that moment. By his turning toward and staying with these moments of suffering, he is demonstrating for participants that it is possible to empathically attend to the experience and know there may be nothing that needs fixing and that simply being present may be enough.

Having described these attitudinal foundations, we can now discuss them at work in the following excerpt from the third session of the MBCT program ("Gathering the Scattered Mind"). The dialogue is taking place after the meditation practice of working with challenging or difficult physical sensations. The teacher is facilitating the inquiry process, using the attitudinal foundations to inform his approach and his responses to what participants volunteer.

Teacher: I'm curious to hear what showed up in this practice? (At the beginning of the discussion, the teacher is inviting an attitude of *curiosity*.)

Participant 1: I had a lot of pain in my back. It's all this sitting.

Teacher: Were you able to explore the sensations?

Participant 1: A little. Some pulsing, tightness.

Teacher: Any other sensations?

Participant 1: I moved my position, which was helpful. And then when you said to return to the original position, I did that, and the sensations were different.

Teacher: So, noticing a change?

The teacher is supporting the ability to track sensations and encouraging *trust* in the ability to do that rather than emphasizing the positive valence that the participant is ascribing to it.

Participant 2: I got a little concerned about this idea of investigating a pain in the body. I have a lot of pain from a shoulder injury that has never healed properly. I did have a go at exploring the sensations, but it didn't help.

Teacher: So, we want to take our time with this investigating and with working with the instructions (*nonstriving and patience*). Can I ask how you went about exploring?

Participant 2: Well, I liked the idea of breathing into the area and out.

Teacher: And what did you discover? (Here the teacher is encouraging *curiosity*.)

Participant 2: I think it got a little easier.

Teacher: Was that from noticing the body sensations, thoughts, or emotions?

Participant 2: I think it was from breathing into the area and out.

Teacher: Interesting, thanks.

Participant 3: My mind just gets so busy with this silent meditation practice. It's hard to notice anything else. I'm finding it really difficult to do the practices, as my mind doesn't shut up.

Teacher: Yes, the mind can get very active when we stop moving and sit quietly, noticing what is going on. It's very normal. So then what happened? (The teacher is *accepting* the difficulty as well as placing *trust* in the process of what he is asking. He is also *not judging* the mind being active).

Particpant 3: I wanted it to stop, so I tried to focus on the breath, but that didn't work.

Teacher: When we want something to happen, like wanting it to stop, it can backfire on us in this practice. So one of the things we are cultivating is the sense of *patience* and *nonstriving*. The patience to keep being present, even when it is challenging, with a sense of not needing it to be different.

Through his inquiry into the participants' experiences, this teacher is implicitly and actively working with several of the attitudinal foundations. He is embodying what is being noticed from practice without needing to identify these foundations overtly. At the point where this excerpt ends, we see him naming two of the attitudinal foundations, *patience* and *nonstriving*, after these participants have spoken. He could have named the others, but these are the ones that seem primary in this dialogue. At this stage, participants are still going to be struggling with what they are meeting due to their engagement with mindfulness practice. If we review what these participants spoke about, it was useful that the teacher decided to highlight *patience* and *nonstriving* as they applied to all three of the participants' experiences, thereby supporting individual and group learning, a helpful tool and attitude to bring to the practice. The attitudes are also essential as we move forward in the program and begin to work with more difficult states.

Using a Key Teaching of Buddhist Psychology

A second foundation that underpins and informs a teacher's embodiment of mindfulness will be an understanding of some central aspects of Buddhist psychology. We see these as crucial to embodying and communicating mindfulness as they will be active ingredients in the teaching of meditation practices and inquiry. It is impossible to do justice to the depth of these teachings here, but we see developing a familiarity and understanding of these as extremely relevant in reinforcing the depth of the teaching, nourishing competency, and promoting best practices. Of note, these Buddhist teachings provide an ethical framework for our instruction that augments any professional code of conduct we may have. They will also provide a frame of reference for those who may be in an occupation that has not identified these professional boundaries. The ethical principle of *do no harm* is a practice embedded in Buddhist philosophy and shared by all health care professions.

Below, we outline the key Buddhist teachings that we think have relevance to MBCT. We will focus on the three marks of existence—viewing experience as imperfect, impermanent, and impersonal—because we see them as central to deepening meaning and reinforcing what we are trying to represent as teachers. Although we discuss these here, they are not talked about directly in the MBCT program. This is because they are underlying a teacher's embodiment and guiding inquiry as the teacher listens for them in participants' responses.

Suffering is an inevitable part of life as we are all subject to loss including illness, aging, and eventually death. An aspect of being human is to encounter experiences that are *imperfect* and unsatisfactory. Compounding this is that we desire certain things and crave others, but find the satisfaction from getting what we want is short-lived. Buddhism theorizes that it is our relationship to these experiences that will largely determine the perception and degree of suffering. Resisting what is being experienced only adds an additional layer of suffering and is a root cause for further anguish and stress. As Shinzen Young (2004) points out, "suffering equals pain multiplied by resistance" (p. 32). For example, if one experiences sadness or back pain for any length of time and then worries that it will never get better, this makes the situation worse.

We have a strong tendency to want to hold on to and repeat things that are being perceived as pleasant, avoid those that are unpleasant, and ignore things that are neutral. But continuing attempts to increase a sense of pleasure by wanting more of the same thing or looking for something else that could offer similar enjoyment reinforces a sense of dissatisfaction. And grasping that which is transitory, regardless of whether it is pleasant, unpleasant, or neutral, produces states that are observed and experienced as inherently unsatisfying, which causes more suffering. For example, the first bite of a chocolate bar produces a heightened awareness and pleasure of the sense of taste. This quickly diminishes, as thinking recognizes that you only have a finite amount to eat, that you think you'd prefer a different type of chocolate, or that you ate too much and feel sick.

Intellectually, we know that nothing can remain the same and that *impermanence* is a fact of life, but experientially and emotionally, we find this hard to accept. We seek permanence. And yet we do not have the same body that we were born with, nor when we were young, nor as an adult of twenty, thirty, forty, and so forth. The cells in our bodies are constantly engaged in self-renewal and deterioration. If all things are constantly changing, then mind and mood states must be subject to the same process. We perpetuate low mind and mood states by avoiding them, hanging on to them, or struggling with experiences or situations that are impermanent. The way we make meaning of the resulting mind and mood states contribute to building an identity as a depressed person. It is also true that whereas we understand the concept of impermanence, we don't believe in it until we have the lived experienced of it through practicing mindfulness.

That experience is *impersonal* is embedded in the concept of *not-self* or *non-self*, a core teaching of Buddhism, though difficult to grasp. There are three aspects to this idea, and these are that we are all connected, we are all subject to the changing nature of experience (causes and conditions), and though we personalize everything, all experience is universal. Ignoring these leads to a fixed sense of self, the trap of identity. We get caught into thinking that there is such an entity as a permanent and unchanging self. If we believe this, we become prone to wanting to hold onto what is "me" or "mine," and this produces unhappiness and suffering. If, on the other hand, we can see that events are impersonal, that we are all interconnected, and that everything is subject to change, then we have more ease throughout life.

Of most relevance to people who are suffering from mood disorders and anxiety is the tendency to personalize their condition. Thoughts and emotions have significant adhesion, as we tend to believe them and what they say about us. Over time, these patterns of thinking and mood fluctuations are reinforced, becoming fixed in the form of identity so that, by example "I am a depressed person" defines me, whereas a more skillful view is "I am a person who suffers from depression." Having a primary focus on self is isolating. It disconnects one from one's resources and the universality of interconnectedness.

In MBCT, the embodiment of not-self is supported by the guidance of mindfulness-based meditation practices (for example, the way a teacher *refers to "the body" versus "your body"*) as well as conversations that encourage a description of what is present, helping participants to be less immersed in their difficulties and the stories about them. Consider a participant who remarks, after the meditation practice in session 4 ("Recognizing Aversion"), "I've always been depressed. I don't think I have ever not been depressed. It's part of my makeup." The teacher picks up on the fact that she identifies with being depressed and responds by returning the participant to the practice she has just completed by asking, "Do you remember when you first became aware of this in the practice we just did?" In this way, he is steadying the focus back to what has just been experienced (the here and now) rather than getting caught up in the narrative of self-identification with depression. "There was a lot of thinking, and I felt sad." The teacher responds with, "Any body sensations?" and she replies, "Yes, a sick feeling in my stomach." She is beginning to track her own experience, supporting being with what was happening and strengthening an observational stance. This is a key aspect of the decentering process and not-self. In breaking up experience into its component parts, there is the opportunity to see the changing nature of experience and be less identified with it.

Although developing a strong sense of self is important for psychological development and function, clinging to a fixed image of self is fraught. Though a stable sense of self is necessary for us to function, we place an overreliance on things outside ourselves as a crutch that props up a fixed and permanent sense of who we are, forgetting that adaptability is required to meet the varied and changing conditions of our lives. This overreliance on being defined by what other people think about us, how well we are doing compared to others, the accumulation of possessions, how much money we make, and so forth will ultimately fail us. The dependence on external conditions for feelings of self-worth can be easily dented the minute the situation, event, or person offers some communication that is negative. We are constantly in process, responding to our internal and external environments—and by understanding that our identity is not fixed, we can be responsive, flexible, and adaptive. We loosen up on the often harsh and unkind criticisms we direct at ourselves and others and have the tendency to personalize. By becoming less attached to our ideas about ourselves, we become less self-centered and more sensitive to the perspectives and needs of others. This is not to say that a sense of who we are should be eliminated but rather that if we hold it lightly, we will experience more ease.

A small digression here will be useful to discuss how the doing and being modes of mind contribute to a fixed and flexible sense of self, respectively. The doing mode, like a fixed sense of self, is necessary for us to function in the world. It provides stability and an enduring and consistent narrative, so we are able to plan, organize, and meet the demands of life. It is responsible for our ability to engage in many activities automatically, which is useful, although it can lead to rigidity and habitual reactivity, which are common. Alternatively, being mode of mind establishes an intentional and attentional emphasis on noticing the range of experiences in the present moment. It is based on an experiential exploration of sensations staying close to the immediacy of an experience that is helpful in counteracting tendencies to get lost in thought or be overwhelmed by challenging emotional moments. This supports adaptation and resilience.

Being mode decreases the tendency toward repetitive negative thinking irrespective of whether one has a mood disorder or not. Instead, it encourages the ability to observe thoughts and emotions without needing to problem solve or fix the situation or oneself (*nonstriving*). We become observers of our patterns, also known as decentering. This lessens the hold that thinking and emotional states have on our narratives (for example, *I am flawed*) and instead enhances an open-monitoring or meta-awareness of experience, which supports discernment of patterns that can lead to further suffering.

If we return to Young's mindfulness equation that suffering equals pain multiplied by resistance, the different forms of resistance are behaviors like avoidance, wanting things to be different, and rumination. What fuels these are the mental traps that life and experience should be *perfect* and free from pain, that what happens to us is *permanent* and not subject to change, and that it is *personal*, viewed from the lens of me, myself, and mine. The MBCT program subtly leads participants to an awareness of this relationship, and the utility of mindfulness practice is to lessen these resistances even if for brief moments.

We can now explore how an awareness that life is imperfect, impersonal, and impermanent and that resisting this creates suffering applies to teaching MBCT through the following case example. In a discussion after a sitting meditation practice in session 6 ("Thoughts Are Not Facts"), participants are talking about their experiences.

The practice has instructed them to be especially aware of how they are relating to thoughts when they notice them.

Participant: It's much easier to be with the breath and the body than with thoughts. I much prefer yoga. It's so much easier not to think maybe because they play calming music.

Teacher: Huh, so liking and not liking was showing up? What did you notice in this practice today?

The teacher is not getting pulled in to the narrative and reflecting on preference.

Participant: I can stay with the breath and the sensations from the body for longer. With thoughts, I start thinking!

Teacher: Do you have a sense of what the thoughts are saying?

The teacher, while ostensibly asking for content, is primarily interested in the externalizing of thoughts and their description as evidenced by his use of the phrase "what the thoughts are saying…" versus "what you are thinking"—language that encodes an understanding of not-self.

Participant: Yes. They're random. One minute it's one kind of thought, the next it's another. I did notice that a lot of the thoughts are about the past. They're not happy memories.

Teacher: So, you are watching them?

The teacher identifies the decentering from self and has elicited a description of thought qualities.

Participant: Well sort of. It's more like I notice I am thinking when I realize that I am thinking. Am I doing this right?

The teacher does not answer this question, reassure, or move away from what the participant is expressing about her experience. Instead he answers, maintaining a focus on what is being revealed *(being present for)*, embodying curiosity and a calm interest and staying current with externalizing the experience. He is also going to stay close to the intention of this practice that is to notice any relationship to thoughts.

Teacher: Thoughts are tough to watch. When you were noticing you were thinking, did you notice anything else?

Participant: (The participant pauses for a moment, obviously thinking about this.) Yeah. Now that you ask…I remember my breath got tight.

Teacher: So, the breath was tight. Do you remember where you felt this?

The teacher is reinforcing change (and by extension, impermanence).

Participant: In my throat.

Teacher: That's interesting. And then what happened?

Again, tracking the changing nature of experience and highlighting impermanence and not-self.

Participant: I think I went back to thinking. That's probably what I did.

Teacher: Noticing the relationship we might have to thinking can sometimes show up in the body.

Participant: Should I watch out for this?

Teacher: Well, not necessarily by looking for body sensations. But checking in with the body from time to time during the meditation practice can give some helpful information about our relationship to what we are thinking. It can also give us a break from getting caught up in those thoughts.

The teacher here is disrupting the narrative and sense of self and shifting attention to the body.

He focuses on *being* with the participant's experience, exploring, and conveying interest and curiosity about it. He is not interested in the content of thoughts per se because the danger there is to fall in to the story that thoughts often produce. He is embodying sensitivity to a nuanced inner world, helping the participant to trace the movement of sensations *(impermanence)* without personalizing them.

In Closing

We have discussed how the embodiment of aspects of Buddhist psychology, namely that life is imperfect, impermanent, and impersonal and the knowledge that suffering results from wanting things to be other than they are, supports a teacher's ability to express a mindful presence in his teaching. From this wisdom, the attitudinal foundations can flourish, particularly curiosity and compassion. This will allow him to meet and follow his participants wherever they might lead. Together they discover the insight and wisdom afforded by the practice of mindfulness in their journey through the MBCT program. In the following chapter, we will address how the teacher expresses an embodied mindful presence through teaching and modeling bare attention, open-monitoring, and discernment.

An MBCT teacher who understands and resonates with the imperfect nature of experience, impermanence, and not-self comes to epitomize mindfulness. This is discernment and has little to do with intellectual knowing. Discernment and wisdom arise from meeting all experience in its various forms with a clear sense of recognition, kindness, and skillful action. This way of being, the heart of the practice, enhances a teacher's ability to embody and express compassion, to be present and responsive to his participants.

Chapter 7

Expressing and Fostering Embodied Mindful Presence

In the previous chapter, we discussed certain attitudinal foundations of mindfulness and aspects of Buddhist teaching that inform its embodiment and impact our teaching of the MBCT program. We can now turn our attention to building upon these foundations to see how they can be expressed by a teacher and encouraged in the participants. Our focus will be about how to best help participants cultivate the embodied mindful presence that the teacher, in the last chapter, has learned how to model. She does this by learning to embody and teach bare attention, open-monitoring (receptivity and tracking), and discernment (the insight that guides skillful responding) through a consistent present-moment orientation. We see these as central to the guiding of mindfulness practices and how this is reflected in the contemplative dialogue that we call inquiry.

Present-Moment Orientation

Entertaining the possibility that the teacher can always maintain and represent a present-moment focus is unrealistic. And yet, this is what we are asking of ourselves because it is what we invite our participants to practice and is what we attempt to embody from the beginning of each class. From the moment we enter the room where the class is being held, we are intentionally slowing down. By doing this, we are encouraging and supporting our intention as teachers to have a focus on regularly checking in (bare attention) and to attend to the experience of the moment, allowing us to discern what to do next, if anything. Slowing down also marks our movement into a period of teaching where we are inviting ourselves and our participants to enter a way of being that is different from our usual ways of interacting and relating.

For many of us who teach MBCT, it is not our only professional responsibility, and frequently we teach at the end of the day. This can affect the energy we bring to our MBCT sessions. Ideally, it is important to allow time before the class begins to give oneself time to review the agenda, set an intention to find ways to settle into acknowledging the currency of the moment (such as tiredness, excitement, or anxiety), and to let go of expectations of how the class will go. Useful ways for the teacher to stabilize a focus on the present moment and reinforce this intention include allowing time for her own short practice, such as a ten-minute breath-awareness practice, or a Three-Minute Breathing Space if time is short. If there is recognition of a lot of busyness of mind or fatigue, then a moving practice can be beneficial; if there is a sense of needing to take some time to be quiet, then a sitting meditation will be helpful; if there is hunger, then bringing a snack and practicing eating meditation will be nourishing.

Being present when a session begins is a complex endeavor for the teacher, and over the duration of each session, there will be times when the teacher's present-moment orientation is inevitably pulled away. This is to be expected, as an MBCT teacher is responsible for facilitating and delivering many teaching elements. She is aware of the narrative arc of the session, supporting and attending to the group and maintaining attention to key learning themes and teaching points (using TRIP). This balance of the doing and being modes of teaching can be difficult. For the novice teacher, challenges such as worrying about the time, perseverating on what a participant said or getting lost in the story, concern about a participant's condition, being too heavily invested in making a teaching point, and her own insecurities about her teaching can be additional concerns.

In the beginning, a teacher will learn by applying a doing mode of mind (a top-down process) employing intellect, or cognitive learning, to understanding the MBCT protocol. This knowledge base is then applied to teaching. Over time, this experience of working with the protocol is valuable, as it builds confidence and skills. Once the teacher is versed in the structure and modules of the program, she then has the freedom to teach from a being mode, one that is experiential and process driven. This is the difference between a purely cognitive and content driven approach to teaching versus an experiential, embodied, and internalized one. What is used to maintain this balance is the fluid interplay between teaching essential aspects of the MBCT program and knowing when bare attention, open awareness, and discernment are needed. This is dependent on the experience and skill of the teacher, what is being elicited from the group, and the degree to which the group is struggling to internalize the learning.

Bare attention, open-monitoring, and discernment are essential practices embedded in the MBCT program that experientially assist in the transmission of teaching. *Bare attention* is the ability to intentionally pay attention to one's internal and external experience, *open-monitoring* is the practice of being receptive to all sensations as they come and go, and *discernment* is the practice of skillfully choosing how to respond to experience, even as we hold it all with compassion and kindness. All three are practices the teacher embraces in her guidance, demeanor, and presence and encourages in participants via the process of inquiry. The evolution of a mindful, embodied presence is a practice and requires the teacher to be attentive to what is showing up in the group and in herself in an open and receptive manner, while being able to discern what is required from moment to moment. This can be an encouragement of a present-moment focus on process over content, gentle guidance toward a teaching point, or space and a container for a participant to endure an emotionally charged moment.

A word here about the risks inherent in any definition that attempts to describe a working understanding of meditation practice: these risks include reification, misunderstanding, and oversimplification of what is essentially a dynamic process. Nevertheless, we discuss these as separate and sequential while understanding there is significant flow and overlap between them.

Bare Attention

Again, bare attention is the ability to intentionally pay and direct attention to one's internal and external experience. For MBCT teachers, this includes the guiding of participants. For example, in leading a breath-awareness practice, a teacher will continue to pay attention to her own experience while setting up a posture for herself and her participants that promotes a sense of wakefulness and comfort. The teacher then directs the participants to the sensations of breathing wherever they are most vividly being felt in the body. To hold this bare attention, participants are invited to bring a sense of curiosity to this direct experience of sensation. When attention is, inevitably, pulled away from the primary focus, they are reminded to notice this and gently escort the attention back to the breath. Part of maintaining this instructional focus of bare attention requires the teacher to pause so participants have time to experience these sensations and to become aware of how frequently the mind or attention is drawn into thinking, other sensations, emotional states, and so forth. As the practice ends, the teacher will use language that facilitates the transition into the next moments. This generally marks the intentional shifting of attention from formal practice to inquiry.

Below is an example illustrating how bare attention is expressed by the teacher and encouraged in the participants through the guidance of a ten-minute meditation practice in session 2 ("Living in Our Heads").

So, let's get started.

The first thing to consider is finding a comfortable sitting position. Choosing to sit in a chair, on one of the cushions, or on a bench.

Whatever your posture, adopting a position that can best convey the sense of being awake, alert, and relaxed. It's helpful, if you are using a chair, to have your feet flat on the ground and your knees hip-distance apart. Also, if it's possible, coming toward the front of the chair, away from the back, so you are supporting your spine. If that is not possible, then having a cushion or a rolled-up blanket in the small of your back to support the arch in the lower back can be helpful as you let the back of the chair support the rest of the spine. Whatever position you decide upon, the key is to be at ease as much as is possible. (The teacher pauses to allow participants time to set up and settle.)

Once you have found a position that is comfortable, allowing the eyes to close, or equally softening the gaze, looking down toward the floor in front of you.

Now, taking a few moments to notice the weight of the body sitting here, the contact points that the body is making with the chair, the floor, with itself. Noticing the physical sensations arising from the body, both from the surface of the skin and from inside the body. (Teacher pauses to allow bare attention of sensation.)

As you pay attention to body sensations, you will become more aware of the sensations of breathing. You might be most aware of the breath coming in through the nostrils and leaving from there as well. You might be aware of the movement of the ribs as you breathe in and out or the movement of the belly, rising with each in-breath and releasing with each out-breath. Taking these next few moments to bring your attention to where you best sense the physical sensations and rhythm of breathing, and allowing the attention to rest right there. (The teacher pauses to enable participants to find a bare attentional focus on the physical sensations of breathing.)

You may be finding, as you pay attention to the breath in this way, that the attention moves to thinking, to sounds, or perhaps to sensations elsewhere in the body. This is perfectly natural. This is what minds do. Once you notice this, the choice is to return the attention to the sensations of breathing wherever you best sense the body breathing. In this way, you are supporting the possibility of letting the focus on breathing be an anchor to the movement of each moment, a way to be present for each moment, rather than be governed by thinking about the past or worrying about the future. (This invitation reminds participants of the intention of the practice, normalizes the pull of attention, and assists them in bringing bare attention to the movement of experience.)

Over the next moments, continuing to practice in this way… Allowing the breath to be in the forefront of your consciousness and noticing when the attention moves off that focus, waking up to that moment, and then gently bringing the attention back to the sensations of breathing. (The teacher pauses here again, allowing participants to continue to practice this present moment focus.)

In a few moments, we will be coming to the end of this sitting meditation practice. Allowing the eyes to open or widening the gaze, taking in the surroundings of the room. Taking a moment or two here before transitioning into the next moments of our time together. (The teacher is stressing that all components of the practice from beginning to end and beyond are worthy of attention.)

In this example, the teacher sets up the practice in a way that creates the preconditions for intentional attention and a move from doing to being mode. She uses invitational, kind language and periods of silence to allow the participants to practice using bare attention. She is guiding them to direct their focus to the sensations of breathing as an anchor, and in a nonjudgmental manner, normalizes the inevitable pull of attention. This is important because the language of the guidance promotes a kind approach to movements of mind that are so easily perceived as failure, often resulting in harsh judgments against the self. This normalization supports the beginning of observing this movement of mind, stabilizing attention, and promoting openness to experience without adding anything else to it.

Open-Monitoring

While the teacher will initially instruct participants in the first few weeks of the program in the training of focusing and directing attention to primary foci (bare attention), in the latter weeks, she will gradually guide the broadening of attention toward a receptive stance of open-monitoring (also known as open awareness or choiceless awareness). Again, this is a practice of being receptive to all sensations as they come, persist, and go. Thoughts and emotions are treated no differently than other sensory foci and are described as events or sensations of the mind. Part of open-monitoring means sequentially tracking one's experience as it arises and passes, both internally and externally. Lastly, this will include an awareness of how one is relating to one's experience, whether that is with reactivity, equanimity, or indifference.

How is the teacher embodying and teaching this practice of open-monitoring? This is most easily demonstrated when a teacher is guiding her participants in a sitting practice in session 4 ("Recognizing Aversion"). This excerpt begins toward the end of the practice.

…having focused in turn on breath, body, and then sounds, now shifting attention to focusing on thoughts themselves. Just as with hearing and noticing individual sounds coming and going, as best as you are able, noticing thoughts in the same way as they arise, develop, and pass away. Thoughts as objects of attention…. as sensations of the mind. No need to search for thoughts or direct your thinking, but allowing for thoughts to come into and pass through the spaciousness of mind. (The teacher pauses to allow participants to practice this.)

And when noticing getting caught up in thoughts or lost in thinking, stepping back, and observing as best you can these thoughts as mental events. Watching them arise, stay for a while, and pass, to be replaced by other thoughts. (Pause.)

It may be hard to watch thoughts in this way, noticing when there is a stream of thinking or there are no thoughts at all. In this case it may be helpful to imagine yourself on the bank of a river watching the water flow by, sometimes gently and slowly, and at other times, faster and with force. If the river is like the mind, then individual thoughts are like twigs or leaves floating on the water being carried into your field of awareness and then passing by. Occasionally you can get "hooked" and caught up in a stream of thoughts, until recognizing that this has happened and coming back to watching thoughts flow by. (In MBCT, we rarely use metaphors, as they can drive conceptualization and thinking. However, metaphors can be useful when encouraging distance and perspective from our thinking because this can be difficult without such imagery.)

Sometimes thoughts may come with an emotional charge; when this happens, noting this. If any thoughts are associated with intense emotions, whether pleasant or unpleasant, as best you can, simply noting these as sensations like any other that arise, stick around for a while, and pass away. It can be helpful in these moments to say quietly to yourself, "Sadness is here; joy is present; frustration, worry, happiness is here." If emotionally charged thoughts are particularly intense, bringing attention to where in the body these might show up as a bracing, tightness, or heat. Holding these body sensations in awareness, bringing attention to where in the body they are showing up, investigating them, perhaps, breathing into or with sensations on an in-breath and softening on the out-breath.

And now choosing to let go of any one particular object of attention, like breath, body sensation, sound, thoughts, or emotions, and letting the field of awareness open to all experience, internal or external. Not directing your attention anywhere, not looking for or holding on to anything but rather receiving sensations. Noticing the movement of experience, sensations arising, staying for a while, and leaving to be replaced by another and another. (Here the teacher, in her instructions, is guiding participants to practice a receptive, open, and effortless stance to experience.)

In this practice, we are noticing whatever comes in the moment as we sit here, observing sounds, thoughts, emotions, and sensations in the body including the breath. (The teacher allows for a long pause to allow participants to practice this.)

> Resting effortlessly in awareness itself. Sitting here awake, breathing, being present.... And now directing attention back to the sensations of breathing for a few minutes.... And now making a transition by opening the eyes if they have been closed or widening the gaze, bringing attention to these next few moments, moving the body in any way that feels helpful.

In this example, the teacher moves from a primary attentional focus on the sensations of breathing to an increasingly broader field that discretely includes body, sounds, thoughts, and emotions as part of the development of an "observer stance." The teacher then shifts the participants' focus to rest in and be receptive to all sensations. This is the open-monitoring of the entirety of experience. The intention of this practice is to enhance the capacity to bear witness to experience as well as to how one is relating to it. This facilitates the participants' ability to receive experience regardless of its charge with less identification, less reactivity, and an embodied understanding of impermanence. This has important ramifications for participants as it helps them to address negative mind and mood states earlier, which is central to developing choice around how to skillfully respond.

At this point, the teacher embodies open-monitoring through her guidance of the practice by using such words as, "Noticing whatever comes in the moment as we sit here, observing sounds, thoughts, emotions, sensations in the body including the breath. Not directing your attention anywhere, not looking for or holding on to anything, but rather receiving sensations. Noticing the movement of experience, sensations arising, staying for a while, and leaving to be replaced by another and another," and using such metaphors as thoughts as clouds in the sky or leaves being carried downstream. All of this reflects the attention to the movement of experience as a participant-observer rather than as the protagonist in his own story.

Discernment

Discernment is a third component of a present-moment orientation. It may be viewed as the capacity to hold all experience with kindness and compassion, supporting skillful choice around how we respond even though we may be experiencing reactivity. This is cultivated within mindfulness meditation practice, which is then generalized to everyday life through inquiry via home practice and home practice review. Participants are guided within the frame of the practice to pause, notice what is present, and to be receptive to whatever is happening. In some practices (such as the Three-Minute Breathing Space–Responsive with action step), the teacher guides participants to discover moments in which they can choose either to continue practicing, keeping the experience in awareness, or to shift their focus as a means of action or self-care. This training provides participants with a portable means of discerning how to approach challenging situations in their lives. The teacher who has worked with challenging moments in this way will provide a container for safely and skillfully enduring these emotionally charged moments within the group. In this way, she is modeling the utility of this approach and its everyday application.

For example, during the Nourishing and Depleting Exercise that takes place in session 7, participants spend time breaking down activities that take place during a typical day and categorizing them into ones that are nourishing (nurturing), depleting (draining), or neutral. They are then asked to count the number of nourishing and depleting activities and reflect on them, noticing any surprises. After a large group discussion, participants are asked whether there is an opportunity for an increase in the former or a decrease in the latter or if a change in attitude might be useful. This exercise is a key to self-care, compassion, and discerning when and what actions may be required at given times. It brings together the practice of mindfulness and skillful response, whether attitudinal or actionable. Frequently, participants find that their daily activities cannot be changed and therefore bringing a shift in attitude can change their relationship to them. This is where the practice can be most useful. For example, on noticing how depleting it was to make dinner, a participant said how she hated it. Bringing awareness to this in this exercise allowed her to step back and consider how she could see it differently. The first thing she recognized was that she was tired at the end of the day and was rushing to make the dinner. Second, she noticed there were times when she enjoyed cooking when she wasn't rushed. Ultimately, she decided that she would make herself a cup of tea before unpacking the groceries. This allowed her to pause in her reactivity and see that there was nothing that was requiring her to act immediately; she could cook calmly, at her own pace, which could lessen the irritation and depletion she would otherwise feel. This provided a moment of self-care and brought the potential for mindful action.

In this process, participants are now engaging with the idea that they can have agency and bring intention and choice to how they relate to and behave in their lives. It starts with noticing, pausing, and bringing mindful awareness to habitual patterns. Cultivating discernment empowers the individual and the group when facing difficult mind and mood states. This is wisdom in action. How can we demonstrate the relationship between discernment and the teacher's embodiment? As in the above example, pausing is an ally for the teacher to attend to her reactions and the responses of the group guiding her when to speak and what to say if she does.

As an example, after the Body Scan in session 2, a participant stated, "I had a lot of fear as we moved up the body." Any teacher, uncomfortable and worried about the participant's experience, might have the immediate tendency to reassure, give advice, or tell the participant to skip the body part without recognizing how her own reactivity may determine her response. By pausing for a moment and noticing these reactions (specifically attending to body sensations, thoughts, emotions, and impulses), the teacher can respond with discernment consistent with the intentions of the program.

Teacher: When did you first notice this fear? (a "when" question, leading the participant to bring bare attention to the experience and explore it)

Participant: When we got to the belly. And it increased as we got up to the chest.

Teacher: And then what happened?

Participant: When we moved past the chest, it started to decline.

Teacher: Okay. So, you had a lot of awareness of the increasing sensations of fear and then it lessened. (open-monitoring)

Participant: Yes, but it's still here, and I had a memory of a similar situation where I tried to figure out what this meant and why I was having it. It's strange, I realized here, that being with the fear and those sensations made it easier.

Teacher: Thank you.

Here, the teacher is staying with and where the participant is rather than projecting or promoting her own agenda. This can be difficult when a participant is expressing distress, as she does not know where the participant will take her. Discernment in this situation requires that the teacher embodies the attitude of trust, staying with where the participant leads, gently guiding the process when indicated with respect to safety, individual learning, and the themes of the session. In this example, ensuring that the participant has moved through the process enough, she then can leave the participant to reflect upon what is being learned as indicated by her response that shows that she is observing the difference between attending mindfully and staying present versus engaging in problem solving or worry.

This reflects one of the important themes in the MBCT program—that through being with challenging moments, exposing oneself to them, and seeing that they shift (if or when they do), it is possible to attend to these moments experientially rather than conceptually. With this in mind, the teacher will be able to integrate this into the discussion around the utility of the practice. Discerning when to incorporate participants' expressions of the teaching points depends on where one is in the program, what the theme of the session is, what has been identified by other participants, and how this learning is to be integrated into everyday life. Ensuring and reinforcing this process as the teacher is an integral part of discernment.

The attitudinal foundations of curiosity, kindness, and compassion are vital supports for teacher and participant when working with challenging patterns of negativity. This is crucial because these offer a different approach to how we typically encounter such taxing moments. In *The Art of Happiness,* the Dalai Lama (1998) comments, "I think that cultivating positive mental states like kindness and compassion definitely leads to better psychological health and happiness" (p. 41). This is not accentuating the positive and ignoring the negative (as in "turn that frown upside down!"), but rather the recognition and tracking of the positive (pleasant), negative (unpleasant), and neutral in experience to highlight interest, steadiness, kindheartedness, and self-care.

The teacher embodies this by encouraging the participants to pay friendly and kind attention to and accepting the movement of experience as it arises from thoughts, body sensations, emotions, the breath, or sounds, which helps participants stay with the evolution of sensations and lessen the "grip" of any one experience. Tracking experience in this way heightens the ability to sustain attention on process and enhances an expanded frame of reference for witnessing internal and external experience. All sensations can be met with interest, kindness, and compassion, and without preference. This is equanimity and is demonstrated in the excerpt that follows. In the discussion in session 4 after a sitting meditation, a participant is struggling with feeling bored during the practice.

Participant: It's no good. I was bored. And agitated. I kept wondering when the meditation would be over. How long was it anyway? I have always found it hard to focus for any length of time. I've never been a good student. I don't think this meditation stuff is for me.

The participant has moved away from the experience of the practice into describing and evaluating something about himself and identifying with it.

Teacher: So, can you tell me something about the boredom? How did you know you were bored?

Participant: I felt antsy. I kept opening my eyes, looking around. I looked at my watch but couldn't remember when we started.

Teacher: This antsy feeling…any sense of how you knew you were antsy?

Participant: I kept shifting my position. I couldn't get comfortable.

It would be easy for a teacher to feel overwhelmed by this amount of information and perhaps not know how to stay close to the experience as it is unfolding. So far, she is doing a good job of tracking the experience by asking for more information. Let's see what she does next.

Teacher: Okay, so we have a lot of noticing of not-such-easy stuff: boredom, agitation, feeling antsy, and uncomfortable?

Participant: Well, if this is mindfulness, I want out! (He is smiling and laughing, and the group is laughing as well.)

Teacher: (smiling) Yup! Sometimes mindfulness practice is all about being with these challenging moments, exploring them, and being kind toward feelings that are difficult. The more we stay present with them, which is what you did, the more likely it is that we can be curious about the experience and develop a friendly interest toward them. You could have gotten up and walked out, but you stayed.

The teacher has managed to ignore the story this participant believes about being a poor student, instead remaining interested in the unfolding nature of the difficulty. Remember, the theme of session 4 is recognizing aversion. She also expressed, at a critical point in the discovery process, the idea of being friendly and kind toward what one is experiencing, bringing this attitude into the forefront of awareness.

Learning to do this is not easy for participants but is assisted by a teacher who waits before responding to a participant who is struggling to understand the mindfulness practices or to absorb how the presented information is relevant. A teacher understands these moments and recognizes the value of waiting, of helping the participant check in with the range of present-moment experience he might be facing and helping to adopt an observational stance to what is arising, over a problem-solving one. At these times, she can ultimately respond in any number of ways: asking for clarification, letting the participant lead, and engaging in a reflective dialogue that steadies a participant to come to fully know his experience as it unfolds in each moment.

As a teacher becomes more experienced and skilled, the teaching becomes a place of participatory engagement, of working with and inside the practice of mindfulness, thus fully contemporizing meditation practice through bare attention, open-monitoring, and discernment. Knowing the primacy of staying close to the currents of each mindful moment, the instructor has no need to control the learning—being a guide, yes; being in charge, no. This is an uncommon place from which to teach but is one of the premises of this book and one we would want all MBP teachers to explore.

We are suggesting that teaching MBCT is a contemporizing of the practice of mindfulness. As a means to succinctly summarize this chapter and the previous one, there are some specific elements the teacher must understand in order to be able to teach MBCT as a practice. We offer the following as a characterization of embodied mindful presence:

- An experiential understanding of the attitudinal foundations
- Understanding the universality of suffering and the changing nature of all phenomena and loosening the identification with a fixed sense of self

- A present-moment orientation, curiosity, and the investigation and tracking of experience as it is revealed

- A practice of bare attention, open-monitoring, and discernment

- Enhancing a participant's ability to access a "being" mode of mind, the capacity to mindfully attend to and track experience increasing self-awareness, and attentional, emotional, and behavioral regulation

- Modeling and supporting an open and receptive stance to all experience (equanimity)

- The primacy of kindness and compassion

In Closing

In this chapter, we have focused on embodiment and how we can map out important characteristics that will contribute to a teacher's mindful embodied presence. This will make it easier to inhabit being a guide rather than trying to be in charge or eliciting teaching points versus lecturing. Embodying mindfulness practice is about a teacher developing the facility to engage in bare attention, open-monitoring, and discernment, leading to a conscious relationship with herself, to others, and to the movement of life. By being present to ourselves and developing kindness and compassion to challenging mind and mood states, we can all be more present. In learning to be attentive to the moment, we become more observant of our internal and external environments and less controlled by reactivity. We are then able to make more intentional and skillful choices about how we think, feel, and act inside the classroom and out. We would argue that the degree to which participants come to be able to do this is dependent upon the teacher's personal mindfulness practice, her embodiment of mindfulness, her inquiry skills, and her ability to follow participants' experiences.

Teaching mindfulness is an iterative process in which the teacher is acted upon and changed during the process of her facilitation of the program. By embodying the practice of mindfulness through her own formal and informal practice, her expression of the attitudinal foundations, and her experiential mode of teaching, the MBCT instructor will be both subject to the transformative process of mindfulness and able to guide participants to that process. Embodying traits of mindful presence, compassion, self-reflection, and humility, she imparts these more powerfully than by talking about them.

Chapter 8

Inquiry as Contemplative Dialogue

Inquiry is the discussion between teacher and participants that takes place following the meditation practices and cognitive exercises. Considering its centrality in MBPs, inquiring into a participant's experience has received relatively little attention compared with other components of MBCT. Until recently, little has been written either discussing or researching the process. Crane et al. (2015) published a qualitative study analyzing the delivery of inquiry by senior teachers. However, the remaining literature consists of relatively short descriptions or chapters in manuals or books of various MBPs (Brandsma, 2017; Crane, 2008, 2017; Woods, 2010; McCown, Reibel, & Micozzi, 2011; Segal et al., 2002, 2013; Santorelli, 2016). This may in part reflect the difficulty in conceptualizing and then describing a highly experiential and interactive process, fluid and contingent on what participants express in the group resulting from their experience and learning.

Inquiry has been defined in a number of ways, including: an "investigative" or "participatory dialogue" (Crane, 2008), "dialogue and inquiry" (Santorelli, 2016; Woods et al., 2016), a "sequence" of "turn taking" (Crane, 2017), a distinct skill of asking questions and dialogue consisting of a "back and forth exchange" while "keeping the space open..." (Santorelli, 2016), or an "exploration of personal practice…reactions… patterns and (their) implications…" (Brandsma, 2017). It is, as Crane (2008) writes, "a key aspect of the teaching…as it facilitates a 'translation' of direct experience arising within the mindfulness practices into learning that participants can apply into their lives" (p. 143). As we can see, there is little consensus about what inquiry is, how to engage in it, whether or not it can actually be explicitly taught (Santorelli, 2016; Crane et al., 2015), or if there is even a fixed structure to it (Brandsma, 2017). This chapter is our attempt to add clarity to this aspect of MBCT that is often cited as the most difficult to learn (Segal et al., 2013; Crane, et al., 2015; Woods, 2010).

We see the process of inquiry as a contemplative practice embodying the mindful presence of the teacher described in the previous two chapters of this book. Inquiry as first elucidated in MBCT was understood as a reflection on practice that has two stages, one of which is to describe the actual experience and the second to comment on it (Segal et al., 2002). The process was subsequently more formally described by Crane (2008) as a practice or skill to be learned consisting of three layers. The first layer entails recognition or noticing experience, the second involves attention to what is salient (what is standing out compared to automatic ways of attending) and tracking the unfolding components of experience, and the third addresses integrating and understanding how mindfulness is relevant to preventing depression and anxiety and staying well. (See also the second edition of the MBCT manual [Segal et al. (2013)], in which inquiry, using the Kolb model, consists of three layers following the experience itself: reflection, context, and invitation.)

In this chapter, we'll explore inquiry as a *contemplative dialogue between teacher and participant(s) that supports the investigation of experience arising from the practice of mindfulness.* Inquiry is the part of the program in which mindful presence is at its most dynamic, interactive, and difficult to embody. It is where the heart of the practice is revealed.

A Contemplative Dialogue

We have chosen the term "contemplative dialogue" as a complement to the word "inquiry" because we think that it is a closer articulation of what is occurring during the interactions between a teacher and his participants. To contemplate upon something is a process that involves observation, examination, and reflection. This process as it pertains to a contemplative dialogue includes both an active agent and a receptive one: the active agent is the one that the MBCT teacher facilitates through conversation, and the reflective agent is the one that becomes internalized by participants as a result of these conversations. By bringing an internal observation, examination, and reflection to the practices of mindfulness, participants have a skill that can be employed to work with challenging mind and mood states and ultimately engage in self-care.

Inquiry with a contemplative focus is an attentive and meditative expression of mindfulness, representing foundational principles and attitudinal qualities that reinforce the ability of both teacher and participant(s) to stay present to what is occurring at any time (Woods, 2010; Santorelli, 2016; Woods et al., 2016). This includes a present-moment orientation, embodying the attitudinal foundations and communicating (in a contemporary manner) the three characteristics or marks of existence as described in previous chapters: suffering (resistance to what is), impermanence (nothing lasts), and not-self (events and experience as impersonal, dependent upon context, and universal).

The intention of these conversations with participants is to support reflection on their experience of mindfulness practices, cognitive exercises, home practice, and the application of mindfulness to everyday life. This interactive process uses a series of open-ended questions, observations, wonderings, and reflections. The objects of investigation are the actual noticing of experience (and one's relationship to it); its components, qualities, and temporal nature; and the integration of what is learned through this exploration into daily life. Through this process of honing the participant's skill of describing direct experience and reflecting on what has just occurred versus narrating (following a storyline), decreased identification with experience is cultivated.

A central theme for the process is to assist and develop the ability to be both participant and observer of one's internal and external environment rather than getting overwhelmed or overly identified with it. By attending to the movement of experience as "sensation" (including thoughts and emotions), the attachment to and importance of the narrative of our lives is lessened. This, of course, is directly tied to the intentions of MBCT, which are to support participants in reducing the suffering so often a part of depression and anxiety and to guide them in developing relapse prevention skills. The participants in the MBCT program learn that their experiences and problems are not personal but rather universal.

A potential pitfall for the teacher articulating the contemplative nature of inquiry is an inclination to conflate the structure or method of the inquiry process (by asking specific and layered questions) with its contemplative character, an embodied mindfulness practice. That is, they engage in question-and-answer about specific and isolated experiences, rather than using the inquiry to convey subtle instruction for the participant about how to move through noticing, tracking, and integrating or understanding experience. It is the difference between the doing mode of inquiry and being in a contemplative conversation with participant. It is, in part, this tendency, in our opinion, that leads to some of the difficulty and confusion around its practice. We use the three layers identified by Crane (2008) as an entry point to our discussion on inquiry.

The Three Layers: A Framework for Inquiry

We think that the three layers of inquiry—recognition or noticing experience, the ability to track the components of experience as it unfolds, and the integration of this experience into one's understanding of mindfulness and how it prevents depression and anxiety and promotes staying well—are useful anchors for initially learning how to best facilitate it via questions and reflections.

The framework of the layers helps organize the teacher's thinking and understanding of the process. It is informed by key attitudes and principles of mindfulness and has at its core an experiential understanding of what is being expressed in the group. It does, however, put the teacher's inquiry at risk of becoming mechanistic or rote. For the novice teacher, facilitating inquiry by moving through these layers and their associated questions and reflections is akin to using a script when first learning to guide a meditation versus guiding from one's own practice. Over time, as a teacher, you will internalize the process of inquiry as a mindfulness practice in its own right.

The First Layer: What Did You Notice?

As discussed in the literature (Segal et al., 2013; Crane, 2008), the layers are in part a heuristic device to help both teacher and participant develop a common language in which to review what occurs in the practice or cognitive exercises. It also provides a structured way of thinking about this process, particularly for novice mindfulness teachers and those in training. In the first layer of questions, which are aimed at helping participants recognize what is present for them, participants are often asked, "What did you notice about this experience (this sitting meditation or this exercise)?"—reflecting the attitudinal foundation of curiosity. Participants often respond with comments about preferences (what they liked or didn't like) or an assumption about causality (this happened because), even though the teacher may have asked specifically about the participant's experience itself. That is, participants default to analysis, rather than describing experience as the teacher is asking them to do. When a participant presents a lot of ideas or interpretations about what happened in the practice, the teacher can respond with a general comment—"Oh, so you noticed a lot of thoughts coming up," or "That's one idea"—then redirect her to this aspect of inquiry: what she noticed. One of the aims for a teacher is to highlight for participants how easy it is to move into narration and to encourage a return of attention to direct experience. What is also gently brought into the participants' awareness is how commonly they engage in negative self-evaluations or other evaluations and the effect of this on mood and behavior. For example, in answering a participant who says, "I'm a lousy meditator," the teacher replies, "It sounds like there are some judgmental thoughts. When you noticed this judgment, what emotions or body sensations were you aware of, if any?" In this way, the teacher is making the link between harsh evaluations against the self and mood.

Awareness of and learning to pay attention to all experience is an important factor of what is being taught in the MBCT program. Neuroimaging studies in both long-term meditators and participants in mindfulness groups have supported this impact of cultivating such attention to present-moment sensations, suspending the immediate judgment or narration about experience. These studies suggest that in response to emotional challenges, there is less reliance on cortical midline regions associated with narrative self-focus and dysphoric reactivity, in favor of a balance between such narration and sensory pathways (Farb et al., 2007; Farb, Anderson, & Segal, 2012).

What this means is that participants learn to interrupt rumination or anxious thinking when needed in favor of shifting attention to body sensations, learning to observe and describe the actual moment rather than getting lost in their ideas or conclusions about it. This is referred to as a shift from narrative self-referencing (storytelling) to experiential self-referencing (moment-to-moment describing of experience). Finally, the first layer begins heightening the awareness of all experience for participants regardless of whether it is joyful, difficult, or neutral.

While the above research can assist the teacher in understanding the value of bringing attention to the body when difficult states emerge, it is equally if not more important to recognize that in inquiry, we are concerned with the entirety of a participant's experience, which includes attention to thoughts, emotions, body sensations, behaviors, and impulses to act. Although attention to body sensations is an initial training, a teacher must recognize other aspects of sensation and experiences in his inquiry. A narrow and default focus on the body in inquiry, common in new MBCT teachers, is overly simplistic.

The Second Layer: How Might This Way of Paying Attention Be Dif\ferent? And Then What Happened? And Then?

What is referred to as the second layer asks participants to reflect upon how they are meeting experience, their relationship to what is being noticed, and how this might be different from how they usually pay attention, eat, move their body, and so forth. This question is also asking participants how paying attention mindfully is different. This is intended to help them recognize that there may be other ways to relate to experience than the ones they typically employ.

After the first couple of sessions the question, "How might this be different?" is dropped, as participants develop an understanding of mindfulness and that another way of paying attention is being learned. From this point, the tracking of experience is emphasized by asking, "And then what happened? And then?" This form of inquiry stresses attention to the internal, sequential, unfolding nature of each moment. Its purpose is to increase the capacity of participants to stay close to their experience, track it, and recognize the relationship between its various components. These components consist of thoughts, emotions, body sensations, impulses to act, and behaviors.

A central feature of this second layer of inquiry is that it enables participants to develop a new perspective on habitual ways of thinking and an enhanced awareness of contingencies. Highlighting these components deconstructs experience; it works to make difficulties more manageable, keeping people in the present and reducing the tendency to fall into a cascade of ruminative or obsessive thinking that may hijack mood or perpetuate stress reactivity. The process of inquiry enhances mindful attending, supporting distress tolerance and enhancing affect regulation.

The Third Layer: And How Might This Relate to Preventing Depressive Relapse, Managing Difficult Mind and Mood States, or Staying Well?

The third layer of inquiry is about integrating, or linking, what has been learned in the group to everyday life and its vicissitudes. It is about helping participants apply and test out what has been learned. Early in the program, group members are asked to consider how the practices might prevent or reduce depression, anxiety, or distress; later, they are asked more generally how the practices might help them stay well. This implies that there is a skillful next step to dealing with problems and that this can be learned. The third layer is therefore hopeful and embodies personal accountability for making change. Early on in MBCT and other MBPs, this line of questioning helps participants make connections between seemingly idiosyncratic practices, like eating a raisin, scanning one's body, or following one's breath, and their reasons for coming to the group. Making these links and applying them to everyday experiences is an essential part of adult learning.

This takes participants well beyond the common misconception that the practice of mindfulness is simply about relaxation or just learning to meditate. The linking to a future where they have more self-efficacy and skills for self-care, with mindful attention allowing them to determine which skill to use and when, is essential. It helps create a bridge from the experiential to the conceptual, increasing understanding and acceptance of the practices by participants. The third layer is about helping participants apply and test out what has been learned. In the example below, we have a conversation about home practice between a teacher and a participant. They are talking about the Three-Minute Breathing Space in session 5 ("Allowing and Letting Be").

Teacher: Let's turn our attention to the Three-Minute Breathing Space. Anyone have a chance to use it this past week?

Participant 1: I was able to use it quite a lot this past week.

Teacher: Yes?

Participant 1: I had a busy week at work and was commuting home, and the subway was hot and stuffy. After a long day, I would have been really irritated and impatient. But I decided to use the Three-Minute Breathing Space. And you know something? It made a difference.

Teacher: How? In what way?

Participant 1: I still felt the irritation and even noticed the tension in my shoulders and jaw, but then I didn't obsess over it, and it gradually eased.

Teacher: (turning to the whole group) This is interesting. So, how is this useful?

Participant 2: I guess this shows that you can use it anywhere. The problem for me sometimes is to remember this.

Participant 3: I use it before speaking to my teenagers!

Participant 4: I have a dental appointment coming up, and I will use it in the dentist chair!

(General laughter in the group.)

As the program progresses, the teacher will move away from the construct of the three layers into a contemplative dialogue commensurate with his own maturation as a teacher *(embodiment)*. In lieu of the three layers, the teacher uses the five agents of change as a conceptual frame to animate the dialogue. He will be holding the themes and agendas of each session *(protocol)* in mind when he is listening to his participants' responses after having facilitated a meditation practice. He is always referring the participants back to that practice when they move into thoughts about the past or future *(mindfulness practices)*. In the meditation practices and the cognitive exercises, he assists them in making the link to everyday life, and during inquiry, he monitors group process and reinforces *individual and group learning*. The fifth agent of change, the *embodied mindful presence of the teacher*, remains salient throughout.

A structured approach to inquiry will also necessitate a teacher attending to the *Themes, Rationale, Intentions,* and *Practice Skills* of any given session or practice to help anchor his attention and inquiry. Moreover, horizontal inquiry (gathering a breadth of responses from participants) will be emphasized early in the program. Later, particularly when difficulties show up, vertical inquiry (deepening dialogue with one participant) is used more often.

As a guide to some of the characteristics embedded in inquiry, we see the following as important aspects:

- The teacher actively engages and embodies what he understands to be the central attitudes of the practice.

- He holds the agenda lightly, becoming comfortable with uncertainty and acknowledging not knowing what may show up in the group.

- He learns to lead his participants by following their responses, being sensitive to the verbal and nonverbal expressions by the group members.

- He actively listens to participants instead of formulating his responses while they are speaking.

- He continually asks himself, "What am I hearing?" "Do I really understand what this participant means?" checking his assumptions and asking for clarification when needed.

- He listens for narration, expectations, interpretations, and explanations, and when these show up, gently interrupts or brings into awareness these habitual ways of relating to experience.

- He engages a participant in conversation while at the same time attending to the rest of the group.

- He elicits key thematic points, helping the group make links to the rationale or utility of any practice or exercise as they apply to life and difficult mind and mood states.

- He brings curiosity to help participants enhance the granularity of their attention and tolerance for distressing events as they occur.

Holding all of this can be overwhelming to say the least, particularly when we are first learning inquiry—when it is being approached from a conceptual perspective or *doing mode*, when one is attempting to master its form. As in tai chi or other martial arts, there is an outer form, necessary to learn to engage in the practice, and then there are what are called internals that arise once one has a foundation in the external structure. So, with the contemplative dialogue that is inquiry, a form is helpful. The internals—a sense of curiosity; the ability to listen actively; the ability to recognize and be with the impersonal, imperfect, and impermanent; and implicitly guiding participants to do the same—come from the embodiment of mindfulness and its articulation.

From the Conceptual to the Contemplative

Curiosity is the greatest ally for a teacher facilitating inquiry and for his participants learning about mindfulness practices. It is the antidote to making assumptions or quick judgments and the need for assurance. When we are curious about our or another's experience, we become interested in exploring and reflecting on whatever is happening. This is a good example of contemplation in action. One of the things this asks of a teacher is that he operate from a place of not knowing, embodying beginner's mind and at the same time holding an agenda and the need for a specific outcome lightly.

By using curiosity as a frame for his inquiry, a teacher elicits verbal descriptions, reflections, and key insights from participants that ultimately make the teaching richer. This is demonstrated by maintaining an open-ended and present-moment focus on the *what*, *where*, *when*, and *how* of experience. The *why* is generally not addressed, as this invariably takes us out of description of experience and into analysis. The teacher works to enhance the participants' ability to stay with what is happening in the practice. This reduces the tendency for them to move quickly into the past or future or to look for reasons why something has occurred, or to come to conclusions about experience that are often erroneous and reinforce a fixed view of self.

Questions, while open-ended, are generally short and simple. The teacher tries to avoid the use of double-barreled questions, questions that ask about two issues but permit one answer—as in: "Were you restless or agitated?"—and closed or leading questions, meaning those that begin with "is," "was," "were" or "do," does," or "did": for example, "Did it change?" "Is this something you normally notice?" "Do you notice your posture is different?" These tend to take the participant out of the experience, shutting down the dialogue.

An illustration of how the teacher can maintain an ongoing present-moment orientation while asking about a practice that has just occurred is described below:

- The teacher waits, listening to the participant response, and selectively reflects back to enhance the group vocabulary of experience.

- He highlights key thematic points that have been expressed when appropriate.

- He also helps participants to enhance their capacity to describe and track their experience. This descriptive process will reinforce the value of attending in this way.

- He asks permission to continue inquiry, particularly when a participant is struggling (vertical inquiry).

- The teacher will frequently express gratitude for the participant's response.

The teacher needs to remember *less is more*, following the participant's lead while at the same time gently ensuring the dialogue stays on track, close to direct experience, and relevant to the theme of the session. He is judicious in his reflections or responses, not needing to speak to every participant response, allowing the ones that reflect direct experience to stand on their own. The teacher exhibits patient attending that embodies the practice. He does his best not to insert his biases, attachment to outcomes, or an agenda into the participant experience.

Finally, the teacher practices modeling that all experience is open to investigation, bringing a curious and kind stance to his inquiry. No experience, "good" or "bad," is privileged over another. This does not mean that some problems don't need addressing: discerning if, when, and how they are to be addressed is required by the teacher, particularly when safety is a concern.

Active Listening

In a contemplative dialogue, the teacher's focus is on listening to the participants' attention to and deconstruction of experience as they describe what is sequentially noticed in practice (tracking). Therefore, within this context, what is valued is description over narrative and explanation to help participants interrupt such thinking behaviors as rumination and worry. A contemplative dialogue therefore requires active listening. This means that the teacher is deeply attentive to the speaker, asking for clarification when needed. He will be able to reflect, paraphrase, and judiciously use summation.

An example of this ability to describe and track experience from a meditation practice is demonstrated when a participant says, "I noticed I felt agitated and restless when you asked me to bring up a difficulty. My jaw was tight, and I felt a bit nauseous. When I brought my attention to my stomach, I felt even sicker. And then it started to lessen. When you said to breathe into overwhelming sensations, I did that, and it changed. It's still there a little." The participant's focus remains on sensations as they evolve and pass. And by maintaining this focus, the participant is discovering that such sensations *do* pass.

This is in contrast to a participant who gets lost in the narrative as in, "I brought to mind a fight I had with my boss yesterday, I realized what a jerk he is, and I started thinking that I should just quit. But then what would I do for money? I noticed my stomach was upset and I was jittery probably because I'm so mad and I drank a lot of coffee before class today. Coffee always makes me shaky. I guess I should stop drinking it."

Another important aspect of listening intently is the way a teacher brings awareness to participant reactions or attitudes. He also attends to wanted, unwanted, and neutral experiences and to the participants' relationship to these. How individuals in the group might shift these reactions and attitudes to help recognize and prevent negative mind and mood states is an important component of changing our relationship to difficulties, particularly those that can't be changed. The teacher should actively listen for this.

Being with the Imperfect, Impermanent, and Impersonal

As a contemplative dialogue, inquiry will utilize the teacher's understanding of the three marks of existence, outlined in Buddhist psychology and discussed previously. We tend to have a view that life should be perfect, that our selves are concrete and permanent, and that what occurs is personal. It is important for the teacher to listen for and identify these themes in his practice of inquiry with respect to what he asks about and reflects back to participants. This is because the suffering we experience will be described from a variety of perspectives including, but not limited to, our resistance to what is. The teacher can, by listening for these moments, help his participants change their relationship to difficulties, for example, "I was so impatient." "I was so bored." "This was so good I didn't want it to end." "This shouldn't be happening." "I shouldn't feel this way." All these statements are about resisting how things are, thinking they should be different, and wanting them to be other.

Likewise, rumination and worry, so much a part of depression and anxiety, may be viewed as thought behaviors designed to get away from, or resolve, these difficult states, as if one might think oneself out of them. A contemplative dialogue gently brings attention to and an awareness of participants' difficulty, resistance, and mental elaboration. In this way, he facilitates an understanding that by being with and exploring these difficult states from the practice of mindfulness, emotional flexibility and resilience are supported and reinforced.

As an illustration, the following excerpt takes place after a mindfulness practice working specifically with a difficulty in session 5 ("Allowing and Letting Be").

Participant: My boss told me I had to do extra work on a project, and I started to panic.

Teacher: So was this what came up in the practice? (locating the participant in the practice)

Participant: Yes. I started to feel anxious, with tension in my jaw and a knot in my stomach.

Teacher: And then what happened? (tracking)

Participant: I stayed with the sensations in my body and used the breath to be with them. I noticed, more sting wasn't added to the situation, and I realized that while something may not be made better, we can make it not worse.

Teacher: So you were able to stay with the challenging sensations of anxiety and tension in the body. And then as you were able to be with that, you recognized it wasn't going away, but you could hold it without making it worse. (reinforcing the practices of turning toward difficulty, being present for it, and allowing and staying with it, without exacerbation)

Here, the teacher is checking with the participant that this reflection came up in the practice just completed. He asks for further observations about experience, reinforcing the participant's ability to track and stay with it, cultivating equanimity in the face of challenging moments.

The next example demonstrates a teacher helping participants be with difficulty in an embodied and experiential way, reflecting the themes that everything changes and passes and that we personalize events. We tend to want to reduce uncertainty and control change. This can show up when a participant talks about his or her depression.

Participant: I will always be depressed, and I will never get better. I'm a depressive. (This will be a key moment for the teacher because it highlights the fixed nature of view. There are many ways a teacher may respond to this. One way might be to externalize thoughts from self.)

Teacher: That's a compelling thought. Hmmm. What else were you aware of in the practice?

Participant: (pauses and looks confused and thoughtful) I noticed I felt sad, and my shoulders and chest were tight.

Teacher: Okay, so there was some thinking, some sadness, and body sensations. And then what happened? (deconstructing experience into components)

Participant: And then the instruction guided us to attend to the entire body. And my shoulders felt less tight.

Teacher: Oh, so it shifted? (reinforcing change, impermanence)

Mindfulness helps us to internalize and embody impermanence. Here, the teacher is bringing awareness to the changing nature of attention, senses, and sensations. Participants are encouraged to pay attention to the range of sensations (tracking), to describe them (exploration), and to notice when they change, if they do, and when they don't. They can then begin to reflect on how such knowledge helps to decrease suffering. They can begin to discover by paying close attention to their direct experience that they can lessen the primacy of any one sensation and that everything is in flux, whether this speaks to changing intensity, severity, or duration. The awareness of impermanence can become a source of hope and reduce the tendency to perseverate or elaborate on problems that cannot be solved through ruminative thinking.

The contemplative nature of inquiry will also illustrate the problematic nature of a fixed sense of self. "That's just the way I am," is a common refrain. While it can be argued that an "I" is a necessary vehicle to express ourselves and to navigate the world with coherence, it becomes problematic (as outlined in earlier chapters) when identified with too closely. A fixed view of self reduces possibilities for change or for developing more skillful ways of interacting with the world. Seeing through this rigid lens in which experience is personalized, "He looked at me because I did something wrong," or "She didn't speak to me because she's jealous," means that it is easy to miss how frequently reality is actually a series of interpretations or constructs dependent upon the context in which we find ourselves. Such a view is narrow and is usually "all about me."

Sometimes a situation really is about the individual, but often people are immersed in their own thoughts and emotions. Their reactions have nothing to do with us. This tendency to personalize is alienating and isolating. In addition, a sense of self is contingent upon conditions (Batchelor, 1998), meaning our view of who we believe ourselves to be is dependent upon what happens to us. Mindfulness practices and reflecting upon them through inquiry helps our participants see that who they believe themselves to be may in fact be a much more fluid rather than fixed notion.

Within the context of inquiry, the teacher also listens for those moments when participants reflect on the commonality rather than the personal nature of their experience. Participants come to realize they are not alone nor are their problems necessarily specific to them. There is often relief in the recognition that their conditions are not a moral failing but part of what it is to be human.

This means that as a teacher listens to the participants' reflections, he will guide them to become more aware of personalizing experience and highlight when they aren't. One example of this is when participants are getting lost in storytelling or explanations about why they are doing what they're doing, as in a participant who says, "I was so tired and sleepy in this body scan and my husband has been snoring so much, so I thought, *Well, why not let go, relax, and fall asleep?* I feel like I missed out, and I didn't do a good job in the meditation."

Teachers can assist participants to decrease their narrative by helping them to label emotions and describe sensations as a means to decenter from self as a fixed entity. This cultivates a view of self as an ongoing process or collection of thoughts, emotions, body sensations, behaviors, or impulses to act. In the above example, the teacher will respond by bringing the participant back to the experience of the body scan by replying, "So, sleepiness was present and then some thoughts about your husband's snoring and some disappointment and judgment about not doing a good job."

Identifying when a participant expresses a shifting view of self will be another focus of the teacher's attention in addition to listening for the universality of experience. For example, in a review of the weekly home practice, a participant says, "I usually really hate the body scan and think I can't do it. I suck at meditation. In fact, during the week, I would turn on the recording and get up after ten minutes. But today, I was able to pay attention to some of the guidance and thought, *That wasn't so bad. Maybe I can learn this, and if it's hard, that's okay.*" The teacher might comment, "Oh, so when you were at home, you had thoughts about how you can't meditate and harsh judgments, and today you had a kinder, more accepting view about what might be possible for you."

The inquiry into and deconstruction of experience using the various modules of the MBCT program reveal how ordinary we are. We are neither so horrible as we suspected or so wonderful as we may have thought (although the latter is not a common problem for those who are depressed or very anxious), and there is a great relief (and reduction in suffering) in letting go of both sides of our self-importance. We can stop holding so tightly to our sense of self and sense of lack (Loy, 2000), worry, dissatisfaction, judgment of ourselves, others and the world, or insatiable wanting.

In Closing

Inquiry assists participants to reflect on experience and develop an observational stance with meta-awareness of difficult mind and mood states that promote the disidentification with a fixed sense of self. Cultivating meta-awareness and insight leads to a view of the self as process, one that is responsive, flexible, and adaptable. Decentering is essential for attention and emotional and behavioral regulation. This ability to lessen the attachment to personal narrative and instead articulate experience without identifying with it or automatically reacting to it brings insight and wisdom. This then allows for intentional skillful responses and actions. Teacher and participant become more skilled at identifying habitual moments of reactivity, leading to more choice in dealing with challenging experiences.

As a contemplative dialogue, inquiry is a relational conversation that has its roots in mindfulness-based principles. It entails being completely present to the experience of another, maintaining flexibility with respect to an agenda exemplified in each session of the MBCT program. It is supported by the guidance of a teacher who is able to be in this mindful interaction with curiosity and compassion. To this end, while a structure is useful to provide a frame of reference for the teacher, ultimately inquiry is experiential, requiring the teacher to step into the unknown, to be open and flexible with respect to whatever his participants offer, whether painful, difficult, joyful, or dull. He embodies the practice of inquiry, present to his own experience and his participants in every moment. Herein lies a taste of freedom that comes from the exploration and acceptance of the full range of experience and the attention and emotion regulation that is facilitated by this contemplative dialogue.

In the next chapter, we focus on considerations for teacher development from initial to advanced training for maintaining competence and beyond.

Chapter 9

Personal and Professional Training and Beyond

Everyone, it seems, is interested in offering mindfulness. One of the reasons mindfulness has caught on in the West in the way it has is that it provides meaning and purpose in a society that is quite fractured, self-focused, and individualistic. Mindfulness entails a way of being and doing, integrating the personal and the professional, supporting the ongoing growth and development of those who would be of service as mindfulness teachers. Not only is mindfulness being facilitated in health care settings through mindfulness-based programs like MBCT, but it is being offered in schools, in the workplace, and via the Internet through apps and videos. The good news is that as a result, mindfulness is reaching a broad constituency. The bad news? These applications of mindfulness may well be missing something vital, a connection to its historical roots with the risk of being diluted, open to misinterpretation, or stripped of its ethical foundations. The contemporizing of mindfulness and meditation practice raises questions about what is being offered, the population being targeted, and what kind of training is necessary for those delivering the various applications to maintain consistency in delivery and fidelity to the tenets of mindfulness.

We have maintained that an important aspect of teaching MBCT and other MBPs is one of embodying the practice of mindfulness. Teaching is then an ongoing process that is deeply relational both with oneself and with another, the foundations of which are firmly embedded in developing and maintaining a personal mindfulness practice. Of course, as discussed, there are other essential components of skill building that will require training, such as gaining facility with the protocol and the honing of key skills to implement it. In this chapter, we discuss professional training trajectories from initial training to maintaining competence, the importance of a personal mindfulness practice, and the interplay of ethics.

Professional Training

The MBCT program was adapted from MBSR. MBSR was originally intended to work across multiple conditions, highlighting the physical and psychological effects of stress (Kabat-Zinn, 2013). It has since been adapted to target specific populations as diverse as parents expecting the birth of a baby, as in mindfulness-based childbirth and parenting (Duncan & Bardacke, 2010), and for people suffering from eating disorders, such as binge-eating disorder (the mindfulness-based eating awareness training; Kristeller & Wolever, 2011). Indeed, the MBSR program has extended its reach to include a variety of nonclinical settings, including education, the workplace, and correctional institutions.

As for MBSR, there is also increasing evidence of the effectiveness of MBCT (Gotink et al., 2015; Kuyken et al., 2016; Goldberg et al., 2018). The U.S. Veteran's Affairs and Department of Defense (2009) Clinical Management Guideline for Management of Major Depression recommends MBCT "should be used during the continuation phase of treatment with patients at high risk for relapse (i.e., two or more prior episodes, double depression, unstable remission status) to reduce the risk of subsequent relapse/recurrence" (p. 73). The Royal Australian and New Zealand College of Psychiatrists clinical practice guidelines for mood disorders (Malhi et al., 2015) cites MBCT as a maintenance treatment for depression and prevention of depressive relapse. Within the National Health Service in the UK, MBCT has been recommended by the National Institute for Health and Clinical Excellence (NICE, 2009, 2018) as a treatment of choice for people with relapsing depression. MBCT is recommended as an evidence-based treatment as part of the Canadian Network for Anxiety and Mood Disorders (CANMAT) Treatment guidelines for preventing depressive relapse (Parikh et al., 2016).

MBCT is also being adapted to multiple conditions and populations and increasingly used both within hospitals and community settings. There is growing evidence that MBCT is effective for patients with a history of recurrent depressive episodes when they are acutely depressed (Van Aalderen, Breukers, Reuzel, & Speckens, 2014), for treatment-resistant depression (Eisendrath et al., 2016), and for anxiety (Goldberg et al., 2018). Furthermore, the MBCT protocol has been adapted to target those with a history of substance misuse and dependence (Bowen, Chawla, & Marlatt, 2011), for people at risk of suicide (Williams et al., 2017), for mood distress in cancer (Haller et al., 2017), and many other conditions.

With this growing evidence base, there is increasing demand for practitioners competent to deliver MBCT. The majority of MBCT teachers have a professional mental health background that requires several years of rigorous training. There remain ongoing discussions about which factors in psychotherapy influence outcomes and how teacher competency fits within these. Shafran et al. (2009) concluded that longer trainings in psychotherapy are positively linked to more effective outcomes for clients. The results from a study (Ruijgrok-Lupton, Crane, & Dorjee, 2018) looking at the impact of mindfulness-based teacher training on participant well-being in the mindfulness-based stress reduction program found that longer time spent training in mindfulness-based skills may well be associated with increased positive participant outcomes.

This seems to be pointing to a training trajectory that would imply that a longer rather than shorter period of training for developing the skills of MBCT teachers is valuable. On the other hand, MBCT has a well-developed manual to follow (Segal et al., 2013). So, it would be reasonable to believe that to be able to deliver the MBCT program, one could familiarize oneself with the manual, attend a one- or two-day workshop, and then proceed to delivering the program. This is a common continuing education training scenario for mental health professionals and is one that is frequently offered to stay current (maintaining competence) with developments in the field.

However, MBCT is atypical from other Western psychological interventions in some significant ways, and the distinction lies in the word "mindfulness-based." Mindfulness is a key component of the MBCT intervention therapeutically as well as is its grounding in a specific philosophy and psychology. Being a mindfulness-based program means that a substantial proportion of what it offers to participants relies on a teacher being able to teach them how to engage in the formal and informal practices of mindfulness and the relevance of this learning to the prevention of depressive relapse and to staying well.

Facilitating a mindfulness-based program is multifaceted and will therefore require that the teacher train in a formal pathway. The tension for her (and for the creation of training programs) is to stay within an identified framework and emergent process. This requires learning the foundation of the protocol along with offering opportunities for practicing mindfulness. One of the major tenets of mindfulness practice is that everything is in flux, constantly changing. Consequently, we must apply this to training programs highlighting that learning to become a teacher is always an evolution requiring an emphasis on processing an inherent understanding of change, of the need for adaptability, of flexibility, of humility, and that learning is ongoing.

We will, rather than become overly proscriptive about content, outline some critical aspects for a training pathway that include its experiential nature as well as more didactic features for skill building. As a part of this, we see the five agents of change and TRIP as a valuable framework that can be included in the training of future teachers.

Foundational Training and Mentorship

For the beginner, having the experience of being a participant or observer in the eight-week MBCT program is essential. This should be followed by a five- to seven-day training that adheres to the protocol of a clearly laid-out curriculum (Segal et al., 2013).

At this juncture, it will also be important for the novice MBCT teacher to have developed a personal mindfulness practice. Having attended an MBCT program as a participant and completed a foundational training program, the trainee teacher may be ready to begin teaching under the supervision of a more senior teacher (mentorship). When teachers first start teaching, it is suggested that they practice the MBCT meditations as they teach the program, allowing them to deepen their understanding of what their participants are going through.

As a part of this training trajectory, having the guidance from a more senior MBCT teacher is a necessary part of one's development. Presenting opportunities for trainees to discuss what they are encountering while teaching and to be observed as they learn how to facilitate the protocol supports critical elements around languaging, pace of delivery, and instructional focus alongside the themes of each session. Learning from an experienced teacher inhabiting the role of a mentor (a trusted guide and advisor) provides a steadying influence. If this relationship is developed early on, not only does it reduce typical teaching challenges but importantly, it supports the building and enhancement of teaching skills, such as teaching the mindfulness practices, the management of group process and individual learning, and the facilitation of inquiry, and prevents protocol drift. Having the guidance of a mentor augments learning for all the agents of change, prevents confusion, provides valuable direction and oversight, and advances the development of best practices and competency.

This apprenticeship model of mentoring is a critical element to nurture teaching MBCT as a mindfulness practice because the mentor will presumably be able to transmit the embodiment of the practice through her guidance and presence. A focus on the process and practice of inquiry and embodying the practice is essential. Developing the ability to engage in inquiry as a contemplative dialogue and the embodiment of mindfulness is a process of maturation that typically takes longer to become integrated into teaching than does an understanding of and the ability to deliver the protocol. Trainees will often be teaching before they have learned to practice inquiry beyond a formulaic level and before they truly understand what it is to embody the practice. It is therefore likely that these skills will begin to be demonstrated toward the end of a training pathway and further developed beyond. This is where ongoing mentorship, supervision, coteaching, and continuing professional development will be especially helpful.

However, mentoring cannot cover all aspects of skill building. As the MBCT program is about delivering a contemporary form of mindfulness, modules that address the historical perspective of mindfulness and its basic teachings will be of value. These components could include the teaching of Buddhist psychology and how this interfaces with cognitive behavioral therapy. For those who have not studied cognitive behavior therapy, training in some of the core elements of that intervention is useful. And last but by no means least, the teacher should acquire a basic knowledge of research that examines the increasing contribution neuroscience is making to the field, that reviews clinical studies directed at MBCT patient outcomes, and that examines the mediators and moderators affecting those outcomes.

Maintaining Competence

As with all professions, maintaining competence is essential. Finding a community of other teachers who can offer peer supervision will be constructive, as it provides the necessary checks and balances to teaching and lessens the likelihood of drift from the protocol. Meeting with others in the field helps the teacher feel supported and have access to resources outside of herself. As the field evolves, adaptations are more frequent, and a community of practice is valuable for the dissemination of this work in different populations and diverse settings. For example, at the Centre for Mindfulness Studies (CMS) in Toronto, there is a large group of faculty who teach MBCT and other MBPs. They gather monthly for faculty development meetings where, after sitting together in meditative silence, a topic is discussed or recordings of a teacher are reviewed. Recent topics have included an update of neuroscience, diversity and inclusion in teaching MBPs, and a discussion of challenging situations in teaching groups.

Other means of maintaining competence include attending conferences that expose one to the latest developments in the field and are valuable to support the current understanding of what is being offered. Continuing professional development is a requirement of all mental health professions, and this is generally accomplished through attendance at accredited continuing education events, keeping up to date with the literature, or problem-based self-study.

Beyond typical continuing education activities, in order to sustain a connection to the essence of teaching MBCT and its embodiment, finding the time to attend silent teacher-led retreats is important. These periods offer teachers the opportunity for continuous practice where stillness, silence, and self-awareness support compassionate acceptance of the full range of mind, heart, and body experience with the intention to be awake and present. It is therefore essential that as part of maintaining these aspects of competence, you find ways to support your practice. This will look different at various times in our lives. Caring for young children or other care-giving responsibilities, such as for elderly parents, may only allow attendance at weekend retreats. Someone without those responsibilities will be able to attend for a longer period. Establishing and supporting a daily practice will also be vital. Having a friend or a group of friends who you can sit with will be helpful in supporting formal and informal daily practice.

To summarize, elements for the training trajectory and maintaining competence are

- to have an experiential understanding of mindfulness through personal mindfulness practice before entering training
- participation in an eight-week MBCT program as a participant or observer
- professional qualification and experience in working with the target population

- participation in an established professional training program that includes a foundational training
- ongoing mentorship with a senior teacher
- advanced training
- a daily personal mindfulness practice and attendance at yearly meditation retreats
- peer mentorship and support
- continuing professional development through reading and attendance at workshops and conferences

Current State of the Field

A review of a number of international training programs showed that professional training in MBCT varies from one to four years. It is likely that this timeframe will be subject to change as we become more knowledgeable as to what exactly promotes and leads to teaching proficiency. How that is structured is wisely left up to teaching institutions in various countries. There are bound to be national and cultural differences that are important to address and that need to be taken into consideration.

In the United States, the MBCT training pathway is a certification course offered through a university (the University of California at San Diego, http://www.mbpti.org) that typically takes two years to complete with two distinct phases. The first phase includes an MBCT teacher training intensive (MBCT TTI) followed by mentorship while teaching the MBCT program. This leads to teacher qualification. The second phase requires attending an advanced teacher training intensive course and further mentorship, leading to teacher certification. In Canada, at the Centre for Mindfulness Studies (http://www.mindfulnessstudies.com), trainees in MBCT attend a series of foundational programs (including the MBCT TTI) along with being mentored in teaching an eight-week program to achieve their facilitation certificate. They then can seek advanced certification with additional training and mentoring. In Asia, Australia, and Europe, there are several centers offering a variety of training formats including similar two-phase certification.

In the UK, there are various centers affiliated with universities that offer graduate degree programs in MBCT (including Bangor University, University of Exeter, and University of Oxford). There are also training centers in the UK that are not affiliated with universities. The time frame for completion of training varies between these UK-based centers. Additionally, there are master of arts programs in the United States that offer programs leading to degrees in mindfulness studies. In Canada, various universities also offer certificates in mindfulness studies. At the time of writing, none of these broad-based programs prepare the student to specifically teach MBCT. One can see from this that there is as of yet no uniform approach to training in this work.

Assessing Competence and Standards

There is also a need to address how we can assess mindfulness-based teaching skills because, to date, professional training programs rely predominately on attendance and mentorship. Assessing competency is complex. As a part of attending to this, "The Mindfulness-Based Interventions: Teaching Assessment Criteria (MBI:TAC)," developed by Crane et al. (2012a, 2012b, 2013, 2016) is one measuring instrument. The "MBI: TAC" divides teaching skills into six domains. They are *coverage, pacing, and organization of session curriculum; relational skills; embodiment of mindfulness; guiding mindfulness practices; conveying course themes through interactive inquiry and didactic teaching;* and *holding the group learning environment.* In addition to the six domains, the "MBI: TAC" draws on the Dreyfus Scale of Competence (Dreyfus & Dreyfus, 1986). The six stages range from incompetent to advanced, and each are assigned a numeric ranking of proficiency.

The "MBI: TAC" is an attempt to address a core question: How is intervention integrity measured? This is significant, as it is a way to gauge that the program is being delivered as it is intended. Intervention integrity comprises the following elements: adherence, differentiation, and competence. Adherence entails facilitating the appropriate modules in the proscribed sequence and resisting the temptation to bring in additional material that is not part of the curriculum. Differentiation is how distinct the method is from others, and competence applies to a teacher's skill in facilitating the program (Crane et al., 2016).

The "MBI: TAC" is a noteworthy aid to looking at the contributing characteristics to building teaching integrity. It is in a formative stage of development and thus requires more use and research. It is but one part of an emerging and important interest in the field of mindfulness-based programs about how to ensure there are credible teachers and maintenance of competence.

The professionalization of any field will result in the development of guidelines and the setting of standards. Relevant to MBPs, there are good practice guidelines that have been published at the Mindfulness-Based Professional Training Institute, UCSD (http://mbpti.org/; 2015) and in other training centers, such as at Centre for Mindfulness Studies (2018); Center for Mindfulness in Medicine, Healthcare and Society; UMass Medical School (Kabat-Zinn et al., n.d.); and in the UK via the UK Network for Mindfulness-Based Teacher Training Organizations (2015). Additionally, the International Integrity Network, a group of senior mindfulness-based teachers around the world are, at the time of press, engaged in proposing standards for training future MBCT and MBSR teachers as well as developing an ethical code. The International

Mindfulness Teachers Association (IMTA) is another attempt at looking at how to maintain teaching standards.

Developing uniform standards inevitably raises issues related to territoriality (national and international), cultural differences, and differing regulatory requirements. We need to be inclusive of all stakeholders. The worldwide interest in governance of MBPs and the training of those who would deliver them is in the purview of many rather than few. It would be tempting to be categorical and possessive of what it means to be a mindfulness-based teacher, attached to a specific way of how to operationalize and regulate this, before we have the evidence to support such policies. This will require sensitivity, deliberation, and patience to ensure that the leaders in the field are given the opportunity to come together in the spirit of mindfulness and to work through the challenges and cultural variations that will be inevitable as attempts are made to develop best practices.

With the increasing professionalization in the field in 2018, several leading developers of MBCT professional trainings created a website for MBCT teachers to be listed on an international registry called Access MBCT (http://www.accessmbct.com). The purpose of this registry is to provide quality assurance to the public, to publish a listing of sanctioned teachers for individuals and researchers, and to support a network for registered MBCT teachers.

We now turn our attention to personal mindfulness practice and its effect on teaching the MBCT program.

The Impact of Personal Mindfulness Practice

It is generally accepted that the influence of a personal mindfulness practice on teaching an MBP is an essential component to developing competence and best practices. What we know less about is how it influences and shapes teaching, what it looks like, and how we can measure it. In a relatively small quantitative study undertaken by Grepmair et al. (2007), psychotherapists in training who practiced for thirty minutes at the start of each day in the Zen tradition were more positively evaluated by their clients than other therapists in training who did not have a daily practice. In a qualitative study of MBCT, Van Aalderen et al. (2014), looking at the role of the mindfulness teacher from the perspective of the teacher and the participant, found that four major themes emerged from their analyses. These were embodiment, empowerment, nonreactivity, and peer support. In this study, the majority of the participants and all the teachers stated that it was vital for the teacher to have a meditation practice so that she embodied the practice from her own experience and demonstrated such mindfulness qualities as nonjudgment, acceptance, and compassion. In addition, and related to embodiment, both participants and teachers mentioned the importance of how the teacher utilized language and the quality of the voice. While these preliminary studies and our own experience support the idea that personal practice is important for the teacher, more research is needed.

In the current literature, emphasis is placed on the embodiment of mindfulness by the teacher (for example, Kabat-Zinn et al., n.d.; Crane, Kuyken, Hastings, Rothwell, & Williams, 2010; McCown et al., 2011). Segal et al. (2013) state that to offer MBCT, teachers "require the depth of practice and perspective that comes only from knowing, from the inside, what mindfulness practice is and what it is not. This means that *teachers* of mindfulness are *practitioners* of mindfulness in their daily lives. Without a teacher having an ongoing mindfulness practice, whatever is being taught is not MBCT" (p. 9). We would agree and add that a personal practice enables the teacher to know, on an experiential level, the variety of states that emerge from the practice, which of these may be problematic and need attending to, when the practice is useful for dealing with difficulty, and when it is not.

How a teacher embodies mindfulness is an essential and potent ingredient for the delivery of MBCT. Indeed, we consider it to be one of the five agents of change that we examined in earlier chapters. In addition, we see the process of embodiment deriving its foundation from an understanding of the historical (and spiritual) roots of mindfulness. In the chapters preceding this one, we looked at embodiment from the perspective of the teacher-participant relationship focusing on the employment of a teacher's understanding of the three marks of existence and its expression in the contemplative dialogue. We highlighted the specific skills of bare attention, open-monitoring, and discernment as crucial qualities of mindfulness. A teacher's intimate and experiential knowledge of these harvested from her own practice (her embodiment) will influence how she teaches them to her participants and be one of the most, if not the most, critical agents of change.

If embodiment is a significant factor in teaching MBCT, then a training program will need to find some way to emphasize this. So how does a professional training program go about creating opportunities within its training pathway for the development of this way of being? It is an unusual feature to emphasize for the acquisition of competency and is not one that is identified as a necessary teaching skill to foster in most other professional clinical programs. Most professional mindfulness training centers tackle this through identifying the value of a personal mindfulness practice but how they go about incorporating it varies.

As a prerequisite, some centers require their trainees to have sat a silent teacher-led meditation retreat before entering training, thus stressing the utility of such training as an important foundation to have before being trained. Other centers request that trainees state they have a self-determined personal practice but not that they have been on a teacher-led silent retreat. Once a trainee has been accepted into a program, most centers then require their trainees to go on retreat at least once a year during the period they are in training. It is then expected that an established MBCT teacher will continue to sit annual silent teacher-lead retreats and maintain a daily meditation practice.

We are fortunate that in many countries, there are mindfulness meditation retreat centers that provide the support for such sustained periods for silent practice. These retreats are often led by experienced teachers in the Buddhist tradition in sequestered settings.

The most common approach to integrate practice into training has been the opportunity for periods for silent practice to be included in foundational MBP teacher-training intensives. To foster this aspect of skill building, these are frequently held in residential settings, enhancing the aspect of quiet and removal from the distractions of everyday life. This is useful, as it allows trainees the opportunity to work within the container of silence, the practice of mindfulness, and the laboratory of their own mind as they are learning the skills of the MBCT program. Being removed from the interface of social discourse so frequently used to process disquiet and anxiety has important ramifications for teaching. This is because silence provides ample opportunity for insights into how we relate to experience and into our own reactivity. If a teacher does not know how to work with her own impulses and reactivity, she will not be well schooled in how to support that in her participants.

Newer to the field of MBPs are *hybrid* silent teacher-led meditation retreats for training novice and established teachers. By hybrid, we mean that these training retreats are offering sustained periods of teacher-led silent meditation practice that are not only being led by teachers from a Buddhist tradition (dharma teachers) but by senior mindfulness-based teachers or a combination of both. The silent aspect of these retreats is still a major component allowing for sustained periods of personal practice. What is being added are specific teaching modules that aim to use the experiences of personal practice by exploring and reflecting on how they inform best teaching practices. When these kinds of retreats are embedded within a formal training trajectory, the training program highlights the necessity of providing silent meditation practice as important rather than leaving it to the individual to find the time to sit a silent meditation retreat.

The Ethics of Teaching MBCT

We have discussed the centrality of establishing a personal practice as a key ingredient for the delivery of MBCT and how it informs an embodied mindful presence. We have also stated that MBCT is a mindfulness-based program that at its core offers a contemporary form of mindfulness meditation.

But we are holding a tension here. How do we adapt the teaching of mindfulness to a context that is distinct from the origins of this belief system and way of learning (the dharma)? Can it be successfully modified and still maintain its Buddhist historical and ethical roots, and does that matter? In the current literature (for example, Monteiro et al., 2015), there is a discussion that argues that mindfulness-based programs are potentially problematic because they have removed mindfulness from its original Buddhist context and its explicit ethical training. This argument is usefully provocative and can assist the field to be thoughtful about what it is appropriating. However, those who are practicing as MBCT teachers are mostly governed by professional bodies requiring practitioners to do no harm. This is consistent with Buddhist precepts.

To this understanding of ethics, we believe we need to add an additional dimension. Depending on the culture (and its beliefs), social systems will determine what is ethical, normative, and therefore sanctioned. In an article by Rachel Naomi Remen (1988), a physician and a contemplative writer, she defines ethics as a "set of values, a code for translating the moral into daily life." We could define this morality as an integrity of purpose and based on several things, not least the relationship we have with ourselves, others, and our environment.

In Buddhism, as in many traditions and religions, the concept of *right relationship* asks that we be aware of our intentions and motivations, as they will determine our actions and their effects on us and others. In terms of teaching MBCT, reflecting on a personal code of ethics is a good start. This is somewhat uncommon and one that is not often overtly considered in professional practice as it is taken as self-evident. In addition, we typically rely on our training and professional bodies to provide these boundaries through regulation. But here, we are making this code of ethics intentional and explicit as the practice of mindfulness incorporates a way of being, as discussed above, so values derived from the practice of mindfulness become guiding principles for the teacher.

Professions that are actively involved in working with psychological and physical conditions have licensing requirements and boards that act as legal parameters for the scope of their professions and guide behavior. MBCT teachers working with mood-disordered populations will be working under their specific professional clinical licenses and following the ethical boundaries outlined by their governing bodies.

In addressing these questions and others along the same lines, our thinking has been influenced by the teachings and writings of Stephen Batchelor (1998, 2017a) who has promoted the idea of secular Buddhism. Batchelor (2017b), in an article for *Tricycle*, proposes that we think of the dharma (particularly the Four Noble Truths) as secular, less of a belief system and more as a series of tasks to be accomplished that supports "an ethical space from which to see, think, speak, act, and work in ways that are not conditioned by reactivity" (p. 70). In this context, we would think of "not conditioned" (conditioned being a common concept used in Buddhism) as not being controlled by the causes and conditions that result in reactivity. In navigating these tasks, we can actively employ them as a way of viewing and guiding the relationship we have toward ourselves, others, and our environment. In so doing, the practice of mindfulness becomes an ethical path, a way of being, and a place from which to teach. This is exactly what we are facilitating and embodying when we are teaching MBCT as well as other MBPs.

These tasks fall into four broad categories:

- To come to know the various components of suffering (basically that life is not ideal; it is imperfect)
- To come to know the causes of this suffering (desire and greed, ignorance or delusion, and destructive urges)
- To come to know that there can be an end to this pain (or at least it can be mitigated) by letting go of attachment, the need to have and hold onto things, or the requirement that life be different
- To come to know that there is a prescription (path) that leads to the end of suffering

The path provides ethical direction on how to alleviate suffering and is categorized as follows: wisdom (right understanding and intention), conduct (right speech, action, and livelihood), and meditation (right effort, mindfulness, and concentration). The practice of mindfulness and active engagement with these tasks becomes a system of self-study, awakening us to our inner wisdom and compassion. As a teacher works with them, mindfulness becomes a way of *being*, and so she embodies the practice. As this process unfolds, this inevitably influences how she teaches. Teaching then becomes a practice of walking this path.

In Closing

Training MBCT teachers to reach competency is multifaceted, and although founded on personal practice and the ethics of best practices, this is not enough. Hence, we are seeing the establishment of training programs with proscribed learning pathways, methods for assessing competence, and ways to support continuing education. Along with these institutional training programs come organizations and associations attempting to standardize and control who can deliver this work. While we agree that it is important to have standards and a way for the public to recognize who is and who is not *qualified* to teach, it remains to be seen whether any one governing body beyond those already overseeing each mental health profession is necessary in the field of teaching MBCT. Best practices in teacher training will evolve, as will ways of assessing and maintaining competence. This will need to ensure the primacy of personal mindfulness practice and the teacher's embodiment of this, which is, after all, the heart of teaching MBCT.

Afterword

Writing this book has been a process and a practice. As we wrote, we found our collective voice and worked to discover how to convey what we thought needed to be said about being a teacher of MBCT (and other MBPs) from the inner landscape of teaching. We had to somehow convey in writing what it means to teach from within an embodied mindful presence and its outward expression, a dialogue that is deeply contemplative.

The work became an incredibly creative and collaborative effort, and little did we realize the process would go on for two years. Our relationship with each other deepened over that time as we grappled with how to best express our knowledge from teaching and practice. As with everything, there is a beginning, a middle, and an end. As we approached the end, we realized that we were moving out of process and were about to deliver a product to New Harbinger Publications, and more importantly to you, the reader.

What had been an intellectual joy with its inevitable brief tussles and disagreements about what ideas should go in and how they should be expressed became more challenging. On reflection and in dialogue with each other, we realized two things. Our work together in this form was ending. This needed to be identified. We were different in some way having been acted upon by the very process of writing. Could that be named? What did it mean for us, both in our personal relationships and in our professional work together? Second, we realized that in this ending, what we had shared with you, our thoughts and ideas, would now be reified no matter how imperfect. We identified anxiety and a sense of ownership. How would the book be received? Could each one of us stand behind what we had written, knowing that it was imperfect and at best captured a small part of what we wanted to say? We recognized from the outset the limitations of a book to encourage a teacher to rely on experiential learning, embodied presence, and teaching as practice. A description of the taste of the apple, no matter how vivid, will never replace the experience and knowing that is the tasting.

Seeing this resistance to letting go brought some ease and the ability to move back into process and practice and to talk about what was happening. Remember, as in the comic strip, Calvin and Hobbes, Calvin says, "Nothing is permanent. Everything changes. That's the one thing we know for sure in this world. But I am still going to gripe about it" (Watterson, 1995).

Susan has often said at the end of trainings, "The end is just the beginning." So, this is an end and a beginning. We hope that this book supports you in your development as a teacher and as a human being because in mindfulness, the two are inextricably tied together if one would teach as a practice. We also hope that this book is in some small way a contribution to the expanding field of mindfulness-based programs and the training of future teachers who would both be and do teaching.

None of us can know what lies ahead. This is important to remember. As the field of mindfulness expands, how it will unfold in the future remains a mystery. What we do know is that the practice of mindfulness will always ask us to continue to return and explore our own interiority, thus revealing the wonder of mindfulness, its wisdom and heart.

In our hearts, we are all hobbits on an unknown journey.

Dedicated to J. R. R. Tolkien.

Appendices

Meditation Scripts

The following meditation scripts are to be used to help guide your delivery of the various mindfulness practices. They are examples and not to be taken verbatim or indeed to be used to read from when you teach. It is important that you develop your own voice that comes from your practice when guiding. Some important considerations include use of language. These were discussed in the book, such as tone of voice, pacing, use of silence, and wording. Tone should be varied and conversational rather than trying to induce a special state of mind in your participants. When guiding a practice, ensure the intention and structure of the different meditations are understood; timing and pacing are then dictated by that. Ample use of silence, particularly as the program progresses, allows participants to experience what you are guiding and for them to develop autonomy of practice. Language should be simple, nonconceptual (minimal use of metaphors), and invitational. It should use present participles and contain few personal pronouns.

Body Scan Meditation Practice

The script that follows is an example of a way to instruct your participants in the Body Scan Meditation. You should not read this script but rather deliver it from your own practice, ensuring that at the same time you maintain awareness of the group.

It is important to leave extended periods of silence when delivering this meditation practice in order for people to have their own experience. Remember that the pauses will be longer as you move through the MBCT program. For example, the Body Scan in session 1 will have much more speaking than the one delivered in session 8. There will be suggested pauses in the following script. These are to let your participants attend to not only your guidance but also what is in the sensorial field for themselves.

It is not necessary to use all of these words, but keep in mind the purpose of the Body Scan is to explore sensations as they arise in the body, allowing participants to experience them. Another important intention is to learn to clearly establish, explore, and let go of attention in each body part.

In this script, we start the practice at the head and end at the feet. However, you can just as easily start at the feet and end at the head. What is important is that the guidance is systematic and that you visit each body part.

Guidance

In a few moments, we're going to be moving into a Body Scan Meditation practice. You can choose to lie down or sit in a chair, whatever is most comfortable for you, as we are going to be practicing for a while.

So, taking a few minutes to settle in, closing the eyes or bringing a soft gaze, allowing the surface you are lying or sitting on to take on the work of holding you up. Bringing attention to the body and the points of contact, noticing pressure and also where the body is not in contact with the surface you are resting on. Now, bringing attention to the entire body, the front body, the back, and the sides. Perhaps there is a feeling of calm or tension, restlessness or maybe even agitation, and simply noticing this and how it is registering in the body.

(Pause for 25 seconds.)

Now, gently bringing attention to the breath in the body, seeing if you can be aware of where the sensations of breathing are most prominent. This may be at the nostrils, the mouth, the throat, or in the rising and falling of the chest, or at the abdomen as the belly expands and deflates. Allowing the breath to do what it naturally does without manipulating it or changing it. Being with the physical sensations of the breath just as they are. Breathing in and breathing out.

(Pause for 30 seconds.)

Now, on an out-breath, letting go of this primary attention on breathing, and on an in-breath, gently shifting your attention to the back, top, and sides of the head. Paying attention to any physical sensations that present themselves as you attend to this part of the body, noticing and exploring them. Keeping in mind that a sensation may involve warmth, coolness, tingling, moisture, or other qualities, and if you experience no sensation or numbness, noticing that.

(Pause for 30 seconds.)

On an out-breath, releasing this focus of attention from the head, and on an in-breath bringing it to the face—from forehead to chin and from ear to ear. Allowing it to move around the face, experiencing any sensation that arises, bringing attention to that area as best you can, and investigating it and its qualities. Then waiting for another sensation to emerge and exploring that. Attending to the chin, the lips, inside the mouth, tongue, the cheeks, the eyes, the eyebrows, the ears, the forehead—letting whatever sensations arise and simply noticing them come, persist, and go. Letting attention linger; noticing sensations as they change, if they do.

(Pause for 25 seconds).

And now, on an out-breath, gently shifting the focus from the face, and on the inhalation, bringing it to the neck and throat, allowing the attention to explore, the front of the neck, the back, and the sides—noticing any sensations that make themselves known, giving them your full attention. Noticing where the neck is and is not in contact with the surface you are resting on.

(Pause for 25 seconds.)

From time to time, your attention will be pulled away by thoughts arising, perhaps into the past, the future, or fantasy—into worry or judgment or critical thoughts—or your attention may also be hijacked by other sensations elsewhere in the body. If this happens, gently escort your attention back.

(Pause for 30 seconds.)

Now, on an exhalation, guiding the attention away from the neck, and on an in-breath, establishing it in the shoulders—the shoulder joint; the top, front, and back of the shoulders; focusing on any sensations on or below the surface; noticing their qualities, including whether they are experienced as pleasant, unpleasant, or neutral.

(Pause for 20 seconds.)

Now, on an exhale, letting go of this focus on the shoulders, and on the inhale, moving the attention down the right arm to the right hand, exploring its position. Attending to any sensation that crops up—exploring the hand in its entirety. There may be tingling, pressure, numbness, or warmth, or no sensations at all. Observing as best you can with an investigative curiosity the quality of these sensations that arise in the hand. And again, if attention is pulled away by thoughts or sensations elsewhere in the body, see if you can let these be in the background and return to the current object of this meditation, which at this moment is the hand.

(Pause for 30 seconds.)

Exploring the front of the hand; the palm, the fingers, and thumb; the back of the hand, its shape, the backs of the fingers, and the nails. Taking in the entirety of the right hand and whatever sensations are showing.

(Pause for 15 seconds.)

And, on the exhale, letting go of this attention to the right hand, and with an inhale, moving attention to explore the wrist joint, the forearm front and back, the elbow joint, and upper arm. Exploring deeply into the joints as well as the front, back, and sides of the arm, noting its position, and where it is or is not in contact with the body.

(Pause for 25 seconds.)

Sensations might be due to clothing as it touches the skin or to the arms making contact with the surface you are resting on. There may also be more subtle sensations below the level of the skin. The intention is to study these sensations with curiosity. If more than one sensation comes up, feeling free to attend to the one that really piques your interest.

(Pause for 20 seconds.)

Exhaling now and releasing this attention from the right arm as you move the attention across the chest to the left arm, allowing it to travel down to the left hand. Attending to any sensation that arises—exploring the left hand in its entirety, its shape and curve, its position. There may be moisture, dryness, coolness, or warmth. Observing as best you can the qualities of these sensations, exploring them as they arise in the hand.

(Pause for 30 seconds.)

Checking out the front of the hand; the palm, the creases of fingers, and thumb; the back of the hand, its shape, the backs of the fingers, and nails. Taking in the entirety of the left hand and whatever sensations are showing.

(Pause for 25 seconds.)

And on the exhale, letting go of this attention to the hand, and moving attention to explore the wrist joint, the forearm front and back, the elbow joint, and upper arm. Exploring deeply into the joints as well as the front, back, and sides of the arm, noting its position and where it is or is not in contact with the body. Perhaps you are aware of clothing or air upon the skin. And whenever the attention moves—to sounds, thoughts, or sensations elsewhere in the body—with gentleness, return to the object of focus, which in this moment happens to be the sensations that arise in the arm.

(Pause for 25 seconds.)

Now, releasing attention from the arm, and bringing attention to the upper back and surveying this area. There may be sensations of pressure or temperature as you explore the shoulder blades, muscles, and spine. Observing and investigating each sensation with a kind and friendly interest, without having to change anything. Exploring each sensation as best you can.

(Pause for 25 seconds.)

Directing attention now to the mid- and lower back, and drawing attention to any sensation that comes up and exploring it in detail. The lower back, particularly, is a region that presents, for many of us, challenging sensations. If these are present, as best you can, exploring them.

(Pause for 30 seconds.)

Now, moving the attention from the back body and shifting it around the sides of the body and coming to rest on the chest as it rises and falls. There may be sensations made by the clothing against the skin as the chest moves with each breath. You may be aware of your beating heart. Attending fully to each sensation as it arises, allowing it to do whatever it does, observing moment-to-moment as you examine the chest and ribs.

(Pause for 35 seconds.)

Now, moving the focus of attention to the abdomen, attending to the belly as it rises and falls with each breath. Noting the full length of each in-breath and out-breath, not trying to breathe in any special way but being with the breath as it is. Letting the breath breathe itself.

(Pause for 30 seconds.)

Releasing the attention on the out-breath from the abdomen and bringing it to the area of the pelvis, the front and sides and the back, including the organs of reproduction and elimination, the pelvic bowl, the genitals, and the buttocks. Investigating any sensations that call attention to this region of the body.

For some of us, strong sensations may arise in the pelvis, and if this is the case, noting them, exploring them as best you can, and always knowing you can return the focus to the breath as a way to stabilize your attention, and when you feel ready, returning attention to this area that we are investigating, waiting for other sensations to arise.

(Pause for 20 seconds.)

Gently letting go of the pelvic region on the out-breath, and shifting attention to the right hip joint and thigh. Exploring the top, sides, and back of the thigh; noting pressure, the sensation of clothing, and the position of the leg.

(Pause for 30 seconds.)

Deeply exploring the right knee and kneecap and its position. Investigating the calf, shin, and ankle joint. Really getting to know the right leg and any sensations that present themselves, exploring them to the best of your ability. Being present as best you can to whatever is arising.

(Pause for 25 seconds.)

Waiting patiently for sensations to arise and then exploring them, and when the attention is pulled into thought or elsewhere in the body, coming back to the object of meditation without a story or judgment. In fact, noticing that the attention has been pulled away is just as much a part of the practice as is staying on the body part itself, which in this moment is the right leg.

(Pause for 25 seconds.)

And now, on the out-breath, releasing this attention on the legs and inhaling, allowing this attention to move into the foot, the top of the foot, the toes, the nails, the sole, the heel—resting here as best you can, attending to the foot, focusing on sensations as they make themselves known, and then exploring, investigating them fully, studying sensations such as moisture, dryness, tingling, pulsating, even numbness. So, attending to the foot moment by moment.

(Pause for 30 seconds.)

Now, moving the attention from the foot on an out-breath, and on the inhalation, directing the attention to travel up the leg, across the pelvis, and into the left hip joint, exploring any sensations here, and then allowing the attention to include the thigh. Exploring the top, sides, and back of the thigh, noting pressure, other sensations, such as tension or ease, the sensation of clothing, and the position of the leg.

(Pause for 30 seconds.)

Deeply exploring the left knee and kneecap and its position. Investigating the calf, shin, and moving deeply into the ankle joint to explore it. Really getting to know the left leg and any sensations that present themselves, exploring them, getting really curious about them. Being present as best you can with whatever is arising.

(Pause for 25 seconds.)

Waiting patiently for sensations and then getting to know them as you are exploring the left leg. And now, releasing this attention on the left leg and ankle, coming to investigate the left foot, the top of the foot, the toes, and the nails, attending to their shape and points of contact. Including the sole and the heel of the foot in your exploration—resting here as best you can, attending to the left foot, focusing on sensations as they make themselves known.

(Pause for 30 seconds.)

Letting go of attending to the foot, and moving the attention along the back of the body, the back of the heels, calves, thighs, buttocks, the spine, the lower, middle, and upper back. Breathing in and out, noticing tenseness, looseness, pain, comfort, vibration—whatever is present—and resting in this exploration, this scan of the entire back body. Continuing to move the attention along the backs of the arms, shoulders, neck and head, attending to the back of the head, and the scalp; noting any sensation that comes up in this moment. And, as sensations come and go, see if you can gently move from location to location, lingering for a moment and attending to one sensation, exploring it, and moving on.

(Pause for 35 seconds.)

Now, bringing attention to include the entire front of the body: the face, neck, shoulders, chest, arms, hands, torso, pelvis, legs, and feet. In a moment or two, releasing the attention from the front of the body to include the length and breadth of the body lying or sitting here. Taking these moments to be aware of any sensations that are appearing from any part of the body, noting them, exploring them with a kind and friendly interest.

(Pause for 25 seconds.)

Now, releasing attention from the entire body and bringing awareness to the physical sensations of breathing; noticing the movement of the breath as it enters and leaves the body. Attending to things just as they are in each moment.

(Pause for 20 seconds.)

In a moment, we will be coming to the end of this Body Scan practice; allowing the eyes to open, if they've been closed, or widening the gaze; bringing this quality of attention to the next few moments. Taking some time to move the body in any way that feels helpful in this moment, such as wiggling the toes, moving the legs or arms.

Please note. Instructions for safety as expressed in the guidance of attending to the pelvis may be used elsewhere in the body depending upon the population with which you are working. For example, if you are working with those who have lung disease or have had breast cancer, you may wish to bring such instructions when attending to the chest or breasts, respectively.

Awareness of Breathing and Challenging Physical Sensations

Please note that timing is approximate. Spend about ten to fifteen minutes on setting up posture and the sensations of breathing. Then, shift attention to the body and guidance about how to be with intense physical sensations for another ten to fifteen minutes, finishing with a return to the physical sensations of breathing.

Guidance

Choosing to sit on a chair or on a cushion on the floor. If you're sitting on a chair, it is helpful to place your feet flat on the floor with your legs uncrossed, sitting toward the front of the chair or using a rolled-up towel or blanket supporting the back. If sitting on a cushion, make sure the knees are lower than hips, and if necessary, supporting the knees with cushions.

Inviting you now to adopt an erect, dignified, and comfortable posture. The chest and spine are rising, and the neck is long, with the chin in line with the navel. Allowing the hands to rest on the thighs or folded in the lap. Gently closing your eyes if that feels okay, or taking a half-open, soft gaze, looking a few feet in front of you.

Bringing your attention to the physical sensations of the body by focusing on where the body is making contact with the floor or whatever you are sitting on, spending a few moments exploring these sensations.

(Pause for 25 seconds.)

Now, turning attention to the sensations of breathing wherever they are most vivid, perhaps at the nostrils, the chest, or at the level of the abdomen, and resting your attention here. Not needing to do anything in particular or to change your breathing, observing what it feels like to breathe. There is simply the physical experience of breathing. If at the nostrils, attending to the cool, dry air going in and the warm, moist air going out; if at the chest, attending to the expansion and contraction of the ribs; and if at the belly, to the stretch of the abdominal wall on the in-breath and the deflation on the out-breath. Picking one place in the body and allowing the attention to be here as best you can.

(Pause for 30 seconds.)

Staying with the movement of the breath as you breathe in and out is the intention of this practice. When the attention moves away from the breath to other sensations of the body, hearing, or thinking, recognize that this has occurred, and simply returning attention back to the breath in the body.

(Pause for 25 seconds.)

Allowing the breath to do whatever it does, making room for each breath, being with it just as it is, attending to the physical sensations of breathing moment-by-moment.

(Pause for 30 seconds.)

When the attention is drawn away, gently bringing it back to sensing the breath in the body without judgment or a story. No need for any harshness, simply attending in this way of being with the body, breathing moment-by-moment.

(Pause for 25 seconds.)

And now, on an out-breath, letting go of this primary attention on the sensations of breathing in the body, and on an in-breath, bringing attention to the entire body, allowing the breath to be present but in the background. Taking an open and receptive stance to experience, to whatever sensations are presenting themselves, lingering, and passing.

When a particular sensation calls your attention, bringing curiosity to it and investigating its shape, depth, parameters, and other qualities. Really getting to know it, and then when it no longer holds your attention, waiting for another sensation to capture attention and investigating that.

(Pause for 40 seconds.)

When you notice that the attention has been drawn to thoughts, stories, or sounds, this is a moment of mindfulness and an opportunity to choose to return to the original focus of attending to body sensations.

At this point, you may be noticing particularly intense physical sensations arising in the body. If this is the case, bringing attention to these sensations, noting them, and getting curious about them, exploring their characteristics.

(Pause for 30 seconds.)

If the sensations are too strong, then breathing with the sensations or trying to expand into them on the in-breath and softening on the out-breath as a way to support continued exploration and to be present.

(Pause for 30 seconds.)

Sometimes, the sensations may be really strong, even painful, and an option is to intentionally shift your position, noticing any sensations that arise as you do this. And then, when and if you feel ready, returning to your original posture, coming back to the focus of this practice, which is on physical sensations and where they are most felt.

(Pause for 45 seconds.)

And now, on an out-breath, shifting attention away from the physical sensations, allowing them to be present in the background, and moving attention to the sensations of breathing in the foreground. Returning the primary focus to where the sensations of the breath are most dominant and, as best you can, maintaining attention here.

And when the attention moves, which it naturally does, simply escorting it back to the breath gently, without rigidity, with a sense of intention, and starting again. Remembering that coming back to the breath is a part of mindfulness just as is the focusing on the breath itself.

(Pause for 40 seconds.)

Maintaining a steady focus on breathing as you sit here. The breath is always with you, always present, an anchor to current experience.

And now, as we bring this practice to a close, opening the eyes or widening the gaze and moving the body in whatever way is needed.

Three-Minute Breathing Space–Regular

The Three-Minute Breathing Space–Regular is a brief practice and can be used as a check-in to current experience.

Guidance

The first thing we do is to take a very definite posture on a cushion or chair. The back is erect, letting the body express a sense of being present and awake.

Now, closing the eyes, if this feels comfortable, the first step of the Three-Minute Breathing Space is bringing attention to what is going on right now. Becoming aware of what thoughts are present, what emotions and body sensations. So, rather than trying to push them away or shut them out, noticing them.

(Pause for 40 seconds.)

Step two of the Breathing Space is to shift attention to focus on the movement of the breath at the abdomen. Becoming aware of the rising and fall of the belly as the breath moves in and out. Noticing the sensations of breathing and bringing your full attention to them.

(Pause for 40 seconds.)

And now, the third step is allowing your attention to expand to the entire body, bringing a more spacious awareness to your experience if possible. Letting the breath be present but in the background. In this moment, noticing the contact points that the body is making with the chair or cushion and with itself.

(Pause for 40 seconds.)

And when you are ready, opening your eyes, letting go of this brief practice and bringing your attention to the next moments.

Mindful Movement

This is meditation in action, an unfolding process with the emphasis on the body in motion. Your instructions will include connecting movement with noticing breathing. Pace is important, but not so slow that your participants find it difficult to maintain interest and stay with the unfolding nature of the practice.

These poses are based on yoga, but the practice is not a yoga class. If you are not a yoga teacher, make that statement, and if you are, then remind yourself that you are not teaching a yoga class.

Make sure you are demonstrating the postures and practicing with your participants while guiding. Please leave enough time between poses and in the poses themselves for participants to experience what they are feeling. Safety instructions are important to state at the beginning of the movement practice and, depending on the population you are teaching, may be modified.

Guidance

In a moment, we will be moving into a practice of mindful movement. So, finding a space where you have enough room to move. (Leave enough time for your participants to move, and if you have yoga mats, give them directions about getting a yoga mat.)

This practice is designed to bring you into an awareness of the body. It is always important to be aware of your limits in any given moment and to allow your own sensitivity of your body to override my instructions. Alternatively, you can modify these movements in a chair. If you wish to skip something we are doing, you can visualize your body following the instructions. You are learning about nourishing and strengthening the body. So, following the instructions as best you can, doing what you feel capable of, and refraining from doing anything that does not feel appropriate. When you practice regularly, you will find that your limits will change. The best results occur by not trying to achieve anything at all, but by fully opening to the experience of the moment.

We are going to start by doing some standing stretches. You can decide whether you would like to do the stretches in bare feet or leaving your socks on. If you decide to leave your socks on, it is important to know that socks on a floor or yoga mat can compromise safety, as they are slippery.

So, let's come to a standing position, with the legs hip-distance apart and the knees slightly bent. Taking a moment to notice any sensations that may be arising from the contact that the feet are making with the floor or yoga mat either through the socks or from bare feet.

Now, bringing attention up into the ankles, the shins and the calf muscles, the knees, up into the thighs, the hips, gently tucking the tailbone slightly forward, down toward the floor. This engages the lower abdominal muscles, a way to protect the spine and bring strength to the core of the body.

Bringing attention to the chest area, gently lifting the spine up out of the pelvis, bringing attention now up into the shoulder blades and the shoulders. Moving the shoulder blades toward each other and slightly down toward the waistband at the back. And now, bringing attention to the length of the arms, into the hands and fingers. Letting the arms rest comfortably alongside the body.

Bringing attention to the neck and throat, releasing the muscles of the face and allowing the head to be gently held, supported by the neck.

Taking a moment here to notice the physical sensations arising from the body as you breathe. This pose is often referred to as mountain pose. Taking our stance. Breathing.

(Pause for approximately 30 seconds.)

And now, gently lifting the shoulders up toward the ears on an in-breath, and on an out-breath, releasing and letting go. Let's go ahead and do that three more times. On an in-breath, lifting the shoulders up toward the ears, and on an out-breath, releasing and letting go.

(Allow time for the participants to complete these movements three times.)

Now, let's go ahead and roll the shoulders forward as you continue to breathe, and then, rolling them gently backward, bringing the shoulder blades back toward each other. And let's do this again breathing as we roll the shoulders forward and back.

(Allow time for the participants to complete these movements.)

So, now let's go ahead and bring the hands onto the shoulders, bending the elbows and making a big circle with the elbows; first in one direction and then going in the opposite direction. Taking a moment here to experiment with this circular motion that we are making, with our hands on our shoulders, with our elbows bent, gently making circles first in one direction and then the other. There is no rush. We are noticing and being present with the sensations from these movements.

(Allow time for the participants to complete these movements.)

And now, bringing the hands down alongside the body. Taking a moment here to notice any sensations that may be present in the body as well as a sense of breathing.

(Pause for 30 seconds.)

Now, let's go ahead, lifting the right arm up toward the ceiling. And then stretching over to the left, sliding the left arm and hand down the left thigh. Noticing the sensations of stretch. Letting the breath move freely. Taking a moment here to notice the sensations.

(Pause for 10 seconds.)

And then, on an in-breath, releasing the stretch by bringing the right arm up toward the ceiling, taking a moment here. And then, on an out-breath, letting that right arm release, returning the arm to rest alongside the right-hand side of the body.

(Pause for 10 seconds.)

Now, let's lift the left arm up toward the ceiling. When you feel ready, stretching over toward the right, sliding the right hand down the right thigh. Stretching, breathing, and noticing the physical sensations that are arising. Taking a moment here and then on an in-breath, lifting the left arm up, and on an out-breath, releasing that left arm down alongside the body and noticing the sensations that may be present.

(Pause for 10 seconds.)

Let's go ahead and visit the first side again. Lifting the right arm up toward the ceiling. Stretching over to the left. Letting the left hand and arm slide down the side of the left leg. Stretching and letting the breath move freely. Noticing sensations that are arising from the stretch. On an in-breath, releasing the stretch as you bring that right arm up toward the ceiling again. And then, on an out-breath, letting go, by allowing that right arm to come back down alongside the right-hand side of the body.

(Pause for 10 seconds.)

Now, let's visit the second side for the second time. On an in-breath, lifting the left arm up toward the ceiling. Stretching over to the right as you slide that right hand down the right-hand side of the thigh. Stretching, noticing sensations, and breathing.

(Pause for 10 seconds.)

On an in-breath, bringing the left arm up toward the ceiling, and then, on an out-breath, releasing the arm down alongside the left-hand side of the body. Taking a moment here to notice the sensations that may be present.

You may have become aware of some thinking that is also present in these moments of movement. When you notice that, that is a moment of recognizing how the attention to what you are doing can be hijacked by thinking. This is normal. No worries. The invitation in these moments is to let go and shift the attention back to the physical sensations of movement and letting those sensations be in the forefront of your interest and attention.

(There are many more standing poses you can teach. A lot will depend on the time you have available—a minimum amount of time for the whole practice needs to be between twenty to thirty minutes and what is possible for your participants.)

For our next pose, we will be coming down on to our hands and knees.

(Allow time for the participants to come down onto the hands and knees.)

So here we are. The hands are underneath the shoulders, a little in front of the shoulders. In this way, we are protecting the wrists. Knees are underneath the hips and hip-distance apart. We will be doing two poses in this position, which is known as tabletop pose. These two poses are often called the cat and the cow.

(Pause for 10 seconds.)

So, let's go ahead, by lifting the spine, arching the back up toward the ceiling. As we do this, allowing the head to gently be released toward the floor. Eyes will probably be looking back toward the thighs. Gently breathing and allowing the body to accept whatever stretch is available in this moment. This pose is called cat pose.

And now, let's go ahead and reverse the arch by gently and slowly releasing the back and allowing the spine to accept a stretch in the opposite direction. We can gently raise the head. We don't want to overarch in the neck area, so the eyes might be slightly looking ahead a few feet. This pose is called cow pose.

So, in the next few moments, gently moving the spine between these two arches. And letting the head be a part of this movement. This is a wonderful pose for the spine. Our spine often holds a lot of tension, and by moving the body in this way, it can help release this tension.

(Allow time for the participants to complete these movements.)

Coming to a pause by letting the spine be midway between these two stretches, back to our original pose, tabletop. Taking a few moments here before coming down to lying on your back on the floor.

(Allow time for the participants to come into a lying down pose.)

Now let the body be completely supported by the floor. On an in-breath, let's go ahead and bend both knees, letting the feet be flat on the floor. Knees are hip-distance apart, arms resting comfortably alongside the body. On an in-breath, gently lifting the buttocks up off the floor. Gently stretching into the feet, engaging the thigh muscles. Breathing, noticing the stretch as you hold the body in this position.

(Pause for 10 seconds.)

On an out-breath, gently releasing this position, by bringing the buttocks and the spine back down to the floor, vertebra by vertebra. Taking a moment here and noticing any sensations that may be present.

(Pause for 10 seconds.)

Let's go ahead and do that one more time. On an in-breath, stretching into the feet as you lift the buttocks up off the floor, engaging the thigh muscles, the muscles of the back, and the abdominal muscles. Gently holding this position and continuing to breathe.

(Pause for 10 seconds.)

On an out-breath, letting this position be gently released as you bring the buttocks back down to the floor and the spine, vertebra by vertebra. And then, stretching both legs down toward the floor, completely releasing and letting go, being aware of your breathing.

(Allow time for the participants to complete these movements.)

On an in-breath, bending the knees once again so that the knees are pointing up toward the ceiling and the feet are resting comfortably on the floor. Feet are together; knees are together. Now, bringing the arms out to the sides, so that the arms are resting away from the body, arms at a right angle to the body.

Then, let's go ahead on an exhale, and drop the knees down to the right-hand side, toward the floor, turning the head to the left. Accepting whatever stretch is possible in this moment. Continuing to breathe, letting the breath move freely. Taking a moment here to notice sensations.

(Pause for 10 seconds.)

Then on an in-breath, bringing the knees back up so they are pointing toward the ceiling, and turning the head, so the eyes are looking up toward the ceiling.

(Pause for 10 seconds.)

When you're ready, dropping the knees down on an out-breath to the left-hand side as you turn your head to the right. Noticing these sensations, steadying attention, breathing.

(Pause for 10 seconds.)

Then on an in-breath, bringing the knees backup so they are pointing toward the ceiling, and turning the head, so the eyes are looking upward, toward the ceiling.

(Pause for 10 seconds.)

Let's go ahead and visit the first side for the second time. Dropping the knees down to the right, as you turn the head to the left. Accepting whatever stretch is available in this moment. On an in-breath, bringing the knees back up so they are pointing toward the ceiling, and turning the head so the eyes are looking upward, toward the ceiling.

(Allow time for the participants to complete these movements.)

Let's go ahead and visit the second side for the second time. Dropping the knees down to the left as you turn the head to the right. Noticing the stretch. On an in-breath, bringing the knees back up so they are pointing toward the ceiling, and turning the head so the eyes are looking upward, toward the ceiling.

(Allow time for the participants to complete these movements.)

(There are any number poses that can be offered in a lying-down position. This will depend on time and what is possible for the participants in your group.)

And now, stretching the legs out, so that they are resting on the floor, and bringing the arms down alongside the body, the feet falling away from one another. If this feels comfortable, allowing the eyes to close or equally to soften the gaze. Taking a moment here to completely let go, letting the body be supported by the floor. Being aware of this lying-down pose. Letting go of any thoughts, letting this sense of the body and breathing be in the forefront of your awareness. A state of relaxed attention, noticing things as they are and experiencing the length and weight the body.

(Allow participants to be in this position for a minute or two.)

And now, allowing the eyes to open or to widen the gaze, taking in the surroundings of the room. Taking a moment here. Go ahead and move the body in whatever way feels comfortable. Wiggling the toes, moving the feet, the hands, and the arms. Perhaps stretching the arms out as you stretch down into the legs.

Rolling over onto the right-hand side, bending the knees. Taking a moment here and then coming into a sitting position.

Walking Meditation

Guidance

In a few moments, we're going to be practicing a silent walking meditation. This practice is asking you to bring the same quality of attention that you brought to the Body Scan and the sitting meditation. The major difference in this practice is that you're walking! However, unlike our usual walking speed, we are going to slow the process down because we're bringing attention to every step we take.

We will be bringing full attention to one foot placed after the other, and how our bodies transfer the weight from one foot to the other. Rather than our usual automatic pattern of walking, we're slowing the pace down so we can more easily pay attention to the sensations of walking.

Coming to mountain pose. Taking a moment here to notice this position of standing. Noticing the sensations from the soles of the feet all the way through the body. This helps set our intention to be present. The arms and hands can be resting alongside the body, or you can clasp the hands behind your back or in front, whatever feels most comfortable and relaxed.

(Pause for 15 seconds.)

So, let's take a moment here in this standing position, bringing attention to the breath and to the body sensations. It's helpful to pick out a path no more than ten to fifteen paces long in which you will walk back and forth. Unlike our regular walking, in this practice, there is no destination. When you get to the end of the path, pause, turn, and then retrace your steps in the opposite direction.

Let's begin to walk slowly and naturally, allowing the eyes to gaze on what's ahead or down toward the floor. There is no need to exaggerate the walking, just going slowly enough so that you can maintain attention to the sensations of the feet as they touch the ground and the movement of the body.

(Pause for 20 seconds.)

It's helpful for some as we practice in this way to say to yourself quietly, "lifting, moving, placing," with each step you take.

(Pause for 45 seconds.)

Remember, we're not going anywhere, just to the end of the path we've chosen, coming to a stop, pausing, turning, and then returning the way we've just come.

(Pause for 2 minutes.)

It is common that we will notice the attention moves into thinking, stories, memories, or things you see or hear. When this happens, we simply return the attention to the sensations arising from the soles of the feet. As we practice in this way, we are bringing the body and mind into each unfolding moment. Being aware of the body in movement, the sensations arising, our breathing; allowing the eyes to be soft and body relaxed. And the focus of the eyes is straight ahead or looking gently down toward the floor, because our feet know what to do.

It can take some time for this slow walking to develop naturally. So, we're trying it out with that same sense of open-hearted curiosity and gentleness about exploring the experience from this practice as we did with the body scan and sitting meditation. There is no right or wrong way to engage in silent walking practice, relaxing into the moment as best you can, bringing a nonjudgmental attention to the walking.

(Continuing in this way for however long you have to practice with the occasional reminder to return the attention to the soles of the feet and the body moving.)

And now, coming back to standing wherever you are in your practice, returning to mountain pose. Taking a moment here before we move into our next practice together.

Breath, Body, Sounds, Thoughts, and Emotions and Choiceless Awareness (Open-Monitoring)

Guidance

In a moment, we will be moving into a sitting meditation practice. Deciding on a seated posture that supports the ability to be awake, still, and quiet. This means taking care of ourselves and listening to what is possible, acknowledging how the body feels and what is needed to support a seated posture. So, taking a sitting position and making any adjustments so that you can be as comfortable as possible in this moment.

(Allow time for your participants to get settled.)

If you're sitting in a chair, it's a good idea to support the back if you need to or sitting slightly toward the front of the chair so you're supporting your spine. The knees are hip-distance apart, lower than the pelvis, and the feet are flat on the floor. If you are sitting on a cushion on the floor, the knees are crossed comfortably in front of you. If your knees are not touching the floor, it's helpful to have some support under them like a cushion or a blanket. Noticing how the buttocks are making contact with the cushion or the chair so you are not tilting to the left or the right or leaning forward or backward.

The spine is erect but not held rigidly, with the head supported by the neck, the shoulders are relaxed, and there is a general sense of ease as you settle into the body. The hands are comfortably resting on the thighs with the palms facing up or down, and the muscles of the face, jaw, neck, and shoulders are not tensed. The eyes can be open or closed, whichever feels at ease for you in this moment. If you choose to have the eyes open, softening the gaze, looking slightly ahead of you toward the floor.

(Pause for 20 seconds.)

Because we can get so easily lost in thoughts and emotions, we're going to bring our attention to the breath and a sense of the body, using the breath and the body as an anchor to the present moment. As we settle into a sense of the body sitting here, gently bringing our attention to the physical sensations arising from the body.

(Pause for 20 seconds.)

There may be sensations of heat, tingling, vibration, coolness, discomfort, ease. Allowing all sensations to be noticed. We can notice sensations arising from the surface of the skin, perhaps a sense of the air passing over the skin's surface. We can notice sensations arising from deep inside the body.

(Pause for 20 seconds.)

And now, bringing attention to the length and breadth of the body sitting here, checking in with the posture, and bringing a sense of ease as best you can.

(Pause for 30 seconds.)

As we gently bring this interested focus to the physical sensations of the body, we will become aware of our breathing. So now, bringing attention to the physical sensations of the breath. Noticing where you best sense the body breathing, and bringing awareness to that part of the body. Being aware of the movement of the breath, the full length of each in-breath followed by the full length of each out-breath.

(Pause for 30 seconds.)

You might be noticing the breath as it comes into the body and leaves the body at the nostrils; you might be sensing the movement of the ribs as you breathe in and out, becoming aware of this gentle rise and fall. You might be aware of the belly moving as it rises on an in-breath and sinks softly back on the out-breath.

So, choosing to bring your attention to where you can best sense the physical sensations of breathing right now and anchoring your attention here. There is no need to control the breath, as breathing happens quite naturally, but rather, we are learning to rest awareness on each unfolding breath with relaxed attention.

(Pause for 30 seconds.)

So here we are sitting, paying attention as best we can, noticing the physical sensations of breathing. Every time you find the attention has moved away from noticing the physical sensations of breathing, don't worry. This is very normal. When you notice that this has happened, gently return attention back to wherever you best sense the body breathing. There is no need to judge this. By noticing this tendency of the mind, we are simply becoming aware of what minds do. Once we have noticed this movement, we have a choice to let go, by returning to our intention and the attention to be present with each breath.

(Pause for approximately 2 minutes.)

As we continue to sit here, being aware of breathing, we can become aware of particular thoughts: thoughts of future plans, worrying thoughts, stories, thoughts about the past, happy thoughts. Thinking is not the enemy! Recognizing that the attention has moved into thinking is helpful and very much a part of the practice and for now, the invitation is to let go of thinking and to bring the attention gently back to breathing, as a way to return the awareness to the present moment. In this way, we can slowly learn to let go of getting caught up in the stories of the mind and any judgments we might have about these.

(Pause for approximately 3 minutes.)

Now, expanding the attention to include the physical sensations arising from the body. Continuing to be aware of your breathing but allowing the breath to be in the background, as you bring your attention to the movement of sensations arising elsewhere in the body. We are simply resting attention on the sensations in the body, and we are learning to be curious and allow for these sensations, regardless of whether they are pleasant, unpleasant, or neutral. There is no need to change the sensations or to judge them. You are steadying attention and being present for and experiencing whatever is showing up. This is mindfulness of body sensations.

(*Pause for approximately 2 minutes.*)

Sometimes, when working with the body, it can be helpful to reconnect to specific contact points as a way to stay present and grounded. You can notice if your spine is still being held gently erect, the contact the buttocks have with the chair or the cushion, the contact of the feet with the floor, or the hands resting on the thighs.

(*Pause for approximately 2 minutes.*)

Sometimes, sensations from the body can be subtle, and sometimes, strong. As the body is held in this still posture, over time, it can reveal a variety of different sensations: tension, stiffness, pain, relaxation, tiredness, aches, dullness, sharpness, tingling, vibration, heat, cold. Bringing curiosity to what is arising is very much a part of our practice. Can we gently turn toward the experience of sensations just as they are right now, without judging them?

Noticing if the sensations change, if they stay the same, if they intensify, lessen, or even leave. Noticing if sensations are being experienced as pleasant or unpleasant, or perhaps there is not much to attend to, and turning our attention to that. Opening to this experience, if that feels okay to do, and exploring what is here.

(*Pause for approximately 1 minute.*)

Sometimes, sensations can be particularly challenging. If this is the case, the invitation is to continue to gently explore the region of difficulty. Is there a sense of bracing or holding or tightening around these difficult, perhaps even painful, sensations? We might even practice breathing with these sensations. And as we breathe out, seeing if it is possible to let go a little, to soften, not because you want anything to change but rather as a way to be present for what is arising. If we are experiencing a lot of pain or discomfort, there is no need to tough it out. Rather, we can set an intention to move, noticing the sensations that arise as you move the body. Then, when the sensations have lessened a little or a lot, returning to your original posture. In this way, we are working wisely with our experienced limits.

(*Pause for approximately 2 minutes.*)

Now, on an out-breath, releasing attention from sensations arising from the body and shifting attention to sounds. Allowing sounds to be in the forefront of your consciousness.

(Pause for 40 seconds.)

Sounds outside the room, inside the room, sounds in front of you or behind you, to the sides of you, sounds above you, and perhaps even sounds arising from the body.

(Pause for approximately 1 minute.)

So here, we are bringing attention to hearing, and resting moment by moment in the movement of sounds, noting their qualities, such as whether they are loud, soft, sharp, dull, pleasant, or unpleasant, whether they are discrete or continuous. You might notice that the attention is being drawn to particular sounds. If that is so, relaxing, releasing, and returning to observing all sounds just as they are in this moment.

(Pause for approximately 1 minute.)

Sometimes, sounds can lead to thoughts, even emotions, and if that happens and we get caught up in the story or the emotion, we can gently note that. Noticing that this is where the attention is being drawn. These moments are moments of awareness, of mindfulness. We are learning we have a choice here, to let go and return our attention to sounds and listening.

(Pause for approximately 1 minute.)

Allowing sounds to be received. Not looking for sounds, not pushing them away, but rather this receptive open listening. This is mindfulness of sounds.

(Pause for approximately 3 minutes.)

And now, releasing sounds as you shift your attention to include thoughts. We began by adopting a sitting posture. We then brought attention to the breath and to sensations arising from the body and then to observing sounds, and now we bring the same sense of open, gentle, curiosity, and attention to thoughts as sensations of the mind, as mental events.

(Pause for approximately 1 minute.)

If you find yourself drawn into a stream of thoughts or a story, gently note "thinking," and then see if it's possible to let go and return to this openness to noticing thoughts.

(Pause for approximately 1 minute.)

Sometimes, thoughts have a particular traction; they keep repeating themselves, going around in an endless loop. What is helpful in these moments is to return to a sense of the breath and body sensations. In this way, we can allow the breath and a sense of the body to be an anchor that brings us back to this moment, anchors us, and helps us not to get so caught up in an endless cycle of thinking. And then, when you feel ready, shifting the attention to once again to be receptive to thoughts, allowing them to be in the forefront of your consciousness.

(Pause for approximately 1 minute.)

Seeing each thought as just that: a thought about the past or the future, a planning thought, a remembering thought. Observing thoughts as mental events passing through the spaciousness of mind.

(Pause for 30 seconds.)

We can liken thoughts to clouds passing across the sky. Some clouds move quickly; others tend to pass more slowly. Thoughts are no different. Some will move quickly, and others will hang around. Our practice is asking us to gently pay attention to this without needing to add anything additional thoughts about what is happening.

(Pause for approximately 2 minutes.)

Thoughts can be neutral or highly charged. They can be peaceful, calm, fearful, anxious, sad, angry, happy, joyful. Thoughts can be agitated, repetitive, or dull. Does the mind contract around these thoughts, or can there be a sense of space? Is there an emotional charge connected to specific thoughts? What are you noticing? Do these thoughts that have an emotional charge change? Intensify? Weaken? Does the sense of these emotions change into a different emotion?

(Pause for approximately 1 minute.)

Regardless of the emotional charge that might be present with thinking, allowing your attention as best you can, to be present with what is arising, and when this no longer claims your attention, returning to a gentle, open curiosity toward thinking and emotions. In this way, we are working wisely.

(Pause for approximately 1 minute.)

It can be helpful when we notice that there is an emotional charge to thinking, to bring attention to the body and to notice if there is a region in the body that is tense, has tightened, or is bracing or holding in some way. If you notice this, bringing attention to this region of the body, bringing a sense of breathing into the area, softening with each out-breath; nothing to hold onto here, nothing to push against or struggle with.

If the thoughts and emotions become too charged to remain being open and attentive to what is arising, seeing if you can relax, and allowing the breath to be in the forefront of your attention; gently breathing, noticing the full length of each in- and out-breath. And then, when you feel ready, returning to this open, curious exploration of thinking and emotions.

(Pause for approximately 2 minutes.)

Sitting with the spine erect and the body relaxed, continuing to be attentive to the movement of thoughts and emotions. This is mindfulness of thoughts and emotions.

(Pause for approximately 5 minutes.)

And now, for the remaining time, letting go of all objects of attention. Allowing awareness and your intention to be present to notice whatever sensations arise, whether from the body, from sounds, or from thoughts and emotions.

If thoughts come, we can be present; if sounds, receiving sounds. If body sensations, then the experience arising from being attentive to the movement of the physical sensations. If breathing, then noticing breathing. Sitting in the stillness, looking for nothing, but remaining gently aware of all sensations as they come and go within the field of experience.

(Pause for approximately 5 minutes.)

Adopting this kind, open curiosity to all sensations and experience regardless of their nature. If you find you get caught up with a particular sensation, gently bring attention to the breath as a way to steady your intention to be present. And then when you feel ready, returning to this sense of receptive open awareness to all experience. We are cultivating a moment-to-moment awareness, a state of nondoing with a friendly warm-hearted interest.

(Pause for approximately 2 minutes.)

And now, on an out-breath, returning attention to breathing. Noticing where you best sense the body breathing and bringing awareness to that place. Noticing the full length of each in-breath followed by the full length of each out-breath, moment by moment.

(Pause for approximately 2 minutes.)

And so, as we come to the end of this sitting meditation practice, taking a moment to extend warm wishes to yourself for taking this time and for making the time to practice in this way.

(Pause for approximately 30 seconds.)

Now, when you feel ready, allowing the eyes to open if they have been closed, or if you have chosen to soften the gaze, widening the gaze, taking in the surroundings of the room. Becoming aware of the room and of the body and breathing. Bringing awareness to this transition and the next few moments in this way. And then, to move the body in whatever way feels comfortable to you right now.

Three-Minute Breathing Space–Responsive

Guidance

In a few minutes, we will be bringing to mind a difficult situation, or recent worry or concern. Please do your best to bring up a situation of manageable difficulty. On a scale from 1 to 10 where 10 is the most difficult, here, we are working with something that would fall along the scale at a 4. Sometimes, something that is particularly challenging may come up that feels overwhelming, and if this does happen, feel free to let go of the practice, open your eyes, and return your attention to the sensations of breathing at the level of the abdomen.

And now, coming into a comfortable position, one that embodies a posture of being alert and awake, closing your eyes if that's comfortable or taking a soft gaze and then turning attention to the body. Becoming aware of your posture, the points of contact, the front body and the back body, and your breathing as you are sitting here.

(Pause for 20 seconds.)

Our first step in this Breathing Space–Responsive is to bring to mind some difficult situation, some worry, some concern, or troubling thought or image…something manageable, versus the greatest stressor you have ever experienced. Noticing what thoughts arise, what emotions, and what body sensations.

(Pause for 20 seconds.)

If there are emotions, then perhaps saying to yourself, "Sadness is here," or "Irritability is present," and then bringing your attention to any associated physical sensations (if there are any), exploring them, investigating them, being with whatever is here, even if it is unwanted.

(Pause for 30 seconds.)

And if these sensations are particularly challenging, noting them. If needed, breathing with them, perhaps expanding into them on the in-breath and softening on the out-breath, saying to yourself, "I can be with this. Let me feel this. It's already here." Staying with these sensations for as long as they are capturing your attention.

(Pause for 30 seconds.)

And now, in step 2, letting go of attending to the sensations in the body and shifting your attention to the sensations of breathing at the lower abdomen, being with the body, breathing in and out.

(Pause for 20 seconds.)

Now, for the third step, expanding attention to the entire body, bringing a more spacious awareness to the physical experience as best you can. Noticing the points of contact that the body is making.

(Pause for 20 seconds.)

And then letting go of this practice, and opening your eyes if they have been closed or widening the gaze.

Note. In session 7, an action step is added to this practice to assist people in self-care (following the Nourishing and Depleting activity). This can take place during step 3 or on reflection after ending the practice.

For example: Now, for the third step, expanding attention to the entire body, bringing a more spacious awareness to the physical experience as best you can. Noticing the points of contact that the body is making. Then asking yourself, can you let the difficulty be? Can you let it go? Does it need addressing? If yes, is this through a shift in attitude or action? If so, what does that action look like?

All-Day Silent Retreat Schedule

The following schedule is an example. The duration of the retreat and timing of the practices will vary. The week before the silent retreat, we suggest that you discuss what the group can expect from the day, what they should bring (extra layers, a water bottle, shawl, lunch, and so forth), and that participants are advised from the time they wake up in the morning to see if they can be in the practice, maintaining silence. It is therefore suggested that you begin the retreat by 9:00 a.m. if possible, as this is easier for group members.

9:00 a.m.	Welcoming remarks and orientation to the day. Participants are instructed that they need to look after themselves as needed and come to the instructor should they experience any difficulty or wish to leave the retreat early. They are also told that it is helpful to maintain custody of the eyes (by not looking directly at other participants) as there are many ways to communicate, and averting the gaze helps to maintain the quality of the practice without the complication of social interaction. Participants are also asked to turn off their cell phones and to refrain from reading or note-taking. They are also invited not to check their emails or phones during lunch unless there are compelling reasons to do so.
9:15 a.m.	Body Scan Meditation Practice
9:45 a.m.	Mindful Movement
10:45 a.m.	Sitting Practice: Awareness of Breathing
11:15 a.m.	Walking Meditation
11:45 a.m.	Sitting Practice: Awareness of Breathing
12:00 p.m.	Lunch (Provide instructions to participants to engage in mindful eating.)
1:00 p.m.	Walking Meditation
1:30 p.m.	Breath, Body, Sounds, Thoughts, and Emotions and Choiceless Awareness Practice

2:15 p.m.   Mindful Movement

2:45 p.m.   Loving-Kindness (Metta) Practice. It is strongly suggested that if teachers are going to guide Loving-Kindness that they have had experience with the traditional form of this practice. Here, the traditional form is adapted. Participants are guided to first bring to mind a mentor or friend and to direct warm wishes and use phrases to convey a sense of kindness, ease, safety, and well-being toward that person. If someone doesn't come to mind or isn't available, one can bring to mind a pet or person admired. This is then followed by directing these same intentions to oneself, to the whole group, and finally to all beings. It is important for teachers to understand that, depending upon their sense of the group, this practice may not be appropriate if the group members are too depressed, if they have trauma, or for religious reasons.

3:15 p.m.   Transitioning out of silence, group discussion, closing remarks. Participants are advised to move back into their regular lives slowly and with care. They may not realize the influence of the day's silence and practices, particularly to a heightened sensitivity to the stimulation in everyday life as they reenter their routines.

3:45 p.m.   Participants leave.

Frequently Asked Questions

How do I manage trauma?

As previously discussed in this book, screening for a history of trauma is important. Adverse effects of meditation may be more common in participants with a past history of trauma. These may include panic attacks, flashbacks, emotional dysregulation, a drop in mood, or various types of dissociation. However, if a participant has done psychotherapeutic work around the trauma, knows how to keep herself safe if she gets triggered, has a current psychotherapist she can turn to for support, and is aware of the risks, then MBCT may be suitable. Participants with trauma should be monitored and encouraged to notify the teacher if any adverse reactions occur. Facilitators may also choose to modify the guidance of some practices (such as the Body Scan or where they place attention in breath practices) that might be triggering. These modifications include skipping some body parts, opening one's eyes, bringing attention to the soles of the feet, or using the breath as a grounding technique.

What to do when someone has an intense reaction?

While rare, if a participant has an anxiety attack, dissociation, or other severe reaction during a meditation, it is often enough to suggest they use one of the safety mechanisms above or to come out of the practice all together, drink a glass of water, or get up and walk. In addition, it can be helpful to sit beside the participant in distress, thus providing reassurance by one's close presence. When this is not sufficient, a grounding technique can be used like the 5-4-3-2-1 coping exercise in which they are asked to count or attending to things they see, hear, feel (kinesthetically), smell, and taste in systematic order (five of each, four of each, three of each, and so on). Participants should be advised not to leave the room (unless there is a cofacilitator to go with them) so they can be monitored while the rest of the group is attended to.

What about strong displays of affect like crying or anger?

By and large, the practice is about being with whatever difficult feelings show up and experiencing that all emotions pass. It is important for the teacher to model this to the participant and the group by showing concern and support without rescuing or excessive reassurance. A teacher's calm and compassionate presence is key here. Through gently inquiring into what is arising by asking open-ended questions about the full range of what is occurring, and steadying the focus on thoughts, emotions, behaviors, and body sensations, he embodies a willingness and encourages his participant to stay with the experience. In some cases, it can be helpful to have the whole group practice a Three-Minute Breathing Space as a way of regulating and defusing the tension for everyone and showing how this practice can be brought to moments of difficulty. If you become concerned about a person's mood state, then checking in with her at the end of class or during the week is helpful, as it provides you and the participant with necessary information about her safety and continuation in the MBCT program. With angry outbursts, if frequent and disruptive to the group, then it would be necessary to talk to the person outside of the group to assess what's behind the anger and whether it is appropriate for her to continue.

How do I adapt MBCT to my specific populations?

This was discussed in chapter 4. If an adaptation is being considered for a special population (for example, those with cancer, traumatic brain injury, bipolar illness, and so on), reviewing the literature and checking to see what has been published is a good first step. If specific considerations and adaptations are discussed, consider getting in touch with the author(s) to see if he or she will discuss the adaptations with you. Generally, you can make minor changes in language and how a practice is delivered to accommodate a specific population as long as it is intentional, has a sound rationale, and remains true to the core features of MBCT. If there are major changes to the curriculum, then it is important to consider if you should be calling it MBCT at all.

What do you do when someone does not seem engaged or repeatedly doesn't do the home practice?

It can be frustrating for the facilitator when a participant does not seem engaged in the group or is not doing any home practice. Taking the participant aside at the end of the class or during the break if you plan to offer one or contacting them during the week to discuss how they are feeling about the group and what is getting in the way of doing home practice can be helpful. Various strategies can be discussed. If the person is coming to class regularly, that can be some measure of commitment, regardless of how much home practice she reports or how engaged she appears. Different people get different things from the group, and sometimes the problem is not the participants but our expectations as teachers that people "buy into" or "get" mindfulness or "get better." On the other hand, if someone is frequently missing classes or coming late for no legitimate reason, then a frank discussion around commitment may be appropriate. Sometimes participants get pressure by family members or clinicians to attend, but their hearts are not in it. Other times, the timing is just not right, and they can consider doing MBCT another time.

How to I deal with cross-talk?

Cross-talk is the offering of advice or reassurance between one participant and another during group. While an important feature of some group therapies, it is downplayed in MBPs to allow everyone to have their own experiences. The rationale for this should be mentioned in orientation and gently pointed out during the group if it happens a lot. Some advice-giving and reassurance by group members is inevitable both during the group and outside of it, so a teacher needs a light hand in deciding when to discourage it.

How do I manage participants who don't talk? Or talk too much?

During orientation, it is common to say that verbal participation is voluntary and that people won't be put on the spot and forced to speak if they don't wish to. However, we also say it is an act of generosity to share your experiences in group discussion even if you are not a talker and an act of generosity to share the airtime with others if you do like to talk. If a person speaks very little yet is still participating in practice and seems engaged, then this is sufficient. Work in dyads can be a way of ensuring all members have opportunities to share and can be used for discussing home practice, territory of depression, relapse signatures, or the Nourishing and Depleting Exercise before general discussion in the large group. If you are worried about someone's level of engagement, you can discuss this with her outside of group to see if something is getting in the way.

For the person who speaks a lot and dominates discussions, you can ask for others' comments before calling on her for her input. It may also be necessary to gently interrupt someone if she is "going on" and lost in the narrative. Indeed, it can be helpful to say at orientation, and repeat occasionally, that our role as teachers is to support direct experience by coming out of storytelling. Therefore, to do this, we may need to interrupt people at times and bringing them back to their immediate experience of the practice.

How much should I self-disclose personal details about myself?

Although self-disclosure can help build rapport and trust as in any professional relationship, it can also lead to role confusion and unclear boundaries. Generally, self-disclosure should be used judiciously to model or give examples related to practice and be guided by the regulated professional body to which you belong or any institutional policies in the setting where you are offering MBCT. It can sometimes be helpful to mention your own struggles in learning meditation to normalize this, but, as with any personal anecdotes, bring awareness of any tendencies to talk too much about yourself and any need for it to be more about you than your participants.

What about graduate groups or participants who want to continue to meet after the group ends?

It is common that at the end of a group, many participants wish to continue. It is our experience that if they manage to create a group following the end of the program, it is usually short-lived unless it is formally organized and teacher-led. The group may choose to share emails or develop a Facebook page to maintain contact; however, it is our suggestion that you let them organize this themselves. If you are willing to lead a graduate group, this can be regularly scheduled drop-in sessions to practice the meditations from MBCT and introduce other practices. Some teachers also invite graduates to attend the silent all-day retreats they run for their current groups. Another model is time-limited "booster" groups (for example, four to six sessions) for participants wishing to reinvigorate their practice some months or years following an MBCT group. You can also recommend participants consider an MBSR or mindful self-compassion (MSC) group to continue their mindfulness practice. Finally, at the end of an MBCT course, the teacher usually gives participants a list of resources that includes books, articles, websites, and apps as well as meditation groups in their locale that provide opportunities for regular practice in community.

Should I teach alone or with a cofacilitator?

There are pros and cons to each. Many times, cofacilitation is not available, and a teacher must learn how to teach alone with all that that entails. If one has the luxury of a cofacilitator, it may allow mutual learning and support and be helpful in managing difficulties or emergencies. However, cofacilitation can also be problematic if people have different ideas of how to run a group or different styles of teaching. Therefore, it is helpful to discuss how coteaching will be organized. As much as possible, coteachers should strive for an open relationship in which they can give constructive feedback to each other without judgment or defensiveness. There should also be a clear delineation of roles if there is a preexisting hierarchical relationship (such as clinical supervisor, manager, and so forth).

How do I build a community of practice?

This is touched on in chapter 9. With increasing numbers of people offering MBCT and other MBPs, there are more opportunities to learn from and support others in the field. Often, the various centers offering training are creating communities of practice for continuing education and peer mentorship online or in person. If this is not available, it may be possible to reach out to other teachers of mindfulness in your community, regardless of the MBP taught, to explore how you may offer support to each other.

Although Access MBCT (http://www.accessmbct.com) is intended to help direct the general public to qualified teachers and people interested in training in MBCT to recognized programs, it may grow to be an international community of practice specific to MBCT.

How Cognitive Behavior Therapy Informs MBCT

In our experience, people who wish to become MBCT teachers often have a good grounding in mindfulness-based meditation practices but may not know a lot about cognitive behavior therapy (CBT) or appreciate how it informs the MBCT program. While there is no need to be a cognitive therapist to be an MBCT teacher, a basic understanding of the CBT model can be helpful, particularly when delivering the cognitive exercises.

There are many definitions of mindfulness, and we have identified as key to the practice the cultivation of attention, curiosity, and inquiry into the present and the awareness and understanding of one's relationship to that experience. Mindfulness helps us shift our relationship to experience using the body, emotions, sensations, and thoughts as objects of attention and as a means of being with difficulty. It does not deal directly with the content of thinking nor primarily manage problems from a cognitive or *doing* mode but rather emphasizes *being* with things as they are. Both these modes are necessary, allowing us to plan and execute as well as to be aware of the changing nature of experience, enhancing our flexibility and adaptability to everyday life.

CBT is a structured model of psychotherapy that examines the meaning ascribed to experience (underpinned by core beliefs about the self, others, and the world); the interaction between thoughts, emotions, and behaviors; and how these affect mood and anxiety and reinforce one's sense of self. One of its primary techniques is the application of the Automatic Thought Record (ATR). This is a chart that is used by clients to record distressing situations and related automatic thoughts (those that pop into one's head unbidden and contain evaluations against the self, for example, *I'm a loser*). Associated emotions, evidence to support and negate a "hot" negative thought (the most believed and emotionally charged), and finally, the construction of an alternative, more balanced way of looking at the situation are also recorded. The ATR assists clients to identify these components of experience, the habitual interpretations, and the conclusions they make and to gather data to address the accuracy or bias in their beliefs. Thus, it directly addresses the content of thinking, is directed toward solving problems, and teaches specific skills to challenge and modify unhelpful thoughts and behaviors with the aim of developing ones that are more functional. In addition, it uses a variety of other techniques to test out healthier thoughts or behaviors to disconfirm deeply held beliefs against the self that limit behavior. One of CBT's core intentions is to help people to not believe everything they think.

Mindfulness and CBT share many similarities and differences, and several of these are outlined here to clarify and deepen our understanding of them.

Both increase self-regulation, enhance mood, and decrease anxiety. These modalities do this by assisting people to recognize, observe, and externalize the components of experience, resulting in decentering from and being less identified with challenging events. Ultimately, one is learning to relate differently to difficult mind and mood states and to integrate this learning into everyday life to prevent relapse of depression, reduce anxiety, and increase resilience.

Similarities between CBT and mindfulness include:

- increasing awareness, parsing, and deconstructing experience—thoughts, emotions, body sensations, and behaviors
- externalizing and decentering from events
- developing a vocabulary around thoughts, emotions, and sensations
- turning toward difficult or anxiety-producing experiences—exposure
- bringing interest and curiosity to distress
- skill building
- involving active participation by the participant
- structured
- using home practice and experimentation

Differences between CBT and mindfulness:

CBT	Mindfulness
explicit	emergent
fast	slow
leading/guiding the client through Socratic dialogue	guiding and eliciting
correcting and challenging	accepting
addresses content of thoughts	relationship to experience
meaning making	experience as an event or process
emphasis on cognition	emphasis on sensorial experience
thoughts as behaviors	thoughts as sensations
doing	being
emphasizes the behavioral	emphasizes the observational and attitudinal
goal directed	experiential

While mindfulness and CBT help people address their suffering in different ways, both reduce automatic habitual modes of mind. People gain distance from their thoughts and come to see their thoughts are not necessarily "me" or true, and this loosens the tenacity of thinking patterns. We can learn to have them rather than be immersed in them.

The way CBT deconstructs experience is embedded throughout the MBCT program. The cognitive exercises and how they are facilitated are some of the key ingredients that make MBCT different from other MBPs. These cognitive exercises consist of:

1. Thoughts and Feelings (a.k.a. Walking Down the Street)
2. Pleasant Events Calendar
3. Unpleasant Events Calendar
4. Automatic Thought Questionnaire
5. Territory of Depression
6. Alternative Viewpoints Exercise (a.k.a. Office Exercise)
7. Identifying Relapse Signatures (Early Warning Signs) and Developing an Action Plan
8. The Nourishing and Depleting Exercise

The cognitive exercises assist in the development of the following skills:

- To become aware of and identify components of experience (thoughts, emotions, body sensations, behaviors)
- To quickly deconstruct and describe experience
- To see congruence between components (thoughts are concordant with emotions, emotions and body sensations, thoughts and body sensations)
- To challenge one's view of *reality* and see thoughts as "ideas," interpretations, and conclusions following appraisal of an event
- To externalize experience from self (decrease fusion, increase decentering)
- To approach difficulty (reduce experiential avoidance)
- To determine next steps when dealing with difficult states or events (let it be, let it go, address—attitude or action)
- To regulate emotions
- To realize that turning toward difficulty increases distress tolerance, builds skills, and builds self-efficacy

All these exercises follow a particular format with some slight variations. Mindfulness and CBT both use a process of discovery and investigation in which one brings both curiosity and interest to any experience whether pleasurable, painful, or neutral. What follows is an example of how a teacher might work with these exercises in MBCT. Notice that a key part of mindfulness-based programs that is significantly different from CBT and bears repeating is that we are working with one's relationship to any situation rather than an analysis about its meaning, content, or causation.

1. Ask participants to consider the particular topic (for example, unpleasant events or depressive and anxious thoughts).

2. They then engage in a specific exercise or home practice where they identify their own experience (for example, unpleasant events, pleasant events, specific thoughts, emotions, body sensations, or impulses to act, such as via the Alternative Viewpoints Exercise or Relapse Signatures).

3. Responses are gathered by the facilitator from the large group and written on the board or discussed and categorized by the components they include (thoughts, emotions, body sensations, or impulses and behaviors, depending upon the exercise).

4. The facilitator then reads the responses back to the group. If these responses have been written across the board, she may read them vertically to express them back to the group by component (all the body sensations, then all the emotions, and so on). This helps participants reduce their tendency to personalize an experience and increase the possibility of seeing it as a phenomenon that comes and goes.

As discussed in earlier chapters, participants are asked to reflect on what they observe about the exercise and their response, what can be learned from it, and what its relevance is to staying well or decreasing depression and anxiety. A reflective, decentered stance in which the group examines its responses and patterns is cultivated to increase awareness, choice, and skillful over automatic reactivity.

With respect to the themes of each session, what follows are the particular skills addressed that are relevant to CBT. It is important, as outlined above, to remember that while there are definitely differences, there is also significant overlap between the aims and outcomes of mindfulness and CBT.

MBCT Eight-Week Session Themes and CBT Skill Building

1. Awareness and Automatic Pilot: vocabulary building, automatic thinking, and experience of sensations

2. Living in Our Heads: identifying and challenging thoughts, reality as a construct

3. Gathering the Scattered Mind: awareness of cascading thoughts

4. Recognizing Aversion: exposure, experiential disconfirmation, identifying thoughts

5. Allowing and Letting Be: exposure, experiential disconfirmation, distress tolerance

6. Thoughts Are Not Facts: context and state-affect thinking and interpretations, externalizing and depersonalizing thinking

7. "How Can I Best take Care of Myself?": activation, reframing

8. Maintaining and Extending New Learning: skill maintenance, self-efficacy

Mindfulness and CBT share many common features that are emphasized in MBCT. Although one doesn't have to be a CBT therapist to facilitate this program, understanding CBT's underpinnings and appreciation of its use in MBCT allows for more effective delivery of key elements of the curriculum.

References

Batchelor, S. (1998). *Buddhism without beliefs: A contemporary guide to awakening.* New York: Riverhead Books.

Batchelor, S. (2017a). *Secular Buddhism: Imaging the dharma in an uncertain world.* New Haven: Yale University Press.

Batchelor, S. (2017b). A Buddhist Brexit: A secular reimagining of the dharma may help us face political calamity. *Tricycle, XXVI* (3), 68–71.

Brandsma, R. (2017). *The mindfulness teaching guide: Essential skills and competencies for teaching mindfulness-based interventions.* Oakland, CA: New Harbinger Publications, Inc.

Bowen, S., Chawla, N., & Marlatt, G. A. (2011). *Mindfulness-based relapse prevention for addictive behaviors.* New York: The Guildford Press.

Brockmeyer, T., Zimmermann, J., Kulessa, D., Hautzinger, M., Bents, H., Friederich, H. C.,… Backenstrass, M. (2015). Me, myself, and I: Self-referent word use as an indicator of self-focused attention in relation to depression and anxiety. *Frontiers in Psychology, 6,* 1564.

Crane, R. (2008). *Mindfulness-based cognitive therapy: Distinctive features.* New York: Routledge.

Crane, R. (2017). *Mindfulness-based cognitive therapy: Distinctive features* (2nd ed.). New York: Routledge.

Crane, R. S., Eames, C., Kuyken, W., Hastings, R. P., Williams, J. M., Bartley, T.,…Surawy, C. (2013). Development and validation of the mindfulness-based interventions—Teaching assessment criteria (MBI: TAC). *Assessment, 20*(6), 681–688. doi:10.1177/1073191113490790

Crane, R. S., Kuyken, W., Hastings, R. P., Rothwell, N., & Williams, J. M. G. (2010). Training teachers to deliver mindfulness-based interventions: Learning from the UK experience. *Mindfulness, 1*(2), 74–86.

Crane, R. S., Kuyken, W., Williams, J. M. G., Hastings, R. P., Cooper, L., & Fennell, M. J. V. (2012a). Competence in teaching mindfulness-based courses: Concepts, development and assessment. *Mindfulness, 3*(1), 76–84. doi:10.1007/s12671–011–0073–2

Crane, R. S., Soulsby, J., Kuyken, W., Williams, J. M. G., Eames, C., Bartley, T.,…Silverton, S. (2012b). The Bangor, Exeter and Oxford mindfulness-based intervention teaching assessment criteria (MBI-TAC). Retrieved from https://www.bangor.ac.uk/mindfulness/documents/MBI-TACMay2012.pdf

Crane, R. S., Soulsby, J. G., Kuyken, W., Williams, J. M. G., & Eames, C. (2016). Mindfulness-based interventions teaching assessment criteria (MBI: TAC). Bangor, UK: Bangor University. Retrieved from http://www.bangor.ac.uk/mindfulness/documents/MBI-TAC manualsummaryaddendums05-16.pdf

Crane, R. S., Stanley, S., Rooney, M., Bartley, T., Cooper, L., & Mardula, J. (2015). Disciplined improvisation: Characteristics of inquiry in mindfulness-based teaching. *Mindfulness, 6*(5), 1104–1114. doi:10.1007/s12671–014–0361–8

Dalai Lama. (1998). *The art of happiness: A handbook for living.* New York: Riverhead Books.

Dobkin, P. L., Irving, J. A., & Amar, S. (2011). For whom may participation in a mindfulness-based stress reduction program be contraindicated? *Mindfulness, 3*(1), 44–50. doi:10.1007/s12671-011-0079-9

Dreyfus, H. L., & Dreyfus, S. E. (1986). *Mind over machine: The power of human intuition and experience in the age of computers.* New York: Free Press.

Duncan, L. G., & Bardacke, N. (2010). Mindfulness-based childbirth and parenting education: promoting family mindfulness during the perinatal period. *Journal of Child and Family Studies, 19*(2), 190–202.

Eisendrath, S. J., Gillung, E., Delucchi, K. L., Segal, Z. V., Nelson, J. C., Mcinnes, L. A.,... Feldman, M. D. (2016). A randomized controlled trial of mindfulness-based cognitive therapy for treatment-resistant depression. *Psychotherapy and Psychosomatics, 85*(2), 99–110. doi:10.1159/000442260

Farb, N. A., Anderson, A. K., & Segal, Z. V. (2012). The mindful brain and emotion regulation in mood disorders. *The Canadian Journal of Psychiatry, 57*(2), 70–77. doi:10.1177/070674371205700203

Farb, N. A., Segal, Z. V., Mayberg, H., Bean, J., Mckeon, D., Fatima, Z., & Anderson, A. K. (2007). Attending to the present: Mindfulness meditation reveals distinct neural modes of self-reference. *Social Cognitive and Affective Neuroscience, 2*(4), 313–322. doi:10.1093/scan/nsm030

Goldberg, S. B., Tucker, R. P., Greene, P. A., Davidson, R. J., Wampold, B. E., Kearney, D. J., & Simpson, T. L. (2018). Mindfulness-based interventions for psychiatric disorders: A systematic review and meta-analysis. *Clinical Psychology Review, 59,* 52–60. doi:10.1016/j.cpr.2017.10.011

Gotink, R. A., Chu, P., Busschbach, J. J. V., Benson, H., Fricchione, G. L., & Hunick, M. G. M. (2015). Standardized mindfulness-based interventions in healthcare: An overview of systematic reviews and meta-analyses of RCTs. *PLOS One, 10*(4). doi: 10.1371/journal.pone.0124344

Grepmair, L., Mitterlehner, F., Loew, T., Bachler, E., Rother, W., & Nickel, M. (2007). Promoting mindfulness in psychotherapist in training influences the treatment results of their patients: A randomized controlled study. *Psychotherapy and Psychosomatics, 78*(6), 332–338.

Haller, H., Winkler, M. M., Klose, P., Dobos, G., Kümmel, S., & Cramer, H. (2017). Mindfulness-based interventions for women with breast cancer: An updated systematic review and meta-analysis. *Acta Oncologica, 56*(12), 1665–1676.

Kabat-Zinn, J. (1990). *Full catastrophe living: Using the wisdom of your body and mind to face stress, pain and illness.* New York: Delacorte Press.

Kabat-Zinn, J. (2013). *Full catastrophe living: Using the wisdom of your body and mind to face stress, pain, and illness.* New York: Bantam Books.

Kabat-Zinn, J., Santorelli, S. F., Blacker, M., Brantley, J., Meleo-Meyer, F., Grossman, P., ... Stahl, R. (n.d.). *Training teachers to deliver mindfulness-based stress reduction, principles and standards.* Worchester: UMass Center for Mindfulness. Retrieved from https://www.umassmed.edu/cfm/training/principles--standards/

Katz, N., & McNulty, K. (1994). *Reflective listening.* University of Syracuse. Retrieved from https://www.maxwell.syr.edu/uploadedFiles/parcc/cmc/Reflective%20Listening%20NK.pdf

Knowles, M. S. (1988). *The modern practice of adult education: From pedagogy to andragogy*. Englewood Cliffs, NJ: Cambridge Book Company.

Kolb, D. A. (2014). *Experiential learning: Experience as the source of learning and development* (2nd ed.). Saddle River, NJ: Pearson Education, Inc.

Kolb, D. A., & Fry, R. A. (1975). Towards an applied theory of experiential learning. In Cooper, C. (Ed.), *Theories of Group Processes*. New York: John Wiley and Sons.

Kristeller, J. L., & Wolever, R. Q. (2011). Mindfulness-based eating awareness training for treating binge eating disorder: the conceptual foundation. *Journal of Eating Disorders, 19*(1), 49–61.

Kuyken, W., Hayes, R., Barrett, B., Byng, R., Dalgleish, T., Kessler, D.,…Byford, S. (2015). Effectiveness and cost-effectiveness of mindfulness-based cognitive therapy compared with maintenance antidepressant treatment in the prevention of depressive relapse or recurrence (PREVENT): A randomized controlled trial. *Lancet, 386*(9988), 63–73. doi:10.3310/hta19730

Kuyken, W., Warren, F. C., Taylor, R. S., Whalley, B., Crane, C., Bondolfi, G.,…Dalgleish, T. (2016). Efficacy of mindfulness-based cognitive therapy in prevention of depressive relapse: An individual patient data meta-analysis from randomized trials. *JAMA Psychiatry, 73*(6), 565–574. doi:10.1001/jamapsychiatry.2016.0076

Lindahl, J. R., Fisher, N. E., Cooper, D. J., Rosen, R. K., & Britton, W. B. (2017). The varieties of contemplative experience: A mixed-methods study of meditation-related challenges in Western Buddhists. *PLOS One, 12*(5). doi: 10.1371/journal.pone.0176239

Loy, D. (2000). *Lack and transcendence: The problem of death and life in psychotherapy, existentialism, and Buddhism*. Amherst, NY: Humanity Books.

Magee, J. R. (2016). Teaching mindfulness with mindfulness of race and other forms of diversity. In D. McCown, D. Reibel, and M. Micozzi (Eds.), *Resources for teaching mindfulness: An international handbook* (pp. 225–246). New York: Springer.

Malhi, G. S, Bassett, B., Boyce, P., Bryant, R., Fitzgerald, P. B., Fritz, K., & Singh, A. B. (2015). Royal Australian and New Zealand College of Psychiatrists clinical practice guidelines for mood disorders. *Australian and New Zealand Journal of Psychiatry, 49*(12), 1–185.

McCown, D. (2016). Stewardship: deeper structures of the co-created group. In D. McCown, D. Reibel, & M. Micozzi (Eds.), *Resources for teaching mindfulness: An international handbook* (pp. 3–24). New York: Springer.

McCown, D., Reibel, D., & Micozzi, M. S. (2011). *Teaching mindfulness: A practical guide for clinicians and educators*. New York: Springer.

Miller, W. R., & Rollnick, S. (2013). *Motivational Interviewing: Helping people change* (3rd ed.). New York: The Guilford Press.

The Mindfulness-Based Professional Training Institute. (2015). MBCT Mentorship Documents. University of California at San Diego. Retrieved from http://mbpti.org/wp-content/uploads/2015/04/MBCT-Mentorship-Packet.pdf

Monteiro, L., Musten, R., & Compson, J. (2015). Traditional and contemporary mindfulness: Finding the middle path in the tangle of concerns. *Mindfulness, 6*(1), 1–13. doi:10.1007/s12671–014–0301–7

National Institute for Clinical Excellence (NICE) (2009; last updated 2018). *Depression: The treatment and management of depression in adults (update)*. Clinical Guideline 90. Retrieved from http://guidance.nice.org.uk/CG90

Parikh, S. V., Quilty, L. C., Ravitz, P., Rosenbluth, M., Pavlova, B., Grigoriadis, S.,...CANMAT Depression Work Group. (2016). Canadian Network for Mood and Anxiety Treatments (CANMAT) 2016 clinical guidelines for the management of adults with major depressive disorder: Section 2. Psychological treatments. *Canadian Journal of Psychiatry, 61*(9), 524–539.

Parsons, C. E., Crane, C., Parsons, L. J., Fjorback, L. O., & Kuyken W. (2017). Home practice in mindfulness-based cognitive therapy and mindfulness-based stress reduction: A systematic review and meta-analysis of participants' mindfulness practice and its association with outcomes. *Behaviour Research & Therapy, 95,* 29–41.

Pedulla, T. (2017). The mindfulness perspective. *International Journal of Group Psychotherapy, 67* (Supl), S154–S163. doi:10.1080/00207284.2016.1218284

Purser, R., & Loy, D. (2013). Beyond McMindfulness. *Huffington Post* (July 1). Retrieved from https://www.huffingtonpost.com/ron-purser/beyond-mcmindfulness_b_3519289.html

Remen, R. N. (1988). On defining spirit. *IONS Noetic Sciences Review* (autumn), 63.

Rogers, C. R. (1942). *Counseling and psychotherapy.* New York: Houghton Mifflin Company.

Ruijgrok-Lupton, P. E., Crane, S. R., & Dorjee, D. (2018). Impact of mindfulness-based teacher training on MBSR participant well-being outcomes and course satisfaction. *Mindfulness, 9*(1), 117–128. doi: 10.1007/s12671–017–0750-x

Santorelli, S. F., (2016). Remembrance chapter 3: Dialogue and inquiry in the MBSR classroom. In D. McCown, D. Reibel, & M. Micozzi (Eds.), *Resources for teaching mindfulness: An international handbook* (pp. 47–68). New York: Springer.

Schön, D. A. (1983). *The reflective practitioner: How professionals think in action.* New York: Basic Books.

Schön, D. A. (1987). *Educating the reflective practitioner:* San Francisco: Jossey-Bass Publishers.

Segal, Z. V., Williams, J. M., & Teasdale, J. D. (2002). *Mindfulness-based cognitive therapy for depression: A new approach to preventing relapse* (1st ed.). New York: The Guilford Press.

Segal, Z. V., Williams, J. M., & Teasdale, J. D. (2013). *Mindfulness-based cognitive therapy for depression* (2nd ed.). New York: The Guilford Press.

Shafran, R., Clark, D. M., Fairburn, C. G., Arntz, A., Barlow, D. H., Ehlers, A.,...Wilson, G. T. (2009). Mind the gap: Improving the dissemination of CBT. *Behavior Research and Therapy, 47*(11), 902–909.

Sorbero, M. E., Ahluwalia, S., Reynolds, K., Lovejoy, S. L., Farris, C., Sloan, J., ... Herman, P. (2015). *Meditation for major depressive disorder: A systematic review.* RAND Corporation. Retrieved from https://www.rand.org/pubs/research_reports/RR1138.html

Tuckman, B. W., & Jensen, M. A. (1977). Stages of small-group development revisited. *Group & Organization Studies, 2*(4), 419–427. doi:10.1177/105960117700200404

UK Network for Mindfulness-Based Teacher Training Organizations. (2015). *Good practice guidelines for teaching mindfulness-based courses.* Retrieved from https://www.ukmindfulnessnetwork.co.uk/guidelines/

U.S. Veteran's Affairs/Department of Defense. (2009). VA/DoD clinical practice guideline for management of major depressive disorder (MDD). Washington, D.C.: Department of Veterans Affairs. Retrieved from http://www.healthquality.va.gov/guidelines/MH/mdd/MDDFULL053013.pdf

Van Aalderen, J. R., Breukers, W. J., Reuzel, R. P. B., & Speckens, A. E. M. (2014). The role of the teacher in mindfulness-based approaches: A qualitative study. *Mindfulness, 5*(2), 170–178. doi: 10.1007/s12671-012-0162-x

Watterson, W. B., Calvin and Hobbes. (1995). Distributed by Universal Press Syndicate, Kansas City, MO: Andrews MacMeel Publishing.

Williams, J. M. G., Fennell, M., Barnhofer, T., Crane, R., & Silverton, S. (2017). *Mindfulness-based cognitive therapy with people at risk of suicide.* New York: The Guilford Press.

Woods, S. L. (2010). Training professionals in mindfulness: The heart of teaching. In F. Didonna (Ed.), *Clinical handbook of mindfulness* (pp. 463–475). New York: Springer.

Woods, S. L., Rockman, P., & Collins, E. (2016). *A Contemplative dialogue: The inquiry process in mindfulness-based interventions.* Toronto, Canada: Centre for Mindfulness Studies. Retrieved from https://slwoods.com/wp-content/uploads/2016/02/acomplentativedialogue-2-2012.pdf

Yalom, I. D., & Leszcz, M. (2005). *The theory and practice of group psychotherapy.* New York: Basic Books.

Yalom, I. D., Tinklenberg, J., & Gilula, M. (1970). Curative factors in group psychotherapy. In I. D. Yalom (Ed.), *The theory and practice of group psychotherapy* (1st ed.). New York: Basic Books.

Young, S. (2004). *Break through pain: A step-by-step mindfulness meditation program for transforming chronic and acute pain.* Boulder, CO: Sounds True.

Susan Woods, MSW, LICSW, is a clinical social worker and was in clinical practice for many years. She is a senior mindfulness-based stress reduction and mindfulness-based cognitive therapy (MBSR/MBCT) consultant, mentor, trainer, and supervisor, and a professional advisor on various MBCT clinical trials. Susan developed the MBSR and MBCT professional certification programs for the Mindfulness-Based Professional Training Institute at the University of California, San Diego, where she was principal curriculum consultant and senior guiding teacher. Susan has been teaching MBSR and MBCT for many years. She is a certified MBSR teacher through the Center of Mindfulness and the University of Massachusetts Medical School, where she was a teacher. Since 2005, Susan has been leading professional training programs in MBSR and MBCT, and has taught at venues worldwide. She has presented on the clinical application of mindfulness at numerous conferences, and is a published author on the training of health professionals in mindfulness-based skills. Susan is a graduate of the two-year Community Dharma Leaders Program at Spirit Rock Meditation Center in Woodacre, CA. She is a certified yoga teacher.

Patricia Rockman, MD, is a family physician with a focused practice in mental health. Her clinical areas of expertise include stress and change management, brief solution-focused therapy, cognitive behavioral therapy (CBT), and mindfulness-based programs, specifically mindfulness-based cognitive therapy (MBCT) and mindfulness-based stress reduction (MBSR). She is cofounder and senior director of education and clinical services at the Centre for Mindfulness Studies in Toronto, ON, Canada, where she delivers and designs mindfulness-based programs, as well as trains and mentors clinicians (she created the MBCT facilitation certificate program, levels 1 and 2). She has delivered numerous workshops and presented at conferences locally, nationally, and internationally on mindfulness in health care and the corporate sector. She is associate professor in the departments of family and community medicine and psychiatry at the University of Toronto, and a part-time staff physician with the Family Health Team at the University Health Network. She is a certified yoga teacher and freelance writer.

Evan Collins, MD, is a psychiatrist who is trained in both mindfulness-based stress reduction (MBSR) and mindfulness-based cognitive therapy (MBCT), and runs groups in both modalities at Toronto General Hospital and the Centre for Mindfulness Studies in Toronto, ON, Canada. In the past, he has assisted in the development of focused MBCT groups for people in cancer recovery and for people living with HIV, as well as for health care worker stress and resiliency. He is senior faculty in the professional development program at the Centre for Mindfulness Studies, where he is involved with curriculum development and creating supervision and mentoring policies in the area of mindfulness-based interventions. He is also a mentor of trainees in mindfulness, and has delivered workshops for health care providers and the corporate sector in Canada and the United States. At present, he is involved in research studying the use of MBCT. He is adjunct assistant professor in the department of psychiatry at the University of Toronto, and staff psychiatrist in the Centre for Mental Health at the University Health Network.

Foreword writer **Zindel V. Segal, PhD**, is professor of psychology at the University of Toronto Scarborough. He is coauthor of *Mindfulness-Based Cognitive Therapy for Depression* and *The Mindful Way through Depression*.

Index

A

about this book, 2–3
abstract conceptualization, 30, 78, 88–91
acceptance, attitude of, 100
Access MBCT registry, 144, 186
active experimentation, 30, 78, 91–93
active listening, 132
active meditations: Mindful Movement Practice, 50–51, 164–169; Walking Meditation, 170–171
adjourning stage of groups, 69, 73–74
adult learning theories, 30–31
advice-giving, 67, 185
agents of change. *See* five agents of change
alcohol abuse, 70, 138
all-day silent retreat: description of, 12–13; sample schedule for, 181–182; teacher training and, 145–146; TRIP applied to, 20
altruism, 67
angry outbursts, 184
Art of Happiness, The (Dalai Lama), 119–120
assessment: prospective participant, 69; teacher competency, 143–144

attention: bare, 112, 113–115; process of training, 11; stabilization of, 77
attitudinal foundations of mindfulness, 98–103
authenticity and potency, 79
authority, sense of, 75
automatic pilot, 11, 14, 15, 16, 29
Automatic Thought Record (ATR), 187–188
Automatic Thoughts Questionnaire, 56
autonomy, 4, 75, 152
aversion issues, 18–19, 72
awareness: breath, 48–49, 51–54; choiceless, 54, 115
Awareness of Breathing and Challenging Physical Sensations Meditation Practice: script for guiding, 160–162; TRIP framework and, 48–49

B

bare attention, 112, 113–115
barriers to meditation, 72
Batchelor, Stephen, 147
beginner's mind, 99–100
being mode of mind, 106, 112, 122
beneficence, 4
body language, 61, 84, 87

Body Scan Meditation Practice: script for guiding, 153–159; TRIP framework and, 46–48
body sensations, 37, 47, 114, 126–127
booster groups, 186
boundary maintenance, 74
Breath, Body, Sounds, Thoughts, and Emotions and Choiceless Awareness Meditation Practice: script for guiding, 172–178; TRIP framework and, 54–55
breath-awareness practices: Awareness of Breathing and Challenging Physical Sensations Meditation Exercise, 48–49, 160–162; Three-Minute Breathing Space, 51–54, 163, 179–180
Buddhist psychology, 4, 9, 27, 37, 103–108, 132
Buddhist teachings, 88, 98, 146–147

C

catharsis, 66
CBT. *See* cognitive behavior therapy
Centre for Mindfulness Studies (CMS), 3, 141, 142
challenges, teacher, 81
choiceless awareness, 54, 115
clarifying questions, 85
closing ceremony, 74
cofacilitation of groups, 186
cognitive behavior therapy (CBT), 187–192; MBCT session themes and, 192; mindfulness and, 188–189, 191
cognitive exercises, 16, 56–59, 190; Automatic Thoughts Questionnaire, 56; Nourishing and Depleting Exercise, 58–59; Territory of Depression, 56–57; Walking Down the Street, 36, 56. *See also* mindfulness/meditation practices
cohesion, group, 65
Collins, Evan, vii, 4
communication skills, 79–80
communities of practice, 186
compassion, 79, 99, 101, 119–120
competence: assessing standards and, 143–144; importance of maintaining, 141–142. *See also* teaching competencies and skills
complex reflections, 88, 90
composition of groups, 67–68
concrete experience, 30, 78
connection and acceptance, 79
contemplative dialogue, 124–125, 136; active listening in, 132; three marks of existence in, 132–135
continuing education, 139, 141, 142
cross-talk, 67, 72, 185
curiosity, 79, 101, 119, 126, 130

D

Dalai Lama, 119–120
decentering, 84, 105, 106, 107, 135, 136
depression treatment, 13, 70, 138
developmental stages of groups, 68–74; adjourning, 69, 73–74; forming, 68, 69–72; norming and performing, 68, 73; storming, 68, 72–73
discernment, 113, 117–121
disengaged participants, 184
diversity issues, 68
doing mode of mind, 106, 112, 130
double-barreled questions, 131
doubt, issues of, 72
drug abuse, 70, 138

E

education. *See* training in MBCT

embodied mindful presence, 97–122; as agent of change, 37; attitudinal foundations of, 98–103; bare attention and, 112, 113–115; Buddhist psychology and, 103–108; discernment and, 113, 117–121; inquiry related to, 61–62; in learning to teach MBCT, 79; open-monitoring and, 112–113, 115–117; present-moment orientation and, 111–122; Raisin Practice example of, 61–62; summary characterization of, 121–122

emotional displays, 183–184

environment, learning, 79–81

equanimity, 85, 91, 120, 122

ethical principles, 4, 104, 146–148

existential factors, 66

experience: facilitating, 78, 81–83; generalizing, 88–91; normalizing, 85, 115; noticing, 126–127; personalizing, 82, 105, 106, 134–135; tracking, 84, 87, 115, 120, 127

experiential learning, 78–81; environment conducive to, 79–81; Kolb's cyclical model of, 78

experiential self-referencing, 127

F

facilitating abstract conceptualization, 78, 88–91

facilitating active experimentation, 78, 91–93

facilitating experience, 78, 81–83

facilitating reflective observation, 78, 83–88

feedback, 30, 186

five agents of change, 27–40; diagram illustrating, 28; embodied mindful presence, 37; group process, 33–37; implementation of, 38–40; individual learning, 29–33; mindfulness-based practices, 29; protocol for MBCT, 28–29; Raisin Practice example of, 59–62

fixed sense of self, 105–106, 121, 134

forming stage of groups, 68, 69–72

G

generalization of experience, 88–91

graduate groups, 186

grounding exercises, 70, 183

group cohesion, 65

group process, 63–75; as agent of change, 33–37; cofacilitation and, 186; composition of groups and, 67–68; developmental stages of, 68–74; explanatory overview of, 63–64; graduate groups and, 186; Raisin Practice example of, 61; teaching skills relevant to, 74–75; therapeutic factors relevant to, 64–67

guidance: language of, 45, 60; as therapeutic factor, 67

H

handouts, 91

hindrances, 72

home practice, 91–93

hope, instilling, 65

horizontal inquiry, 84, 129

human suffering, 104, 121, 148

I

identification process, 66
imitative behavior, 66
imperfect nature of experience, 104
impermanence, 24, 104, 108, 134
impersonal nature of experience, 105
individual learning: as agent of change, 29–33; Raisin Practice example of, 60–61
informal meditation practices, 29
information, imparting, 66
inquiry, 123–136; active listening and, 132; characteristics embedded in, 129–130; contemplative nature of, 124–125, 136; definitions of, 10, 123; embodied mindful presence and, 61–62; listening for three marks of existence in, 132–135; reflective observation and, 84, 88; three layers framework for, 124, 125–130
instilling hope, 65
intentions, 14, 15; of cognitive exercises, 55–59; of individual sessions, 16–21; of mindfulness/meditation practices, 43–55
International Integrity Institute, 143
International Mindfulness Teachers Association (IMTA), 143–144
interrupting participants, 87
intrapersonal struggles, 72

K

Kabat-Zinn, Jon, vii, 3, 5, 98
kindness, 67, 119–120
Knowles, Malcolm, 30
Kolb, David, 30, 78
Kornfield, Jack, 3

L

language: body, 61, 84, 87; conventions used in book, 4; of guidance, 45, 60
leadership role, 75
leading questions, 131
learning: environment for, 79–81; experiential, 78–81; individual, 29–33, 60–61; theories of adult, 30–31
letting go, 101
Lewin, Kurt, 78
life cycle of groups. *See* developmental stages of groups
listening: active, 132; reflective, 84–85

M

MBCT. *See* mindfulness-based cognitive therapy
MBI:TAC assessment instrument, 79, 143
MBPs. *See* mindfulness-based programs
meditation: discernment cultivated in, 117; formal vs. informal practice of, 29; guiding of exercises and, 81–83; potential adverse effects of, 69, 70, 183
meditation scripts, 152–180; Awareness of Breathing and Challenging Physical Sensations, 160–162; Body Scan Meditation Practice, 153–159; Breath, Body, Sounds, Thoughts, and Emotions and Choiceless Awareness, 172–178; Mindful Movement, 164–169; Three-Minute Breathing Space–Regular, 163; Three-Minute Breathing Space–Responsive, 179–180; Walking Meditation, 170–171. *See also* mindfulness/meditation practices
mentorship process, 140, 142

Mindful Movement Practice: script for guiding, 164–169; TRIP framework and, 50–51
mindful self-compassion (MSC), 186
mindfulness: attitudinal foundations of, 98–103; cognitive behavior therapy and, 188–189, 191; contemporizing of, 137; embodying the practice of, 1, 27, 97–122; formal vs. informal practice of, 29; impact of personal practice of, 144–146; impermanence embodied through, 134; movement practice based on, 50–51, 164–169; TRIP framework and, 44–46, 50–54
mindfulness/meditation practices, 15–16, 44–55, 153–180; Awareness of Breathing and Challenging Physical Sensations, 48–49, 160–162; Body Scan Meditation Practice, 46–48, 153–159; Breath, Body, Sounds, Thoughts, and Emotions and Choiceless Awareness, 54–55, 172–178; Mindful Movement Practice, 50–51, 164–169; Raisin Practice, 44–46; scripts for guiding, 152–180; Three-Minute Breathing Space, 51–54, 163, 179–180; Walking Meditation, 170–171. *See also* cognitive exercises
mindfulness-based cognitive therapy (MBCT): assessing competence in, 143; cognitive behavior therapy and, 187–192; contraindications for, 69–70; embodied mindful presence for, 97–122; ethics of teaching, 146–148; five agents of change, 27–40; group process, 63–75; maintaining competence in, 141–142; practices and exercises, 43–62; professional standards for, 143–144; protocol overview, 10–14; research evidence supporting, 13, 70, 138; special populations and, 184; teaching competencies and skills in, 77–93; training and mentoring in, 138–140, 142–143; TRIP framework, 14–24

Mindfulness-Based Cognitive Therapy for Depression (Segal, Williams, and Teasdale), 9, 28, 51
Mindfulness-Based Interventions: Teaching Assessment Criteria (MBI:TAC), 79, 143
mindfulness-based practices: as agent of change, 29; Raisin Practice example of, 60
mindfulness-based programs (MBPs), 1; contraindications for, 69; diversity issue in, 69; embodying mindfulness in, 27; professional training in, 139
mindfulness-based stress reduction (MBSR), 3, 138
modeling, practice of, 122, 131
mourning stage of groups, 73–74
moving meditations: Mindful Movement Practice, 50–51, 164–169; Walking Meditation, 170–171
mutuality, 79

N

narrative self-referencing, 127
neuroimaging studies, 126
nonjudging, 100
nonmaleficence, 4
nonstriving, 100–101
normalizing experiences, 85, 115
norming stage of groups, 68, 73
noticing experience, 126–127
not-self or non-self, 105
Nourishing and Depleting Exercise, 58–59, 118

O

observation, reflective, 78, 83–88
observer stance, 117
obstacles to meditation, 72
open-ended questions, 131
open-monitoring, 112–113, 115–117
orientation session, 11, 71

P

participatory engagement, 121
patience, attitude of, 99
peer mentorship, 141, 142, 186
performing stage of groups, 68, 73
personal pronouns, 81–82
personalizing experience, 82, 105, 106, 134–135
pitfalls, teacher, 81
placebo effect, 65
potency and authenticity, 79
Practice Skills, 14, 15; of cognitive exercises, 57–59; of individual sessions, 16–21; of mindfulness/meditation practices, 43–55
preclass interview, 11, 69, 71
present-moment orientation, 88, 98, 111–122; bare attention and, 112, 113–115; discernment and, 113, 117–121; inquiry and maintenance of, 131; open-monitoring and, 112–113, 115–117
professional training, 138–139
pronouns, use of personal, 81–82
protocol for MBCT: as agent of change, 28–29; explanatory overview of, 10–14; Raisin Practice example of, 59–60
psychosis, participants with, 70

R

Raisin Practice: five agents of change and, 59–62; TRIP framework and, 44–46
rationale, 14; of cognitive exercises, 55–59; of individual sessions, 16–21; of mindfulness/meditation practices, 43–55
reactions, managing severe, 183
reassurance, 67, 183, 185
recording log, 91–92
reflective listening, 84–85
reflective observation, 30, 78, 83–88
reflective practitioners, 30
reframing process, 85
relational skills, 79
Remen, Rachel Naomi, 147
resistance, 104, 106
respect, 4, 79
responding, appropriate, 85
restlessness, 72
retreat. *See* all-day silent retreat
right relationship, 147
Rockman, Patricia, vii, 3
Rogers, Carl, 84

S

Santorelli, Saki, vii
Schön, Donald, 30
screening process, 69, 71
scripts. *See* meditation scripts
secular Buddhism, 147
Segal, Zindel, viii, 3, 4, 5
self: decentering from, 105, 107, 135, 136; fixed sense of, 105–106, 121, 134
self-care, 13, 21, 118
self-disclosure, 185

self-understanding, 66
sensation, experience as, 125, 126–127
Session 1: Awareness and Automatic Pilot: described, 11; TRIP applied to, 16–17
Session 2: Living in Our Heads: described, 11; TRIP applied to, 17
Session 3: Gathering the Scattered Mind: described, 11; TRIP applied to, 18
Session 4: Recognizing Aversion: described, 12; TRIP applied to, 18–19
Session 5: Allowing and Letting Be: described, 12; TRIP applied to, 19
Session 6: Thoughts Are Not Facts: described, 12; TRIP applied to, 20
Session 7: "How Can I Best Take Care of Myself?": described, 13; TRIP applied to, 21
Session 8: Maintaining and Extending New Learning: described, 13–14; TRIP applied to, 21
silent retreat . *See* all-day silent retreat
simple reflections, 85, 86, 88
sloth and torpor, 72
slowing down, 111–112
special populations, 184
standards, professional, 143–144
storming stage of groups, 68, 72–73
substance abuse, 70, 138
suffering, human, 104, 121, 148
suicidal ideation, 70, 138
summarizing learning points, 85

T

teaching competencies and skills, 77–93; abstract conceptualization and, 88–91; active experimentation and, 91–93;
challenges/pitfalls related to, 81; experiential learning of, 78–81; facilitating experience and, 81–83; group process and relevant, 74–75; impact of personal practice on, 144–146; importance of maintaining, 141–142; learning environment and, 79–81; personal styles related to, 88; reflective observation and, 83–88
Teasdale, John, vii, 5
Territory of Depression exercise, 56–57
themes, 14; of cognitive exercises, 55–59; of individual sessions, 16–21; of mindfulness/meditation practices, 43–55
therapeutic group factors, 64–67
therapy sessions. *See specific sessions*
three layers of inquiry, 124, 125–130
three marks of existence, 104–105, 132–135
Three-Minute Breathing Space–Regular: script for guiding, 163; TRIP framework and, 51–52
Three-Minute Breathing Space–Responsive: script for guiding, 179–180; TRIP framework and, 52–54
Tolkien, J. R. R., 150
tracking experience, 84, 87, 115, 120, 127
training in MBCT: continuing education and, 139, 141, 142; mentorship following, 140, 142; professional, 138–139, 142–143; summary of, 141–142
trauma, meditation and, 69, 70, 183
TRIP (Themes, Rationale, Intention, Practice Skills): benefits of using, 25; cognitive exercises and, 55–59; explanatory overview of, 14–16;

mindfulness/meditation practices and, 44–55; practice example of using, 22–24; session-by-session application of, 16–21

trust, attitude of, 99

U

universality, 65, 135

Urbanowski, Ferris, vii

V

verbal participation, 185

vertical inquiry, 84, 129

vipassana, 3, 4

W

Walking Down the Street exercise, 36, 56

Walking Meditation, 170–171

wanting, issues of, 72

warmth and compassion, 79

Williams, Mark, vii, 5

Woods, Susan, vii, 3

Y

Young, Shinzen, 104

MORE BOOKS from
NEW HARBINGER PUBLICATIONS

A CLINICIAN'S GUIDE TO TEACHING MINDFULNESS
The Comprehensive Session-by-Session Program for Mental Health Professionals & Health Care Providers
978-1626251397 / US $49.95

A CONTEXTUAL BEHAVIORAL GUIDE TO THE SELF
Theory & Practice
978-1626251762 / US $49.95
CONTEXT PRESS
An Imprint of New Harbinger Publications

ACT MADE SIMPLE, SECOND EDITION
An Easy-To-Read Primer on Acceptance & Commitment Therapy
978-1684033010 / US $44.95

HANDBOOK OF CLINICAL PSYCHOPHARMACOLOGY FOR THERAPISTS, EIGHTH EDITION
978-1626259256 / US $59.95

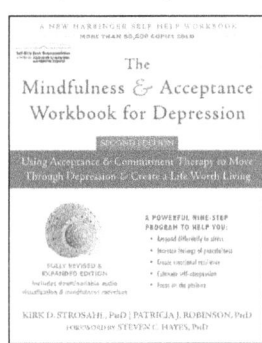

THE MINDFULNESS & ACCEPTANCE WORKBOOK FOR DEPRESSION, SECOND EDITION
Using Acceptance & Commitment Therapy to Move Through Depression & Create a Life Worth Living
978-1626258457 / US $24.95

A MINDFULNESS-BASED STRESS REDUCTION WORKBOOK
978-1572247086 / US $25.95

newharbingerpublications
1-800-748-6273 / newharbinger.com

Follow Us

(VISA, MC, AMEX / prices subject to change without notice)

QUICK TIPS for THERAPISTS
Fast and free solutions to common client situations mental health professionals encounter every day

Written by leading clinicians, Quick Tips for Therapists are short e-mails, sent twice a month, to help enhance your client sessions. **Visit newharbinger.com/quicktips to sign up today!**

Sign up for our Book Alerts at **newharbinger.com/bookalerts**